THE BORDERLAND OF FEAR

Early American Places is a collaborative project of the University of Georgia Press, New York University Press, Northern Illinois University Press, and the University of Nebraska Press. The series is supported by the Andrew W. Mellon Foundation. For more information, please visit www.earlyamericanplaces.org.

BORDERLANDS AND TRANSCULTURAL STUDIES

Series Editors   Pekka Hämäläinen, Paul Spickard

THE BORDERLAND OF FEAR

Vincennes, Prophetstown, and the Invasion
of the Miami Homeland

PATRICK BOTTIGER

University of Nebraska Press
LINCOLN AND LONDON

Portions of this book were original published as "Prophetstown for Their Own Purposes: The French, Miamis, and Cultural Identities in the Wabash-Maumee Valley," by Patrick Bottiger, *Journal of the Early Republic* 33, no. 1 (Spring 2013): 29–60. Copyright © 2013 Society for Historians of the Early American Republic; and "Stabbed in the Back: Vincennes, Slavery, and the Indian 'Threat,'" by Patrick Bottiger, *Indiana Magazine of History* 107 (June 2011): 89–102.

Manufactured in the United States of America ∞

Library of Congress Control Number: 2016936617

To Julie Bottiger and Paul Schwietz

CONTENTS

Figures, Maps, and Tables

Figures

Maps

Tables

Preface

Why do we need another book about Prophetstown and the Battle of Tippecanoe? Originally, I had hoped to write a book about everyday experiences of the diverse Indian peoples at Prophetstown in order to understand how the town evolved—and survived—from 1808 to 1812. I thought that examining these peoples' relationships through time would help us understand the complicated nature of Indian nativism. But as I delved into the primary evidence, I was struck by the fact that Miami Indians and French traders—two sets of people adamantly opposed to Prophetstown—were also the key authors of much of the archival material. This piqued my interest. What fueled such animosity? It was hard to know where rumor ended and truth began.

To this end, I set out to consult as much of the source material as I possibly could—newspapers, treaty negotiations, personal letters, oral histories, and diplomatic correspondence. The more I read, the more I realized that perceptions of the town differed widely. I was not sure whom to believe. Anglo-Americans and Frenchmen could agree neither on the meaning of the town itself nor on the intentions of its residents. Indians felt the same way. How could I write about Prophetstown if the source material was so widely divergent in perspective?

In trying to understand the town, I came to appreciate the complicated history of the surrounding region. There was a history of the Miami homeland that needed to be told—and it was integral to what happened at Prophetstown. After all, the nativist movement at Prophetstown was not simply a reaction to American nationalism. It was also the product of a centuries-long history in which white people played scarcely any part. And while the many biographies of Tecumseh, Tenskwatawa, and William Henry Harrison do an excellent job of investigating those historical actors' connection to Prophetstown, historians doggedly situated Prophetstown within a larger discussion of nationalisms, both American and Native. But when it came to the settlement at Prophetstown and its eventual destruction, no one had examined what it meant for Prophetstown to exist in Miami country and therefore the role the Miamis and French might have played in its existence and destruction.

Thus, I decided two things: one, I would need to understand the longue durée of Miami history to recognize the traditional patterns and relationships that shaped the region that would eventually become the home of the Shawnee Prophet; and, two, discussions of nationalism could only be part of the historical picture rather than its frame.[1] Only then could I really come to understand the causes of the violence at Tippecanoe in November 1811.

Revising the history of Prophetstown to include this new perspective meant that I had to rethink the scale and boundaries of my study. The local and the national—not just one or the other—would have to guide my work. People in the Miami homeland envisioned their ethnic and national initiatives on the local level, and it was on the local level where these would succeed or vanish. In moving beyond "state-centered" histories and looking to the many Native and non-Native residents of the Miami homeland, I hoped to show that their histories were intertwined in ways not yet imagined.[2] The subsequent chapters face east from Indian country not necessarily to tell the story of the Miamis, but to better understand a culture of violence that was central to the physical and psychological contest for sovereignty in the western Ohio Valley during the first years of the early republic. The fight for Prophetstown cannot be understood simply by looking at American expansion or Indian nativism. By looking east, this book brings together multiple historical narratives—Miami, imperial, national, community, nativist, and republican—to comprehend how various communities used violence to protect their sovereign interests.

This template assumes that both Americans and non-Miami Indians were settlers and that their aims posed a threat to the Miamis' world. The Miamis and the French influenced regional diplomacy and shaped the course of American nationalism and Indian nativism despite the fact that their power was beginning to wane. Taking inspiration from David Preston's *The Texture of Contact*, this model demonstrates "the weak grasp of distant colonial capitals and the [relatively] hollow nature of [national and nativist] claims of sovereignty over border lands and Native nations" while pointing "toward Native understandings of boundaries, human movement, the landscape, and historical change."[3] Despite the efforts of influential leaders like William Henry Harrison and the Shawnee Prophet to destroy the Miamis' borderland in order to create bordered American and Indian places, these two men found themselves at an impasse. As the Miamis and French witnessed the collapse of the Miami borderland, they maintained the ability to guide the flow of information, trade, and people through their part of the world.

Looking east from Miami country means trying to understand a Native world on Indian terms. Gregory Dowd's seminal work on Indian nativism helps us understand the perspective of Indians who lived at Prophetstown and other similar settlements. But for the Miamis, supporting Prophetstown or accommodating the Americans were perilous enterprises. Native peoples throughout the Ohio Valley used unique approaches to defend their cultural and political hegemony, including strategies for revitalization and methods for dealing with outsiders. While it might be accurate to identify one faction of Miamis as accommodationist, not all fit neatly into these categories. The accommodationist-nativist interpretive framework risks situating all Indians within the context of American nationalism by presupposing the inevitability of territorial expansion in the United States. Such a perspective implies that Natives were more concerned with American aims than their own struggles. But the power and dominance of the United States was not necessarily the primary threat to Native identity or sovereignty. In fact, sometimes the threat came from within Native communities. Such disputes kept Native peoples from unifying against one another, which in turn prevented the sort of accommodationist-nativist dichotomy that frames so much of the current scholarship.

Facing east from Miami country also helps us understand an Anglo world on local terms. Rather than simply an extension of the republican state farther east, the Anglo settlements of the Illinois country and Indiana Territory were remarkably parochial, factionalized, and dysfunctional. At times they certainly dreamed of a republican world but acted in ways that undermined if not ignored it. Much like the Native communities around them, quarrels within the Anglo communities prevented the sort of national coherence that is typically ascribed to territorial Indiana. The Indian "threat" was certainly a powerful force in shaping Indiana territory, but it has for too long silenced the deep and sometimes bloody divisiveness that wracked western Anglo communities.

Using the perspective of the Miami homeland to understand violence in the early republic allows us to see that nativism and republicanism were just two of many strategies used by Indian and non-Indian people to forge stability in times of tremendous change. Identities—national, racial, political—remained contested and weak, and ethnic and cultural debates dominated native-white relations. By narrowing our focus to the community level, I wish to move beyond labels and to understand Indians and non-Natives in the ways they understood themselves.[4] The result is a multilayered contest for sovereignty far deeper and richer than expansionist Americans fighting nativist Indians. It was a world where personal relationships and the lies binding them together determined the fate of the American republic.

Writing this book would not have been possible without a number of key professional and personal relationships of my own. While completing my graduate studies at the University of Oklahoma, I was lucky to study with Professor Joshua Piker. With all due respect to the written word, I cannot properly express in this short space the gratitude and appreciation that I have for him as a scholar and as a human being. The readings he selected for seminar helped me to appreciate historians who took risks and to recognize that one cannot possibly comprehend early America without understanding the history of American Indians. Our meetings during the writing stages of my dissertation were short, but packed with questions and critiques that made me think more deeply and critically. As a colleague, he has been there every step of the way, sometimes to tease me about my love for the Minnesota Twins, but mostly to remind me that writing history is a deeply introspective process that requires a strong commitment to placing yourself in the period in which you study. Every time I think of Joshua Piker, I think of the small notecard he had on his desk that read, "Work, work, work!"

Paul Gilje introduced me to the complexities of the American Revolution and the debates that surrounded it. Our discussions began with the American bid for independence, but a turn toward the War of 1812 drew me to the roots of violence in the Ohio River Valley, and thus the subject of this book. Terry Rugeley challenged me to think about the provincial nature of violence in North America and to situate my story within a North American past; in doing so, he helped me step away from the tendency to reinforce the inevitability of the American nation-state. I am indebted to Paul and Terry for showing me how it was possible to approach the history of the Ohio Valley from multiple perspectives. In addition, I would like to thank Faye Yarbrough, Robert Shalhope, Warren Metcalf, and Robert Griswold for cultivating such a positive learning environment at the University of Oklahoma. So too did Cathy Kelly, who has since become a trusted mentor and friend.

Professor Catharine Franklin, a dear friend and colleague, has been part of my scholarly journey from the very first day of graduate school. She has read this manuscript several times and offered great advice at each stage of revision. Most of all, I am deeply grateful to her insistence that I tell an engaging story, that I write to both a scholarly and popular audience, and that I insist on writing a narrative. Bringing back to life the sometimes horrifying and at other times comical events central to my story has been a very rewarding experience. But certainly, meeting such a great friend in Catharine has been the real triumph.

When I began to delve into eighteenth- and nineteenth-century manuscripts, the Indiana Historical Society and Indiana State Library proved to be the center of my archival orbit. The Lilly Library at Indiana University, the Bentley Library at the University of Michigan, the Filson Society, the University of Wisconsin libraries, the Center for French Colonial Studies, and the libraries at the University of Oklahoma, Florida Gulf Coast University, and Kenyon College gave me the time and space to puzzle out historical questions. A summer seminar funded by the National Endowment for the Humanities at the Library Company of Philadelphia was a crucial part of the revision process. I was fortunate to join a group of fabulous scholars who devoted six weeks to the problems of governance in the early republic. Directors John Larson and Michael Morrison, Melissa Bullard, Christopher Childers, Thomas Cox, Andrew Fagel, Scott King-Owen, Helen Knowles, Albrecht Koschnik, Gabriel Loiacono, Daniel Mandell, Patrick Peel, Andrew Schocket, Nora Pat Small, and Sarah Swedberg made that summer a memorable one. It was a real joy to be introduced to such fine scholars and their compelling work, and to find my voice among them.

Several people have provided much-needed advice as this project moved from one stage to the next. Professor Carol Berg introduced me to the history of American Indians when I was an undergraduate at St. John's University in Collegeville, Minnesota. The first book she assigned was R. David Edmunds's *Tecumseh*. I keep the same copy of it near my desk as a reminder that one book can upend our ideas about the past. Professors Elizabeth Wengler, David Bennetts, Kenneth Jones, and Gregory Schroeder also welcomed me into their classes, where they shared a deep love for history. At a number of academic conferences, R. David Edmunds, Tracy Leavelle, John Larson, Richard White, John W. Hall, Christina Snyder, A. Glenn Crothers, and other scholars have offered pointed advice that helped me refine my arguments. At the Filson Society's Conference on the "Long Struggle for the Ohio Valley," Christina Snyder urged me to include a more thorough examination of the Miami homeland, which blossomed into a deeper appreciation for the ways in which the Miamis maintained their lands despite circumstances that appeared impossible.

Matthew Bokovoy at the University of Nebraska Press has been a good shepherd to this book and its author. Editorial comments from Matt, Pekka, and Paul have helped me immeasurably. Matt's thoughtful and diplomatic advice allowed me to shorten the manuscript considerably without taking away from the whole. Pekka's generous comments allowed me to hone the broader conceptual framework of the book by challenging me to consider the relationship between imperial and ethnic borders. This involved me making a much deeper evaluation of the scholarship on borderlands, throwing in relief the differences between Stephen Aron and Jeremy Aldeman's analysis in "From Borderlands to Borders" with that of Pekka Hämäläinen and Samuel Truett's "On Borderlands" so that I could craft a more nuanced discussion of sovereignty. Thanks to them, the final product is far improved. Comments from Lucy Murphy and an anonymous reviewer were equally beneficial, and I am grateful for their many suggestions. Equally so, the keen editorial eyes of Tim Roberts and Susan Murray have helped me polish this book for press.

It is remarkable how much my community of scholar-friends has grown over the years. Many of the people from my cohort at the University of Oklahoma have remained key sounding boards during the last six years. Professors Catharine Franklin, Sunu Kodumthara, Patti Jo King, Larry Mastroni, Sam Stalcup, Michele Stephens, Stephen Martin, Emily Wardrop, Matthew Bahar, Paul McKenzie-Jones, Damon Akins, and Mandy Taylor-Montoya are dear friends with whom I studied and celebrated. To them I offer a loud and proud "Boomer Sooner!" Former colleagues at Mount Allison University in New Brunswick, Canada, include the ever-gracious David Torrance, Hannah Lane, Kathleen Lord, Roberta Lexier, Dave Thomas, Tamara Small, Jane Dryden, Leslie Kern, Kirsty Bell, Sean Fitzpatrick, Owen Griffiths, Bill Lundell, Elaine Naylor, Will Wilson, and Marie Hammond-Callaghan. They helped to cultivate in me a love for the liberal arts that I now share with my students at Kenyon College. Nicola Foote, Frances Davey, Erik Carlson, Mike Cole, Eric

Strahorn, Habtamu Tegegne, Irvin D. S. Winsboro, Mari DeWees, and Paul Bartrop cheered me on as I left the history department at Florida Gulf Coast University. Although many miles now separate us, I find it still so easy to pick up a phone to pop into their offices.

Finishing this project in the halls of Seitz House at Kenyon College has been quite special. One could not imagine a better department at a better school. And crafting the final pages of one's book so close to where the events occurred is a rare opportunity for historians. Sharing space and ideas with Glenn McNair, Sylvia Coulibaly, Wendy Singer, Janet McAdams, Ruth Dunnell, Nurten Kilic-Schubel, Eliza Ablovatski, Peter Rutkoff, Bruce Kinszer, Austin Porter, Will Scott, Bill Suarez-Potts, Roy Wortman, Andrew Ross, Pamela Burson, and two fellow Minnesotans, Jeff Bowman and Stephen Volz, made finishing this project a joy. I have spent a great deal of time along the Wabash, Maumee, and Tippecanoe Rivers researching and writing about the history of the Ohio Valley. It is a real privilege to add the Kokosing River—where I live and work—to that list.

Much of my interest in storytelling and history comes from my family and friends. Stories were a key part of reunions, backyard parties, and road trips. My father, Gary, and mother, Mary, made sure to provide me with the best education possible. They always reminded me that education was richer if accompanied by a strong sense of empathy—that studying the history of humanity mattered little if I checked mine at the door. Jim, Dan, Katie, Katryn, Kevin, Molly, Brian, Evan, Aurora, Aiden, Emory, Danielle, Edward, Liam, and August were spared from having to take part in the crafting of this work, but they shaped in innumerous and positive ways the man who wrote it. Many thanks to my extended family—the Bottigers, the Hobans (especially Tom and Mary Kay), the Durnings, and the Gaffneys—who have welcomed me into their homes during my research trips. All historians should be so lucky as to share their archival discoveries around the dinner table. And all human beings should be so lucky to have such dear friends, including Tom and Mary Fitzpatrick, Noah and Michelle Markon, Nick and Elizabeth Dittrich, Brian and Jill Gilmore, Patrick and Stacey Malley, Michael Calcagno, Kenny and Megan Wolf, Jeff and Vicki Jurek, Ellen and Cecilia Ingham, Steve and Katie Bigus, and Peggy Hoban Chinoski.

The Borderland of Fear

Introduction

It was early June 1812, and open war with Britain was only weeks away. But John Badollet, a settler in the Miami Indian homeland, was far more concerned with his neighbors than the threat posed by any outsider. As Badollet penned yet another letter to his longtime confidant Albert Gallatin, he detailed a deep-seated fear that one of his neighbors "under the appearance of an Indian" might murder him in the streets of Vincennes, Indiana.[1] In a town supposedly stalked by indigenous enemies and a powerful British menace to the north, such a fear might seem irrational. It was not. In fact, the idea of a white man dressing up as an Indian to kill another white man made perfect sense.

Badollet's feelings were not simply the product of nameless fears or personal animosities. Instead, his attitude reflected the legacy of troubled relationships in the Ohio River Valley. Born from decades of contested boundaries, these tensions were brought on by complicated diplomatic efforts between empires, nations, and local settlements. Failed diplomacy often produced violence as Native and Euroamerican communities vied to assert themselves. As a result, boundaries and borders were in constant flux, presenting almost daily challenges to Native peoples and non-Natives alike as they struggled to make their way in a world that was at times bewildering.

In the first years of the nineteenth century, Anglo-American and American Indian settlers flocked to what Americans called Indiana Territory and other places in the Old Northwest. Many great rivers, including the Wabash, Maumee, and Tippecanoe, lay in the heart of the western Ohio River Valley. These rivers and the lands that bordered them would be hotly contested by Americans, the French, and numerous Native peoples. The Miami Indians had controlled this area for almost a century; with the arrival of newcomers, their sovereignty came under attack. Native leaders such as Tenskwatawa, Tecumseh, Main Poc, Little Turtle, and Pacanne watched warily as whites invaded Indian lands in present-day Indiana and Illinois. And Anglo-Americans did not intend to come to Indiana Territory alone. Governor William Henry Harrison hoped to bring a republican system to the territory. He also hoped to bring slaves, but to do so he would have to wrest power from the hands of diverse Native peoples.

It is a commonplace that non-Native settlers feared American Indians. But just as important, white and Indian settlers *understood* that their neighbors feared American Indians. In a world where the fear of Indians and violence shaped daily life, manipulating one's fear, or even that of a neighbor, could prove empowering. Scholars traditionally frame descriptions of western violence through two monoliths: whites and Indians. Yet the situation was much more complicated. Communities, rather than races or nations, defined the western Ohio Valley. These communities—social groups perceiving themselves as distinct from the larger society and inhabiting a specific locality—used fear, lies, distortions, and the threat of violence to advance their political and cultural agendas at the expense of their race and nation. Violence also served to reinforce nascent boundaries that formed in the western Ohio Valley. Violence was personified in the persons of the Shawnee Prophet, his brother Tecumseh, and their pan-Indian endeavor at Prophetstown. Indians and white factions constructed representations of Prophetstown to attack one another—attacks that culminated at the Battle of Tippecanoe in 1811.

How did this place known as Prophetstown come about? In early 1808, Tenskwatawa and his brother Tecumseh trudged west into Indiana Territory. A host of followers accompanied them on their journey through the woods bordering the Miami and Maumee Rivers. Here they built a new kind of community. Three years earlier, in the spring of 1805, Tenskwatawa slipped into a deep trance in which the Great Spirit revealed a plan that would allow Indians to renew their culture. Tenskwatawa hoped that all of his followers would follow the guidelines "that [had] come immediately from the Great Spirit through [him]."[2] Tenskwatawa declared that Indians needed to unite politically and militarily in order to resist the destructive forces of Euroamerican culture. These visions became the basis for Tenskwatawa's plan.

That pan-Indian alliance would require Indians to segregate themselves from Euroamericans in almost every way; the brothers hoped this alliance would lead to what one historian has called "the revitalization of Native American communal life."[3] The Shawnee brothers believed that Indians throughout North America needed to consider themselves as one; otherwise, solitary Native communities would find themselves at the mercy of a white onslaught. But the two leaders' historical fame belies the reality of the situation they faced. The brothers failed to prevent American encroachment into the Ohio River Valley. Communities of French, Miamis, and Americans exaggerated, manipulated, and misunderstood the Prophet's nativist message. They did so to empower their own agendas, which ultimately led to the weakening of the pan-Indian experiment at Prophetstown and subsequent violence.

By looking at the network of lies and rumors that developed in the Wabash-Maumee Valley, we are better equipped to understand the fluid identities, social upheaval, and sociopolitical disagreements within Indian and white communities but also conflict between Indians and whites. As Joshua Piker has demonstrated, identifying these lies allows us to trace "the intimate and powerful connections that constituted the all too fragile worlds out of which they emerged," and the ways in which Natives and whites used lies and violence to stabilize their communities.[4] Communities in the Miami homeland seized every possible opportunity to protect themselves, even if they had to create those opportunities by lying.

The history of violence surrounding Prophetstown was in fact the product of years of lies and rumors that shaped how outsiders understood the nativist town. Simply put, much of what we know about Prophetstown was invented. Interpreters, traders, Indians, and territorial settlers used Prophetstown as a foil for their own political and economic purposes in order to influence the development of society in the Ohio River Valley. From this process, new questions arose: What sort of threat did the Prophet pose to Miami identity? Would the French be included in the American community or shut out of it all together? Would Indiana Territory be slave or free? The ever-simmering threat of conflict in the territory meant that the answers to these questions could lead to real and destructive bloodshed, and they did.

Lying about Prophetstown led to dire consequences. Lies shaped reality, then became reality, and soon residents of the Miami homeland began to depend on those lies to marginalize their enemies and empower and protect their communities. In Indiana Territory, lies and exaggerations appeared in newspaper debates, secret meetings, correspondence, diplomatic disagreements, speeches, and false intelligence. These falsehoods—Michel Brouillet's lies, Elihu Stout's untruths, William Henry Harrison's fabrications, Natives' falsehoods—served as the intellectual context through which settlers made decisions central to their safety. Lies tell us much about settlers' views of themselves as well. Fears of Prophetstown were largely unfounded, but fear served as an impetus to seize Indian lands, attack political enemies, and protect trade. Prophetstown informed a system of thinking that dominated the everyday actions of Anglo-American residents; lies became the interpretive context through which settlers—Native and not—thought about borders.

Yet the violent events that transpired because of the Shawnee Prophet's settlement at Prophetstown during the early nineteenth century were as much a part of the colonial legacies of the western Ohio Valley as they were the expansion of the American republic and the War of 1812. Historians have been too quick to tie one arena of violence to another. Decades-old relationships coupled with divisive cultural and ethnic disputes among Native and white settlements primed the region for violence at Tippecanoe in November 1811, while, according to Paul Gilje, the United States went to war against Great Britain in 1812 to "defend the commerce that sustained the growing consumer revolution" and to "secure its trade and to prevent the impressments of American seamen."[5] As a result, fighting in the War of 1812 erupted along the eastern seaboard, on the high seas, and along the Canadian/American borderland.

While the conflict carried over to the Miami homeland, it only complemented decades of violence that had been commonplace and did not fundamentally alter the motives of the French, Miamis, and American settlers who continued to use the violence of the region to defend local rather than national and international interests. In fact, the violence that Anglos, Europeans, and Indians unleashed upon the Miami homeland demonstrated the inability of the American nation-state and the British Empire to control regional relationships. Although the British and Americans were intimately involved in the many "Battles" for Tippecanoe and the War of 1812, these violent episodes were rooted in fundamentally different causes. We must look beyond the mythology of the Battle of Tippecanoe to access the true historical narrative.[6]

If we are to understand the extent to which the legacy of colonial relationships in the Miami homeland shaped violence and fear toward

Prophetstown, we must place the settler communities within their proper spatial and historical context. Central to this new understanding is situating the Miamis and French within the worlds that they understood. Dan Richter's seminal work *Facing East from Indian Country* challenged scholars to look at Indians outside of a traditional Euroamerican and nationalistic interpretation by asking readers to imagine events from indigenous points of view. Such a task means that in order to understand the Miami world, one must examine eighteenth- and nineteenth-century sources that rarely included Miami voice and testimony. Much of what we know comes from secondhand Euro-American sources. In the colonial era, Miamis were often subsumed with other Native groups, meaning that their voices tend to be described in collective form as one entity, as part of a larger Indian confederacy, or silenced altogether. However, in later years, violence wrought by the Revolutionary War and land cessions with the Americans forced the Miamis to be more vocal about their concerns and made the Americans more keen to observe Miami behavior. The historical record reflects this change in circumstances. I examine the growth of Indian and American nationalisms and the resulting violence between these entities within the context of the Miami homeland. Instead of pushing the Miamis and French to the margins of this region's history, I place them front and center and examine the ways in which American and Native settlers such as the Prophet and Harrison reacted to them.[7]

In order to understand those reactions, we must comprehend the patterns of settlement, diplomacy, and violence within the Miami world of the eighteenth century. These patterns demonstrate that the Miamis routinely pursued village and community interests and rarely if ever operated as a singular political entity, despite the intrusion of European imperial agents. The Miamis, like many Indian communities, eschewed centralized political leadership; that is, they did not all adhere to the same leaders. They forged alliances and relationships with Native and non-Native outsiders and manipulated regional violence to their advantage. Yet the culture of violence that existed in the western Ohio Valley was not simply physical conflict wrought by imperial armies and their Indian allies engaged in battle. It was also the threat of violence that proved empowering. Through deception and overt lies, unreliable alliances, and localized conflict, the Miamis fostered a regional atmosphere of fear and violence to protect their settlements, trade interests, and diplomatic reach.[8]

As Pekka Hämäläinen and Samuel Truett have argued, "We must link borderlands to European and indigenous power, envision new cores, and embrace more nuanced definitions of power."[9] The Miamis did not enjoy a martial culture with which they could seize territory and dictate terms through force, but their ability to use trade, information, and alliances to shape the behavior of others was equally persuasive. These patterns of violence continued to function as a convenient tool in the decades after the collapse of the middle ground, paving the way for the Battle of Tippecanoe and the War of 1812.

Fear made Indians and non-Natives question their physical security and porous borders, but it also forced inhabitants to question the ways in which those borders would be constructed, governed, and imagined. In a sense, fear made them see themselves. Expansion, trade, and diplomacy became dependent upon these perceptions. When the French demonized the Prophet to protect their trade interests, their lies complemented those of the Miamis, who sought to discredit Tenskwatawa in their own way. As the lies built upon one another, so too did the threat posed by the Prophet. This behavior in turn shaped larger physical and conceptual borders; all at the same time that discussions about the nation, race, and British intrigue became more prevalent.

A borderlands analysis is crucial to understanding the ways in which fear and violence reshaped the western Ohio Valley during the early 1800s. *Borderland of Fear* looks beyond the histories of present-day national borders and to understand the means by which community relationships defined borders of the Ohio River Valley. These borders were not national in the sense that they reflected the dictates of a nation-state or imperial power. Instead, these borders reflected a much more local process of ethnogenesis that played a central role in the crystallization of ethnic, racial, and political borders.

This study joins two models of borderlands studies to understand how the inhabitants of the Wabash-Maumee Valley used violence to create more stable physical spaces. The Miamis benefited from the larger imperial contest between Britain and France; their history mirrors an idea now canonical to borderlands studies—borderlands were the "contested boundaries between colonial domains." Yet the Miamis' influence in the region is often dismissed as a simple patina of Indian autonomy. Such a perspective rests on the assumption that Native sovereignty (and therefore borders and borderlands) are only the by-product of imperial-state competition. Pekka Hämäläinen's study of borderlands allows us to strip away the "patina" by recognizing the multiplicity of ways in which Native peoples and nonimperial actors could wield real power. This study connects Aron and Aldeman's study of imperial sovereignty with Pekka

Hämäläinen's discussion of cultural sovereignty to better understand the formation and violent contest over boundaries in the western Ohio Valley. Political power over space was often illusory or at least contingent upon cultural frameworks imposed by Indians. The French, British, and American empires struggled to "maintain distinction and hierarchy as they incorporate[d] new people" because Indian peoples, in particular the Miamis, were able to coerce Europeans into their own systems of power.[10]

Imperial projects shaped Native spaces in the American West, but only as one factor within a larger process of borderland formation. Kinship, interethnic, and even interracial relationships were just as important, often superseding imperial policies mandating political and social hierarchies because they promised the best avenues to facilitate trade. This book looks beyond the study of European colonial domains and state-centered polities to what Pekka Hämäläinen has identified as "other turning points" of power where the "future was far from certain." Indians and Euro-Americans often operated outside the boundaries of empire, state, and race. Instead they relied upon personal and often cross-racial relationships to create stability. These relationships were ignored or often misunderstood first by contemporaries and recently by historians. As Hämäläinen argues, such relationships "functioned at scales that were often too small for centralizing institutions to control, contain, or comprehend."[11] With such a community-focused outlook, we can better recognize how rarely these imagined national and racial spaces came to fruition.

Despite the fact that the Miami homeland, the frontier republic, and Prophetstown existed in the minds of settlers as discrete and powerful entities, they remained weak and difficult (if not impossible) to defend after 1800. In order to determine the physical boundaries (or borders) of the territories that they claimed as their own, inhabitants had to first conceptualize and then to make clear who they were as a people. They had to make real their sovereign identities. This was an enormously difficult task given the complicated history of kinship and trade in the region. In the late eighteenth century, Miami communities began to fight for diplomatic recognition, which forced them to announce their physical and cultural boundaries to outsiders. Yet factionalism and disagreements within the Miami communities often undercut any success that they might have enjoyed in defending their borders. As Americans and refugee Indians flooded the Wabash-Maumee Valley, the Miamis lost the ability to incorporate outsiders into their communities. Outsiders no longer respected Miami authority; many of the Miamis were partial to the Americans, who were part of a much larger trading market. Americans, the French, and Indians fought to impose their will upon each another. No one party was successful, meaning that accommodation and alliances, rather than force, became the tools through which communities protected themselves after 1795. Settlers began to vocalize their rights to the lands and to define their status in order to carve out cultural niches for themselves. People defined themselves by their relationship to local trade networks, alliances, and conflicts rather than racial or political philosophies.

But it would be a mistake to speak of this region after 1795 as either an American or Miami borderland. The region bound by the Maumee and Wabash Rivers ought to be called the Miami-American borderland because both Miami and American interests were central to the area's trade, the development of violence, and settlement. Borders remained weak and contested because no one community had established itself as sovereign. The rhetoric of Indian nativism along with Revolutionary republicanism provided the tools through which settlers defended evolving notions of sovereignty. Yet both groups routinely used the language of nationalism to hide ambitions that were far more local. People understood their sovereignty—the ability to maintain independent spatial and cultural boundaries—as contingent upon their relationships with outsiders, in particular imperial state projects, *and* their relationships within their communities. Sovereignty was not simply about political power but also about cultural continuity. While France, Britain, and the United States settled parts of the Miami homeland, their imperial ambitions remained dependent upon cultural outliers who were key to trade and diplomacy. Dependence upon these cultural go-betweens eroded most efforts to extend political sovereignty over the region.

Thus the relative weakness of the imperial state allowed communities and individual actors to exercise their own interests in ways that made clear the contingent nature of sovereignty. Michel Brouillet, a French trader, claimed to be in league with the American imperial project when in fact he was carrying papers of marque from both Britain and the United States. Brouillet wanted his family and community to profit from trading and was not interested in extending trade for a European or American empire. Miami Indians and French traders continued to shape trade and diplomacy, two key ingredients for the sort of sovereign nations that Indians and Americans alike envisioned.

Discussing sovereignty is a difficult task when looking at the multi-ethnic and multinational settlements in the Ohio River Valley. Most scholarly examinations of the Battle of Tippecanoe and the War of 1812 tend to focus on assessing the sovereignty of the French, British, or American empires. Sovereignty is often only a point of concern for historians of American Indians after Indians have lost it. *Borderland of Fear* looks at the ways in which people strived to build sovereign spaces that were sometimes collaborative and sometimes in opposition. Focusing on sovereignty rather than empires, nation-states, or nativism allows for a more balanced assessment of power relationships in the Wabash-Maumee Valley. Groups such as the Miamis did not have an empire, nor did they wish to build a nation-state, but this should in no way suggest that they lacked influence and power.

It is important to remember that Native and non-Anglo agendas have a continuity and a history of their own that is often little remarked in the current scholarship. Native and French agendas played an important role in shaping and weakening American colonialism by providing fragile American communities with convenient alliances that were often self-serving and short-lived. Despite decades of marginalization following the Revolutionary War, the French and Miamis discovered avenues through which they could protect themselves, even if that meant amplifying the threat posed by an Indian community that was also at odds with the Americans. The French and Miamis were simply unwilling to subvert their ethnic and cultural identity to a larger racial and/or national polity, whether it be at Vincennes or Prophetstown. Their actions require us to recenter our understanding of power and boundaries on communities rather than ideas of nation and race that developed years later.

Moreover, these convenient alliances were the tools through which communities began to assert themselves and to create relationships that would be central to Native and American territorial borders. While European and American governments demarcated their possessions through the use of maps and laws, the residents of the region tended to see things differently. They respected boundaries that were produced by familiar people rather than distant political entities. Whether it be a Native community's ability to control trade at Kekionga or the Americans' ability to regulate alcohol sales out of Vincennes, the boundaries of the Miami world were local in nature. It was one thing to claim lands of the Ohio Valley and something else entirely to control them. To understand the boundaries that governed the western Ohio Valley, one must understand the realities faced by all communities in the region, not just the imagined tale of monoliths that has for so long dominated our memory.

Making real the social and political spaces imagined by the various ethnic factions was a difficult process. It required both the control of physical space and the power to attract followers through homogeneous cultural values. The growth of a more rigid and definable American nation did not occur simply through population growth and territorial acquisitions, but through a complicated process of mis-remembering. The American "nation" was not a product of the white conquest of Indians, but a chance result of ethnic factions creating a borderland of lies, a social space contingent on misinformation and exaggeration designed to protect interested parties and factions. Collectively, their lies created what one scholar calls a "shared nationalism." Through lies, the French, Miamis, and Americans created an official history that transformed a "terrain of local and regional autonomies into a more homogenized and nationalized domain." Residents of the Wabash-Maumee Valley created a borderland by creating a narrative the nation-state would soon employ to justify and mythologize westward expansion. In effect, local residents of the Valley empowered a floundering state by creating a narrative state officials used to tie citizens to a central "hegemonic strategy."[12]

As diplomats, politicians, governors, and territorial officials defended American interests in western territories, they routinely used the tropes of expansion, racism, and violence born out of the Tippecanoe conflict to justify their endeavors. They continued a process of mis-remembering initiated by ethnic factionalism on the Miami homeland. Growing regional instability also played an important role in the ethnogenesis of Indian and non-Native communities because it forced these peoples to vocalize their ethnic identities as they defended their physical boundaries and material interests. These communities constituted social groups that inhabited similar locales and that shared a distinct identity and governing system based upon common economic and political goals. As these communities began to defend their shared interests, they typically pointed to physical spaces (homelands) that were the birthplace of an imagined identity (ethnicity) based upon categories such as common culture, language, ancestry, race, and nationality. This work identifies Americans, British, and French as ethnic groups but also uses the same term to describe the Shawnees, Miamis, and Kickapoos. The challenge to understanding this period of ethnogenesis among Indian and non-Native communities lies in recognizing that there are myriad definitions of these two terms, which were both different, evolving, and contested at the same time.[13]

The complexity of this story demands a microhistorical approach. This work builds on Patrick Griffin's *American Leviathan* and Peter Silver's *Our Savage Neighbors* to demonstrate that the causes for Native-white violence were rooted in intraracial factionalism, not interracial disputes. Although white settlers certainly feared Indians, much of that fear was a by-product of political and ethnic factionalism within white border communities. Although whites undoubtedly spoke of an Indian menace, they often did so to demonize their own white neighbors. As settlers realized that they could control the development of the republic by managing the growth of their territory, they seized upon Indian affairs as a means to a broader end. Taking a microhistorical approach to the early republic's frontier is not simply about the "world writ small," but in fact a demonstration of how the larger world—the territorial one—was a product of national ideals redefined and made whole on the local level. Settlers victimized each other by creating images of Indians divorced from actual realities. As war with Great Britain approached in 1812, those images fueled violence at places such as Tippecanoe, which also shaped the growing diplomatic crisis between the Americans and British.

Little has been written about the relationship between national ideologies and local realties. Particularly important are the ways in which local communities refashioned, resisted, and even ignored territorial laws and ideas of republican nationalism in order to protect local relationships. Prophetstown and the territorial capital at Vincennes represented two examples of the competing nationalisms "imposed" by peoples not indigenous to the territory. Some recent scholars have challenged the nationalistic dichotomies that have framed examinations of Native-white relationships on the Miami homeland. Robert Owens in *Mr. Jefferson's Hammer* examines the extent to which territorial governor William Henry Harrison, rather than President Thomas Jefferson, shaped and defined Indian policy for the western territories. Owens challenges scholars to examine how local actors reshaped national ideologies. Jay Gitlin's *Bourgeoisie Frontier* looks beyond the Americans to the French and asserts that the French as an ethnic group should be considered as an important influence on local society and regional identities. Rather than see the French as subsumed into the American nation-state, Gitlin demonstrates that they found ways to defend their interests despite the influx of American settlers.[14]

Though the Battle of Tippecanoe was fought in 1811, in some ways, the struggle for that place—and what it represented—had begun one hundred years earlier and would continue into the 1840s. Resistance and violence defined the Miami and American borderlands, and these borderlands were as much the result of conflicting ethnic boundaries and cultural disputes as they were lines drawn by competing nations and races.[15] Accommodation certainly took place, but to what end? Indian and European peoples undoubtedly coexisted, but to support ulterior motives. Their overtures at collaboration concealed their own interests, which were hidden beneath a veil of misinformation.

Yet non-Indians suffered from the same cultural factionalism prevalent in Native society, which allowed "third peoples" to play a powerful role in the shaping of boundaries. By looking at the ethnic differences of Indian and Euroamerican groups within the Ohio Valley—and the pervasive lying among Indian, French, and American communities—traditional monolithic portrayals of racial and national conflict vanish in the face of what Joshua Piker calls "the fragility—the inherent, bone-deep, all-pervasive weakness—of power in both Indian nations and [Euroamerican] nations."[16] In such a world, groups such as the Miamis were able to gain traction just as the Americans were able to do the same. In eerily similar ways, they both won the battles for Tippecanoe.

1 /   Facing East from Miami Country

It was a bloodbath. As described by nineteenth-century ethnographer C. C. Trowbridge, two Seneca warriors ran furiously to their village "crying out, we are undone, lost, killed, throw away your kettle and stop the dance!" Yet no one listened. This despite the fact that each Seneca warrior, bloodied and maddened, had a blood-soaked human head swinging from his neck. In their vengeful wrath in retaliation for the destruction of one of their villages, a Miami Indian war party had also cut off the hands, noses, and lips of the two still-living Seneca warriors whom the Miamis had surprised, making sure that the gruesome disfigurement would pierce the other Seneca with deep and unrelenting fear. The intensity of the Seneca celebration over their supposed victory against the Miamis drowned out the desperate cries of their two brethren. Eventually a few Senecas spied the absolute horror before them and screamed for the dance to stop, but the noise of song and drum drowned out their voices. Within minutes, elation gave way to fear. Horrified at seeing the decapitated heads of their friends, the Senecas panicked. As the Miamis recounted years later, "all was horror & confusion" once the Seneca realized what was going on. They threw the kettle aside, scattered in fear, while the dance "changed into raving and horrific extravagancies."[1]

After decades of displacement and suffering, the Miamis had seized the moment. By surprising a Seneca force deep in celebration, the Miamis had found a way to turn the table on their well-armed enemies. No longer would they tolerate the Haudenosaunee destroying their towns, murdering their elders, and ritually eating their children. Like many Indian communities stalked by the Haudenosaunee, the Miamis had no other choice but to respond in kind and to turn celebration into chaos. In doing so, the Miamis had also asserted their right to defend both their brethren and their homeland in the western Ohio Valley.[2] They stood as proud Miamis.

Such violence typified the deep-seated animosities Great Lakes Indian peoples had toward the Haudenosaunee, a confederacy of five Iroquoian peoples responsible for the mid-seventeenth-century cataclysm now known as the Beaver Wars. Fueled largely by a competition over furs (and the access to guns that pelts provided), the violence wrought by the Haudenosaunee had remade the Ohio Valley by forcing Indian peoples to abandon their ancestral homelands and to seek shelter in multiethnic Indian villages throughout present-day Ohio, Indiana, Illinois, and Wisconsin. Preyed upon by much larger Indian confederacies to their east and west, plied by imperial powers for alliances and trade goods, and confronted with disputes in their own communities, the Miamis used their geographical location and trade power to shape diplomacy and regional violence to their advantage.[3]

The Miamis continued this behavior throughout the eighteenth and into the nineteenth century, working diligently to deflect violence wrought by European colonialism by incorporating traders, missionaries, and diplomats into their communities. The Ohio Valley was in reality a no-man's-land for non-Indians, a place where French, British, and American imperialists imagined themselves to be sovereign despite having limited influence over both Indians and Euroamerican settlers. With each failed colonial thrust, the Miamis responded. When the British and French fought over trade with the Miamis in the mid-1740s, the Miamis made sure to trade with both groups, never completely isolating one or the other in order to maintain European competition for the Miami market. When British emissaries ventured into the Illinois country in midcentury, the Miamis constructed an umbrella of protectionism over these agents to facilitate a broader system of reciprocity. And when the British and American rebels fought to displace each other from Miami country during the Revolutionary War, the Miamis did not fully engage in the conflict, for it was obvious that British and rebel claims to sovereignty—no matter the victories they imagined themselves to have won—were empty.[4]

By forging trade and kinship connections with Native and non-Native interlopers throughout the 1700s, the Miamis built a system of reciprocity that was as much cultural as it was economic. This spirit of reciprocity was readily apparent at Kekionga (present-day Fort Wayne, Indiana), the Miami cultural capital. One could visit the Miami settlement and expect to see numbers of Lenapes, Shawnees, Potawatomies, French, and British living in relative peace, trading and interacting within Miami parameters of diplomacy. Miami leader Le Gris (although "very polite in manner") acted like a "general or commandant" by ordering French children to assist him and by determining in which traders' homes Indian visitors would lodge. Le Gris tempered his authoritative nature by providing meat—turkeys, deer, bison—for non-Native visitors at Kekionga, often only expecting some rum in return. Expectations for proper behavior extended outside of Kekionga as well. Traders felt the need to meet with Miami leaders to learn the proper etiquette "when they went into the Interior Parts of the Indian Country" to trade.[5]

One American soldier described Kekionga in 1790 as made of "several tolerable good log houses, said to have been occupied by British [and French] traders; a few pretty good gardens with some fruit trees, and vast fields of corn in almost every direction." A Miami leader commented that Kekionga was a "glorious gate which the Miamis had the happiness to own, and through which all the good words of their chiefs had to pass from the north to the south, and from the east to the west."[6] Central to their success were able leaders such as Pacanne, Le Gris, and Little Turtle who deftly navigated decades of complicated imperial and intertribal diplomacy to maintain and expand Miami influence in the Wabash-Maumee Valley.

Surviving the Beaver Wars and the subsequent spread of disease and refugees in what one scholar has called the "social and cultural transformation" of the Great Lakes region was contingent on a number of factors. The fate of the Illinois Confederacy, a grouping of thirteen Algonquian Indian communities that dominated present-day Illinois and portions of eastern Missouri, Iowa, and northern Arkansas during the seventeenth century, loomed large; the combined onslaught of smallpox and warfare had ravaged that group, thinning their numbers from ten thousand to one thousand by 1770. Yet the population of the Miamis remained stable during the same time period, and within the first few decades of the eighteenth century, the Miamis were able to assert themselves along the Wabash and Maumee Rivers. They periodically raided Indian communities for goods and expanded their agricultural production. As the Beaver Wars ended and the fur trade became a liability, Indians and Europeans alike sought to trade at Miami villages such as Kekionga where they could enjoy relative stability. The Miamis could use such trade to secure their influence from the St. Joseph River of modern-day Indiana and Michigan to the Maumee River in present-day Ohio and down the Wabash River to present-day Vincennes, Indiana.[7]

Oral traditions reflect the centrality of the western Ohio Valley to the Miami people. Although contemporary Miamis connect their emergence as a people to the St. Joseph River, the Miami-speaking communities of the Weas and Piankashaws left their kinsman in the late seventeenth century and migrated southwest along the Wabash. Oral tradition states that the Miami peoples at St. Joseph were so numerous (close to three thousand people) that migration of a part of the tribe was necessary. The Miamis at Kekionga, the Weas at Ouiatenon, and the Piankashaws at Vincennes developed a vast trading network along the Wabash and Maumee Rivers. Here, according to the ethnographer C. C. Trowbridge, the Miamis were "very industrious." One Frenchman remarked that although the Miamis lived among Potawatomies, Wendats, Sauks, Foxes, and others, the Miamis were the "long residents at the place." One scholar has more recently framed *Myaamionki* (place of the Miamis) by differentiating between a core area (the Wabash River corridor) and the hinterlands surrounding it (an area bound by lands east of the Illinois and north of the Ohio and Scioto Rivers) that were shared by a variety of different Native communities.[8] He, too, considers both of these geographical areas as Miami ancestral homelands.[9]

Although the Miamis had linguistic ties to the Illinois and suffered their fair share of displacement, the former were fewer in number and thus better able to handle the disruptions wrought by the Haudenosaunee. Rather than compete solely for finite resources such as furs, the Miamis favored trading corn in particular and other foodstuffs such as bison and deer. According to a French report from 1718, they grew a special corn that was "unlike that of our tribes at Detroit" in that it was "white . . . with much finer husks and much whiter flour." By concentrating their efforts on subsistence goods needed by both friend and foe, the Miami positioned themselves in a way that made it difficult for any one group to displace them. More important, corn was central to Miami customs and traditions, so by allowing Europeans and Indians to participate in the corn trade, the Miamis used European trade missions to reinforce their sovereignty.[10]

Corn was not a mere crop to the Miamis; *minjipi*, or "corn spirit," played an important role, for they believed that *minjipi* determined the success of their bison hunts and safety as a people. The Miami seasonal

MAP 1. The Miami homeland in the mid- to late 1700s.

calendar and many traditions, including celebrations marking the three annual communal harvests, revolved around corn. One French-to-Miami/Illinois dictionary authored by a Jesuit priest in the late seventeenth century listed "over 71 variously inflected lexical forms related to corn," while only citing 32 terms for tobacco.[11]

Although Miami women were increasingly marginalized from diplomatic and trade negotiations, they nonetheless played a central role in the functioning of diplomacy. Women were central to the production of corn; they controlled the planting, harvesting, and processing of thousands of bushels a year, which became more pronounced after the Beaver Wars. They were in charge of and facilitated the distribution of goods that were necessary for diplomacy to take place. Such actions allowed the Miamis to shape an interdependent trade network.[12] Miami agricultural surpluses fed refugee Indian communities, fur traders, and even diplomatic councils.

As early as 1715, Europeans were orienting themselves around Miami corn. According to a report filed to the French minister in 1715, when the corn "so completely failed at Detroit," the French sent a small deputation "to the Miamis to buy some." Corn and other grains could also play a key role in diplomacy. One scholar notes that "the agricultural surplus produced by Native women also supported military operations in the western Great Lakes." French voyageurs described the vast amounts of food available and the important role that women played in agricultural diplomacy. One Frenchman remarked, "Indian women daily brought in something fresh, we wanted not for watermelons, bread made of Indian corn . . . and other such things." More significantly, foodstuffs Native women provided would then be used to facilitate diplomatic negotiations and agreements through important community gatherings and feasts, such as when Le Gris's wife prepared a thirty-pound turkey for the English traders at Kekionga. Their capacity as agriculturalists and horticulturalists was empowering. Women could exert influence in terms of how trade was negotiated, and this influence was long-lived, lasting into the nineteenth century. If wronged, Native women could even persuade their communities to abandon alliances with European powers.[13]

Most importantly, the centrality of women and agriculture in Miami society provided insurance against the volatile fur trade by providing the Miamis with a commodity (corn) that was needed by various Native and non-Native peoples. According to Governor Vaudreuil in the fall of 1716, the English, too, sought commercial relations with the Miamis, offering them merchandise at half the price of the French. Vaudreuil realized that pro-English Indian couriers were "incessantly sending" the Miamis offers to "gain them over" to English trade, and he hoped they would remove from English influence. Despite Vaudreuil's pleading, the Miamis did not abide.[14]

That the Miamis enjoyed such influence over trade does not necessarily suggest that they adopted European norms. In fact, the control of Kekionga and trade along the Wabash River reflected the continuity in Miami customs. Even as late as the 1770s, the lieutenant governor of Detroit, Henry Hamilton, wrote of the important role that Native women played in regional affairs. In recording his venture south to Fort Sackville in Vincennes, Hamilton described Methusaagai's (an Ojibwe leader) envoy to the Miamis when he delivered a belt from "the Women living upon the lakes . . . exhorting them to work hard with their hoes, to raise corn for the Warriors who should take up the Axe for the Father the King of England."[15] Agriculture was power. By controlling corn, the Miamis—and in this case Miami women—could facilitate both their cultural and diplomatic stability. This was especially important and evident at places such as Kekionga. By controlling movement through the portage, the Miamis managed trade, and while the Miamis allowed outsiders such as the French and British to move goods, European traders did so in line with the Miamis' wishes. If not, Europeans risked at best an abandonment of this convenient alliance and at worst a violent display of Miami power that might be aimed at the destruction of their settlements.

Europeans recognized the potential power of the region and their inability to harness it. The Sieur de Vincennes remarked that he was "not in condition to prevent [the Miamis] from trading with the English, because it would be necessary to bring them altogether," that he did not possess the merchandise to appease them, and that the French garrison was "too feeble to constrain this nation." His inability to "bring them altogether" reflects the localized nature of Miami society, that they did not function as one cohesive group, and that by refusing to function as one group, the Miamis gave preference to whom they pleased and enjoyed the independence that the regional trade provided. Furthermore, no substantive destruction of the trade network occurred during the eighteenth century. Few in number, French and British traders could not risk alienating themselves from the very people who made trade possible. One Frenchman remarked that the region bound by the Wabash was "one of the more important ones of [New France], since it is a barrier to obstruct the advance of the English." The British, too, recognized the potential might of the western Ohio Valley. Sir William Johnson, the British superintendent of Indian affairs, described the area as "one of the finest Corn countries in the World" that could supply the various forts throughout the region, along with Florida and Louisiana. Aware of the imperial competition between Britain and France, the Miamis successfully imposed a set of limits along the Wabash-Maumee corridor that forced outsiders—Native and otherwise—to adjust to Miami needs. In some cases, the Miamis even demanded that the French lower prices.[16]

Controlling the Portage

The location of the Wabash and Maumee Rivers provided a central thoroughfare through which trade goods and people could travel from the Great Lakes south to the Ohio River and then into the trans-Mississippi West. The Wabash ran on a southwesterly course, stretching nearly five hundred miles from present-day Fort Wayne, Indiana, to Vincennes. Some seventy miles south of that town, the Wabash emptied into the Ohio River. This made it possible for boats to navigate from Lake Erie on the Maumee River to Kekionga, the major trading center of the Wabash-Maumee Valley, then down the Wabash River to Vincennes, and eventually into the Illinois country. It was a fluid waterway except for an eight-mile portage connecting the Maumee to the Wabash River. This key portage is where the Miami established Kekionga, guaranteeing contact with any trade missions from Detroit or Pennsylvania. It was also a place of residence, where traders could live and profit. Veteran trader and diplomat George Croghan described "forty or fifty cabins, besides nine or ten French houses," and "soil rich and well watered" framing the town.[17] Traders and settlers could buy and sell corn, cloth, guns, liquor, and pelts that they had collected from Canada to Illinois.

Such a world was not always peaceful, but in most circumstances, the Miamis managed violence to their benefit. When war broke out between Britain and France in King George's War during the 1740s, the Miamis were quick to use the violence to expand their trade interests, even if that meant attacking their fellow Miamis. For instance, Memeskia, the Miami leader at Vincennes, abandoned his pro-French Miami community and attacked a pro-French Miami community at Kekionga in 1747 in order to court British influence and trade. Memeskia stopped short of destroying the pro-French community and instead convinced its residents to move to Pickawillany, a pro-British Miami settlement numbering close to two thousand people. The British made the apt decision to welcome Memeskia. Although such behavior might lead one to believe that the Miamis were pawns of the French and British, this was not the case. The violence that Memeskia created at Kekionga was not about destruction, but about control. One Frenchman reported that the Miamis who had been living at Kekionga "promised . . . to abandon their village to settle them at Pickawillany." As the population of Memeskia's community grew, so too did his standing with their British trading partners. In fact, the British planned to build two forts on "each side" of Memeskia's settlement that would also include a blacksmith for his use.[18]

Despite actions by the Miamis that demonstrated their regional autonomy and influence, the French and British each imagined claims to the Ohio Valley by the 1740s. The French justified their claim through La Salle's seventeenth-century explorations of the region and the British through more recent Indian treaties. In 1748, the French governor of Canada attempted to check the growing influence of British traders by sending veteran commander Pierre-Joseph Céleron on a mission to mark the physical boundaries of French control. At key river tributaries throughout the Ohio Valley, he nailed a copper plate to a tree and buried an inscribed lead plate in the soil below as a marker of French authority and influence. Yet it was the actions of the Miamis such as Memeskia, not those of the French or British, that defined the boundaries of trade. On the surface, such violence seems to be the logical product of Indian competition for European trade goods. In reality, factors—localized Miami communities facilitating trade with Europeans—central to Miami society were in play. As disparate Miami communities sought to strengthen themselves by displacing others, they willingly attacked neighboring Miami peoples if necessary; however, such violence was not overly destructive and was designed to disrupt rather than to destroy. Despite the apparent anger and deep frustration evident in French communications, one French leader said that Memeskia's community needed only to "return to their duty and settle down in their villages" and their "Father Onontio would pardon their past faults."[19] In reality, the French had few options left other than to make their trade more attractive and to hope for the Miamis to return.

Indians routinely reconsidered European alliances, which were part of the fluid and ever-evolving nature of Miami society. Thus, the Pickawillany Miamis remained receptive to French overtures, even welcoming Céleron into their communities in 1749. Céleron begged the Miamis to return to Kekionga and received nominal assurances that the Miamis would visit that spring when their hunts drew them near. Memeskia considered rejoining the French in subsequent months, but finally decided to remain with the British. Remaining open to French overtures was key because it allowed Miami leaders to shape the regional market by making themselves a commodity to be courted. The French and British remained on the periphery while Miami communities jockeyed for control of places such as Kekionga and overall influence on the Miami borderland. In fact, the Miamis continued to settle according to local needs and circumstance. As a result, there remained four primary Miami settlements in 1749. Charles de Raymond at Kekionga identified Le Pied

Froid (Piedfroid), which was pro-French; Memeskia at the Great Miami River with the English; another headed by Le Gris along the Tippecanoe; and one near the Potawatomies at the St. Joseph River. Despite their allegiances, Raymond complained, "Every Indian is a rascal, and practically no reliance can be put on their promises."[20]

If the French wanted the Miamis to return, they would have to fight for them. Indeed, they did. After the French under Charles Langlade captured Pickawillany in 1752 along with 3,000 pounds sterling worth of trade goods, the Miamis quickly migrated back to Kekionga. The pro-French Indian force supporting Langlade killed the British supporter Memeskia and ritually ate him after boiling his body. It took very little for Memeskia's followers to reestablish their ties to the French; according to the Marquis Michel-Ange, the Duquesne de Menneville, they had only to send "two English scalps which the rebel Miamis had taken by way of proof of their complete return to the will of their Father Onontio." To the marquis, such an overture "seemed to indicate a sincere repentance of their past fault."[21]

By the 1750s, the Miamis inhabited a cultural and economic borderland of their own making; this place was one around which Europeans and Indians oriented themselves. In 1750, a surveyor for Virginia colony named George Mercer who traveled throughout Miami territory commented that the Miamis were "the most powerful People to the Westward of the English Settlements, & much superior to the six Nations with whom they are now in Amity: their Strength and Numbers are not thoroughly known, as they have but lately traded with the English." Their influence was evident as "other nations or Tribes still further to the Westward daily coming in to [the Miamis] & tis thought their Power and Interest reaches to the Westward of the Mississippi." Indeed Kekionga was "one of the strongest Indian Towns upon this Part of the Continent." It was clear that the Miamis would determine with whom they traded and would alter alliances if their terms were not met.[22]

British participation in the regional market benefited the Miamis as well. The British tried to induce Native peoples to trade with them by offering inexpensive products. While this benefited the British and Indians, it undercut the French. One French trader commented that the "English spare nothing to keep [the Miamis] and to draw away the remainder of those [who were working with the French]. The excessive price of French goods in this post, the great bargains which the English give, as well as the large presents which they make to the tribes, have entirely disposed those tribes in their favor and induce them to go off

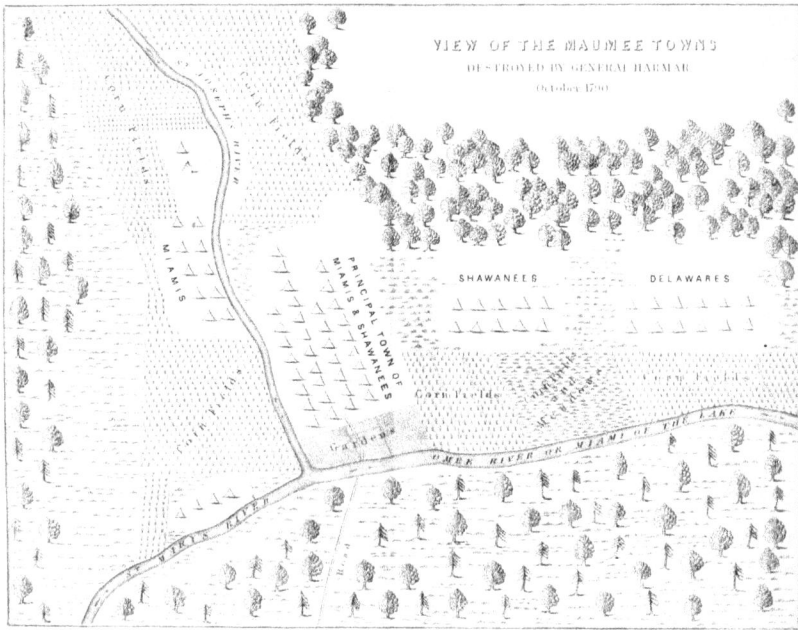

FIGURE 1. "A View of the Maumee Towns Destroyed by General Josiah Harmar in 1790, Modeled after a Drawing by Major Ebenezer Denny." Ebenezer Denny, *Military Journal of Major Ebenezer Denny, an Officer in the Revolutionary and Indian Wars*. Philadelphia, Historical Society of Pennsylvania, 1859 (STATES Va 62 v.7). Courtesy of the Pennsylvania Historical Society.

to the English."[23] The contests to win control of the Indian trade forced Europeans to lower their prices, keeping the market in the Indians' favor. When French trade goods became too expensive, the Miamis extended their trade east into Pennsylvania, and the British responded in kind by sending emissaries west.

Even the physical trading posts were in Miami country. Both French and British traders made sure to build their forts in the heart of Indian country. The French had constructed Fort Ouiatenon near present-day Lafayette in 1717; this small garrison was home to a dozen traders and their métis families. The British had settled at Pickawillany on the Great Miami River, a post that quickly developed into a key trading center for Pennsylvanians and a key departure point for English traders looking to trade in the heart of Miami country. Many of the Indians in the Wabash Valley had familial and diplomatic relations with the French. But when the British offered cheaper prices, the Miamis could ignore kinship and clan connections without fear of repercussion.[24]

It was possible to avoid meaningful repercussions because often European traders were behaving in ways similar to the Miamis. Empire simply did not operate on the ground in the ways that many policy makers in France and Britain wished it had. Many traders, in particular the French coureurs de bois, abandoned the strict rules of their mercantilist empires to trade with whom they pleased. French woodsmen sought out the best market for their goods, which often meant trading with the British. Not only were the French and British powerless to level any sort of real punishment upon the Miamis for trading with the enemy, but they were increasingly trading with them.

As a result, the Miamis did not facilitate their own decline through violence or by incorporating certain aspects of European culture, but instead empowered themselves at the expense of neighboring Indian and European peoples. And by maintaining relationships with both the French and the British, Miami peoples effectively appeased imperial powers that might have otherwise forced their way into the region. Despite efforts by outsiders to control regional trade, the geographic and cultural borders of trading in Miami country—that is, the rules of trading—remained clearly Miami. The Miamis used their unique position in the Ohio Valley to build a borderland by playing off rivalries, to benefit by not simply "occupying the lands 'in between'" in order to survive, as suggested by some scholars, but to evolve as a people who were *culturally* in between. By treating corn as a commodity and by adapting an assortment of European trade goods such as hoes, guns, capes, hats, bed lace, mirrors, and tea into their society, the Miamis, in particular Miami women, used European goods and even oriented themselves toward European markets to maintain Miami independence.[25] Although the Miamis were not quick to join a European war, they certainly recognized—as did other Native peoples—their ability to shape such violence through the trade network they helped to facilitate.

The reality of Miami life necessitated that they trade with outsiders—Native or not—which meant that the Miamis never really saw their "in between" status as a position eventually to be undone. The movement of both the British and French into Miami country was so limited, and those two imperial powers often so weak, that neither group ever truly represented a threat to Miami hegemony. Instead, they accepted it as permanent and necessary. In that sense, their identity was contingent upon including the British and French in their communities because they were key to the regional trade market. Thus, their ability to play imperial powers against each other was not, as some scholars conclude, a "patina" of Indian autonomy but instead a reflection of Miami identity and sovereignty.[26]

It is important to consider that the borderland was not the product of any centralized political system through which the Miamis mandated diplomatic and economic alliances. In the Wabash-Maumee Valley, empires and nations, whether native or non-Native, never controlled physical space in the manner in which the colonizers intended. The Miamis were not so cohesive as to be able to dominate the entire region politically. Rather, small but stable Miami groups exerted power through incorporation and manipulation of Indian communities weakened by disease and warfare, as well as fairly small and localized French and British communities searching for trading partners and military alliances. Mercer recognized as much in his journal when he described the Miamis as being "Very numerous" but "consisting of many different tribes under the same Form of Government," noting that each tribe had a "particular Chief or King."[27]

This was clearly the case for the Miamis: local needs and identities persisted despite the efforts of imperial powers. Miami communities sought to protect their important Maumee-Wabash trade portage and riverine settlements by cultivating individual relationships rather than imperial ones.[28] Face-to-face meetings were far more important than dictates from distant political capitals. And deflecting violence endemic to the region and using it to defend their interests, the Miamis allowed the French and British, as well as Kickapoo, Shawnee, and Potawatomi Indians to live among them without fear of conquest and displacement. The Wabash-Maumee Valley was not an enormous battlefield on which the French, British, and Americans fought for dominance. Nor was it a place where Indian people could only react to imperial intrusions. Although it seems counterintuitive, the Miamis' lack of military power during the first half of the eighteenth century would make them more powerful in the following decades by allowing them room to maneuver and manage European and Indian communities.

Just as Memeskia's former Miami community returned to Kekionga, a new phase of violence extending from the mid-1750s through the mid-1790s increasingly militarized the Miamis as they fought to protect their trade interests. This meant that they were increasingly orienting themselves around British, French, or American armies, and mobilizing themselves in relationship to those armies, not just trade. Although the Seven Years' War and Pontiac's Rebellion ravaged the eastern Great Lakes region during the late 1750s and early 1760s, the Miamis used this violence to once again assert themselves diplomatically through captive exchange and trade. For instance, some Miami warriors participated in the disastrous defeat of Edward Braddock at Fort Duquesne in 1755. And while they resisted any substantive role in the frontier violence that erupted at the close of the Seven Years' War, they did reassert their hold over the region by capturing the British garrison at Kekionga in 1763, an event often portrayed by scholars as evidence of a Miami-French alliance. The seizure of the British soldiers, however, should not be seen as an affirmation of the larger fight by Great Lakes Indians against the British during Pontiac's Rebellion. This was more a corrective, a use of violence by the Miamis to maintain control of a waterway and portage area in a period after the Seven Years' War when the British were occupying forts once controlled by the French.[29] Given that the Seven Years' War ended with the expulsion of the French from the Great Lakes, some Miamis may have believed it necessary to remind the British that they remained.

Capturing the British garrison at Kekionga was one aspect of the Miamis' ability to restrict the efforts of British officials throughout the region. This was increasingly necessary after 1763, when the British occupied formerly French forts such as Detroit and began moving west to access trade once only the privy of the French. Their capacity to protect and even rescue British emissaries also reminded the British that the Miamis controlled diplomacy and could revoke their benevolence when needed. Increasingly convinced that they could not govern the lands west of the Appalachians, the British sent diplomats into the Miami homeland to negotiate peaceful relations. One such emissary, Captain Thomas Morris, had the permission of the Miamis to visit the Illinois country in 1764, yet he met with grave danger when Miami Indians at Kekionga captured and imprisoned him.

Such kidnappings proved quite common and often served as a key part of regional diplomacy. Seizing the opportunity presented by Morris's capture, Miami leader Pacanne rode in on a horse, grabbed his neck, and then freed him from certain execution. Quite possibly he had planned the stunt. Pacanne's entrance suggests that this was more than a last-minute attempt to save Morris's life. As Pacanne untied Morris, he proclaimed that he gave him "his life." Morris remarked that Pacanne was "just out of his minority," suggesting that the Miami leader may have used the threat of violence (and his ability to save Morris's life) to assert his newfound authority. It was skillful political theater. The grateful

FIGURE 2. Miami leader Pacanne, ca. 1776–1778, by Henry Hamilton (MS Eng 509.2 [4]). Courtesy of Houghton Library, Harvard University.

Morris gave a note to Pacanne "entreating all Englishmen to use [him] kindly." The relationship paid off when Pacanne visited Detroit and the English gave him "all our blankets and shirts" and a "very handsome present to lay at his feet."[30] Morris abandoned his mission and quickly returned to Detroit, reminding the British that Pacanne and the Miamis not only possessed sufficient power to control diplomatic affairs in the region, but that the region was not to be traveled, let alone governed, by the British.

Miami influence over regional affairs was just as apparent in lands farther west. In 1765, when Indians from the Illinois country kidnapped the British diplomat and trader George Croghan, the Miamis came to his rescue as well. Croghan hoped to stop the independent and self-sovereign settlers of the region—namely groups such as the Black Boys—from completely destroying the expanding Indian trade out of Philadelphia. Disgusted with violence they blamed on "savage" Indians, the Black Boys disrupted imperial trade between the British and Indians because they saw it as simply enabling if not encouraging violent Indian attacks. Instead of negotiating with the Indians, the Black Boys reasoned that the British should be killing them. Croghan, who was working for his own trading firm in Philadelphia, tried desperately to help contain the violence that erupted between settlers and Indians. After his capture and release, Croghan joined other Englishmen at Kekionga who had been rescued by their Miami allies, demonstrating to the English that the area was simply ungovernable. The Miamis remained the key power brokers and would have to be recognized as such, yet, beneath the release of prisoners and even the theater of Pacanne's actions likely stood Native women. In the Great Lakes region, Native women wielded power over the fate of captives similar to the influence that Miami women enjoyed in agriculture and trade. Women exercised a great deal of control over the adoption, enslavement, and even death of their captives, which meant that the saving of Morris and the release of Croghan may have been the decision of Miami women.[31]

Such complicated diplomatic maneuvering made little sense to the British and French. Europeans had a difficult time understanding the motives of the Miamis because they often interpreted Indian behavior through homogeneous tribal identities; if one Miami polity favored the British, then they must all be so inclined. The Miamis deftly balanced shared ethnic histories with their desire to maintain local trading relationships. They would pursue connections with both imperial powers but would not allow those relationships to cement permanent divisions within the Miami polity. Pro-French Miamis welcomed the pro-British Miamis into their communities at Kekionga and Ouiatenon after the destruction of Pickawillany. Collective action by the Miamis was not necessary or even possible, particularly because the Miamis routinely encountered small trading parties from the British and the French into their villages. More importantly, the fact that the Miamis made Europeans adjust to their terms often meant that Europeans were forced to travel to Indian villages, which only reinforced the local nature of Miami life. By residing in relatively autonomous communities, the Miamis incorporated and satisfied French and English demands without undermining their kinship networks, traditions, and rituals. In fact, they vacillated between attacking the French and British as though it was a seasonal activity. One was Miami because they traded with Indians and non-Natives alike. In many instances the Miamis, by deciding with whom they would trade and live, self-selected the ways in which they would change.[32]

By the late 1770s, a new war had broken out, this time between the British and their former colonists. Neither the British nor the rebels maintained a large military presence in the western Ohio Valley in large part because neither one had the capacity to displace the Indians of the region. Yet both would wage a bizarre contest for control of Cahokia, Kaskaskia, and Vincennes as though controlling the physical forts somehow determined the actions of the Indians. Although rhetorically, some British and rebel leaders would speak of the Miami homeland as a key part of the larger war effort, the presence of small British and rebel forces benefited the Miamis by presenting them with productive albeit temporary alliances. In late 1778 the British, led by the lieutenant governor of Detroit, Henry Hamilton, and George Rogers Clark, who led a small force of Virginian rebels, fought for control of the Illinois country. Although the Virginians under Clark successfully pushed the British out of these trading forts, the overall significance of the wartime violence was minimal. In fact, one scholar refers to the fight for Illinois country as a "costless victory."[33] The taking of these forts mattered little to Indians who continued to trade and manipulate both the rebels and British.

After learning of Hamilton's mission to recapture Fort Sackville (Vincennes) from Clark, the Miami leader Pacanne decided to travel south from Kekionga to accompany Hamilton's force. By the late 1770s, Pacanne had become an influential Miami leader at Kekionga and a friend to the British. Pacanne likely recognized Hamilton's mission to Fort Sackville as an opportunity to affirm Miami influence. The area was hotly contested by Native peoples and non-Natives alike, and the rebels need not gain any new allies that might exacerbate the violence. Pacanne located Hamilton on his march from Detroit and seemed to poke fun at the fight that was developing between the British and the rebels.

According to Hamilton, Pacanne told him that the "Rebels honor [Hamilton] with the title of the Dog. That they mean to use [him] as such—that [he] is to be hawled like a fish out of the water." Pacanne's comments appear to bait Hamilton and to make light of the impending fight between the British and Virginians. Such a conflict might make the British even more concerned with the loyalty of their Indian allies and therefore more generous in trade. By prodding Hamilton, Pacanne may have been reminding the British officer of his own importance. Although the source material on the subject is limited, Pacanne worked to reinforce Miami influence by reminding various Indian communities to stay loyal to the British in the face of Clark's rebel force. He warned his fellow Indians not to break the chain of friendship with Britain by engaging in "imprudent conduct." Likely convinced that his efforts had paid off, Pacanne returned north to Kekionga in January 1779, shortly before Clark's second attack on Fort Sackville that February. However, he promised to return "in the Spring by way of the falls of Ohio [present-day Louisville, Kentucky]."[34]

Instead of risking costly violence, the Miamis played both sides. That March, some Miamis guaranteed Clark of their "fidelity &c. to the Americans and [to] beg their Protection." A year later in Detroit, Miami leaders informed the British that they "would all rise & assist their elder brothers [the British], and act in conjunction in future for the good of the King's Service." Pacanne went so far as to boast that he would not return to Vincennes unless he was attacking it. The Kickapoos behaved much like the Miamis. They declared their support for the British at Detroit in June and July 1778 after they met Henry Hamilton in conference. A Kickapoo leader declared that his people had "no other will" than that of British officials." This was not entirely true, for the Kickapoos had also professed allegiance to the Americans when they marched with Clark to Kaskaskia that summer. When Clark attacked Vincennes in February 1779, the Kickapoos failed to aid the British even though nearly one hundred warriors had joined the British defensive positions. Battles in the Wabash-Maumee Valley had little effect on the Revolutionary War as a whole. Nevertheless, most Indian communities were well aware that Britain and the American colonies were at war, and many capitalized on the resulting opportunities. One British officer remarked that the

Indians "promise well but seem to come [to councils] more on account of trading than otherwise."[35]

Within this vacuum of imperial authority, ambitious individuals and disaffected communities vied for control over the important trade network. Pacanne had successfully established himself as a leader, and soon another Miami leader, Little Turtle, would do the same when a disenchanted Frenchman tried to seize Kekionga. Despite serving as inspector general of the cavalry for the Continental Army, Augustin Mottin de la Balme resigned his post and ventured west three years later of his own accord. Possibly angry that Kasmir Pulaski would be replacing him in the Continental Army or simply an opportunist, de la Balme believed that he could seize Kekionga and its trade with the help of French settlers. Kekionga would then serve as a springboard to attacking Detroit, the heart of British influence in the northwest. Sidelined after the Seven Years' War, French traders and settlers were attracted to de la Balme's plan to resurrect French influence in the region and to secure their property rights in Wabash and Illinois country.[36] French traders at Kekionga, de la Balme hoped, felt the same way.

In the fall of 1780, de la Balme marched into Kekionga with a small force and was relieved to find that most of the Miamis were gone. The French eagerly looted the settlement, unaware that they were being watched by Pacanne and the newcomer Little Turtle. De la Balme and thirty of his men died in the ensuing ambush, which put an end to French efforts to retake the vital trading center. According to a well-known merchant of Vincennes, de la Balme's force was "attacked by the Miami nations who killed the bravest of them." Despite the fact that Pacanne had probably killed de la Balme, Little Turtle used the victory to increase his influence within the Miami nation. His heritage likely made such a move necessary—his father was Mohican and his mother Iowan, which meant that not all Indians considered him a member of the Miami nation. Nor had Little Turtle proven himself a defender of Miami interests like Pacanne. Nonetheless, he solidified his position in the 1780s by welcoming Shawnee and Lenape refugees who had fled vengeful American frontiersmen. Although Little Turtle disliked the disturbances within the Wabash-Maumee Valley, he benefited from them nonetheless. He had failed to establish himself as a Miami leader at Kekionga, but the Revolutionary War provided such an opportunity along with the subsequent violence resulting from American intervention in the region.

Scholars have interpreted these violent episodes at Kekionga as simply a by-product of European imperialism. Such an interpretive framework ignores not only the power of the Miamis but also the disagreements that prevented unity on the part of any group, whether European or Native. For instance, de la Balme lost nearly half his followers on the march to Kekionga. Reinforcements from Vincennes and other quarters also failed to materialize.[37] De la Balme's efforts, like those of British emissaries, did not determine the fate of Kekionga. Rather, it was the Miamis who maintained control. Pacanne had made it clear that the portage area, along with Kekionga, belonged to the Miamis. This was especially apparent when Pacanne's sister Tacumwah divorced Joseph Drouet de Richerville (Richardville), a French fur trader, in 1774. Tacumwah enjoyed a great deal of influence at Kekionga, but her French husband claimed her property as his own in the divorce proceedings. Pacanne and a British court determined that Tacumwah's marriage to a European man did not automatically transfer her property. This was especially important given that she would eventually marry Charles Beaubien, a Canadian-born fur trader who eventually became the British agent for the Miamis. One historian has suggested that the fight to control the portage at Kekionga was solely a conflict between the British and the American rebels. In fact, the British commander of Detroit recognized the authority and hegemony of the Miamis; he understood, like the French, that the Miamis were the "key to the Settlement" of the region because they controlled the portage at Kekionga and were therefore in a position to dictate diplomacy.[38] British dependence meant that the Miamis could defend their interests without fear of reprisal, making the Miamis beneficial but also fickle allies.

Nonetheless, increased interference by the Americans and movement of refugee Indians into the region forced the Miamis to articulate in greater detail than ever before both the terms of trade but also to define the boundaries of their homeland. In the 1780s and 1790s, westward-bound Americans created a flood of refugee Indians who flocked to Miami settlements for protection. While the Miamis welcomed these peoples, they were quick to remind them of their limited rights. When groups of Shawnee and Lenapes settled near Kekionga in 1786, the Miamis told them that "the Ground they occupied now is not theirs."[39] The Miamis allowed these outsiders to grow corn, build villages, and to conduct trade, but only insofar as it reinforced Miami hegemony.

To that end, the Miamis saw fit to limit or temper the American intrusion. The Confederated Congress had recently passed both the Land Ordinance of 1785 and the Northwest Ordinance of 1787, two policies that outlined the sale and future governance of lands in the Ohio Valley. The war with Britain demonstrated to American leaders that the Miamis were indeed powerful and that the West would erupt into costly violence if squatters and land speculators continued to murder Indians. Always the diplomat, Pacanne accompanied Josiah Harmar, who had served in the Continental Army, on an expedition into the Illinois territory in 1787, much like he had when Hamilton marched through the region almost a decade earlier. He did so to allay American suspicions that the Miamis plotted war but also to gauge Harmar's intentions, if not draw him in to the Miami orbit. Pacanne and possibly his confidant the Owl (Hibou) accompanied Harmar to Kaskaskia, supplying the "party with meat (buffalo and deer), both on the march and upon [their return]." Neither the U.S. forces nor the French could control the increasingly hostile environment in the valley. American troops were stationed at Vincennes in 1787 under the command of Major John F. Hamtramck as part of Josiah Harmar's effort to placate the French and to cultivate friendly relations with the Piankashaws, Weas, Kickapoos, and others. But violence continued to grow. In an attempt to protect Miami interests, Pacanne assisted Harmar and the Americans as an intermediary. He found himself their victim instead. Patrick Brown, a Kentuckian, attacked Miami settlements near Vincennes during the summer of 1789 in an effort to avenge recent Indian raids.[40] A large contingent of Kickapoos then attacked an American force near the mouth of the Wabash, forcing French traders into a desperate policing action.

Despite periodic violence and the intrusion of imperial traders into the Ohio River Valley, the Miamis protected their influence by adapting to and incorporating outsiders into their world. Their homeland demonstrated this eclectic blending. As long as outsiders who changed the dynamics of the valley (Native and not) could be successfully incorporated into Miami communities, the commodification of corn, refugee Indians flooding the region, and European settlers proved empowering. The tenor of violence was key to the stability of the Miami homeland, which is why the arrival of the Americans in the 1770s increasingly undermined the Miamis' capacity to protect their homeland.

Miami Sovereignty Challenged

Although the Miamis appeared well positioned to assert themselves as the Americans began to settle the region, difficulties soon arose. The obvious power of the Miamis and their allies necessitated several American missions to the region during and shortly after the Revolutionary War. Knowing that the intentions of the Indians in the Ohio and Wabash Valleys were of paramount importance to the young United States because the Americans hoped to maintain peace in the Northwest Territory, a major area of settlement. In 1789, the governor of the Northwest Territory, Arthur St. Clair, instructed the federal commander at Vincennes to identify the intentions of the Wabash Indians. The Wea and Piankashaw Indians of Ouiatenon would not commit to either the British or the Americans because, as St. Clair concluded, they needed to consult "their eldest brethren" at Kekionga.[41] The Eel River Miamis gave a similar answer. Indian communities worried about the prospect of American settlement in Ohio, but Hamtramck's force in Vincennes caused them special concern, for it led them to question the Americans' professions of peace. Moreover, the Indians were troubled by the Americans' ambiguous motives and their refusal to respect Miami boundaries. Although the Miamis and French used diplomatic channels to ask about the increasing number of American troops in the region, they were ignored.

In addition to American military intervention in the region, the Miamis lost one of their most capable leaders at a crucial point in time. Pacanne left Kekionga in 1790 for the Illinois country not to return for a decade. Pacanne's young métis nephew Jean Baptiste Richardville; Le Gris, a fellow pro-British Miami leader; and the newly arrived Little Turtle administered trade and diplomacy at Kekionga in his absence. Pacanne and some of his followers ventured west in response to a raid by Kentucky militiamen, but such violence does not fully explain his relative permanence in the region for almost a decade, especially when he would return east in the late 1790s after the Americans destroyed Kekionga.[42] His reasons for moving west are more complicated than a desire to flee the destructive Virginians.

Given Pacanne's history, it seems likely that this was part of a larger diplomatic effort. Eight years earlier, Pacanne had warned the Miamis against any alliance with a foreign power other than the British. He encouraged his fellow Miamis to visit "wrath against those who are the authors of all your miseries and all your misfortunes" and to "open your eyes and ears" at the intrigues of the French, Virginians, and Spanish. In what must have been a rousing oration, he told the Miamis to take the tomahawk and "try it on the head of the Virginians or the French who are of their party."[43] Pacanne's distaste for and outright hostility toward the Americans was soon cemented when a group of Virginians attacked his settlement near Vincennes and killed his father-in-law.

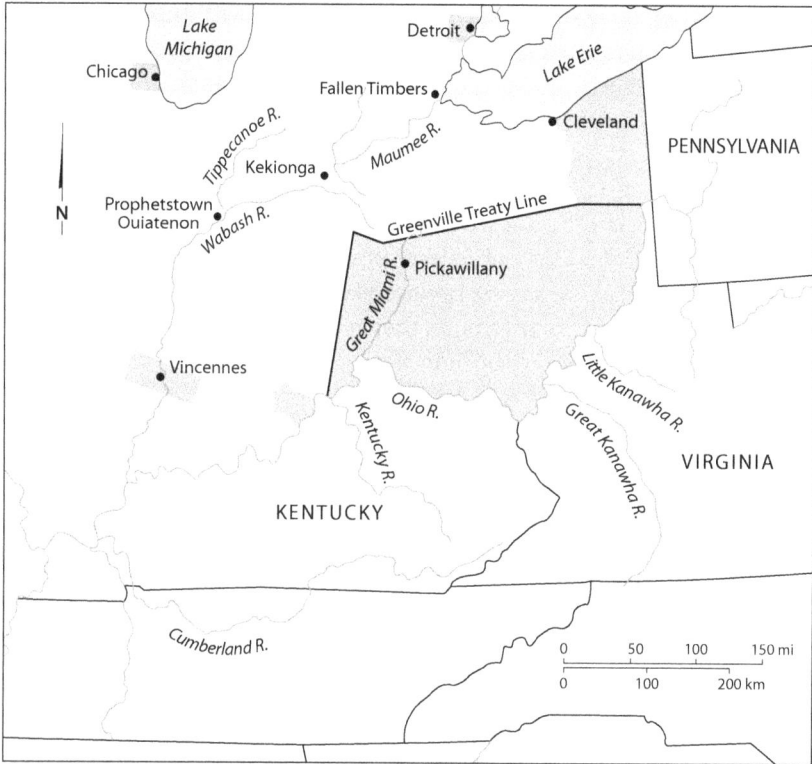

MAP 2. Various Indian and non-Indian settlements within the Miami home-land. Shaded areas mark Native land cessions to the U.S. under the treaty of Greenville of 1795.

By traveling into the Illinois territory, a region that had been at least nominally Miami, Pacanne could reconnect with a close ally, the Owl, and build relationships with the Spanish and other Indian peoples who might prove useful foils to the greedy Virginians. Pacanne needed allies (and sta-bility) in case the violence at Vincennes engulfed the entire region. Ever the diplomat, Pacanne recognized the need to remain independent and will-ingly exchanged his British medal for a Spanish one when he moved west. One British officer had remarked just a few years earlier that it would entail "some difficulty to restrain" the Miamis. Here was yet another example. Like many Miamis, Pacanne exchanged imperial identities in order to fur-ther Miami interests. Yet Pacanne's tenure near Ste. Genevieve resulted in limited success given that he was only able to engage Quapaw and Chicka-saw leaders thanks to the hospitality of Spanish intermediaries.[44]

By 1790, the Americans were equally concerned with the tenor of violence developing in the Miami homeland. Desperate to secure the Ohio Valley, Governor Arthur St. Clair decided that an attack on the Miami settlements was needed. He suspected that a great "meeting of warriors" had taken place at Kekionga between the Miamis and their supporters and that "some of the Chiefs of the Creeks & Cherokees" had attended as well. His decision to attack was also in response to angry frontier settlers whose condemnation of federal power had reached a fevered and uncontrollable pitch. Squatters opposed land surveyors who might seize their ill-gotten lands; furthermore, they made every attempt to ruin federal efforts to negotiate with Ohio Valley Indians, whom they considered bloodthirsty and savage. After years of prolonged and destructive violence, western settlers increasingly thought of Indians as deer: both were wild animals that needed to be contained. In their minds, the Ohio Valley would not enjoy any peace until an American army stopped negotiating with and instead destroyed the Indian settlements.[45]

Arthur St. Clair remarked in a letter to President George Washington that the Indians of the western Ohio Valley did not wear "a very favorable complexion" in large part because they were "guided entirely by those of the Miami Village." St. Clair feared that waiting any longer would give the Miamis and the hundreds of refugee Indians time to organize against the Americans and to "hide their corn before war." Yet he also worried that the Miamis and the "renegade [Shawnees], Lenapes, and Cherokees that lay near them" would destroy an American force that was not yet "prepared to chastise them." One of his lieutenants, Major Hamtramck, warned that any peace overtures made by the Americans to the non-Miami Indians would be fruitless, given that they were all "governed by the Miami Indians" who opposed such a peace.[46]

In the eyes of men such as Arthur St. Clair, defeating the Miamis was essential to the survival of the republic. President George Washington and Secretary of War Henry Knox both hoped to force concessions from Kekionga, but limited military successes proved problematic. Despite recognizing the strength and ambition of the Miamis, St. Clair ordered an attack on the stronghold at Kekionga at the same time that he ordered the destruction of Miami villages along the Wabash. He hoped the latter would distract the Miamis, yet, much to his surprise, he learned that many of these villages were already abandoned. Frenchmen who served with the American forces had warned their relatives of the impending attack; that same French presence may have led the Miamis to refrain from confronting the Americans, although Indians outnumbered whites two to one.[47] Such a collaborative effort by the French and Miami hinted at a relationship that would create a near disaster for the Americans in the early 1800s.

The fighting in the late 1780s occupied hundreds of Indians around Ouiatenon who could have otherwise been guarding the portage area near Kekionga, where troops burned gardens, orchards, and vast fields of corn. These military expeditions culminated in the 1790s, when Indians attacked and defeated two American armies under Josiah Harmar in 1790 and Arthur St. Clair in 1791. Harmar requested a trial by courts-martial after his defeat to clear rumors that he had run a drunken command. St. Clair was in equally rough shape after his command of nearly one thousand soldiers suffered a disastrous defeat with a casualty rate of 97.4 percent. The humiliating defeats of Harmar and St. Clair left the American army in shambles; the government could not enforce its policies upon the Indian communities in the Ohio and Wabash Valleys. Indigenous military victories placed the Indians of the Northwest in a unique position to influence and even dictate policy in the late 1780s and early 1790s. The Miamis refused to treat with the Americans in 1792 and likely murdered two American emissaries who were traveling to Kekionga to start negotiations.[48]

If ever there was a threat for the western republic to collapse, this was it. Shocked by these defeats and the growing division between the eastern and western United States, John Marshall warned that the rebellious settlers and western chaos "threatened to shake the government of the United States to its foundations."[49] Not only had the Whiskey Rebellion exploded in western Pennsylvania, but the "Miami Confederacy" presented a real threat to the expansion of the young republic. Anglo-Americans used this term to indicate a united front of Indians based largely in western Ohio and the Wabash Valley. Yet the Miami Confederacy as a singular political entity did not really exist; it was merely a product of American perceptions. The Miamis were not necessarily an ally of the British, nor were the many other Indian communities. Yet the deep hatreds born from frontier strife with the Americans elevated the Miamis into a diplomatic and political status that Americans could only explain within their conception of centralized political authority. The Miamis likely seized upon the pervasive anger Indians had toward the Americans and then directed it to defend their homeland. Moreover, given their history of incorporation, the Miamis had hundreds of willing supporters living among them.

As chaos spread throughout the western territories, the American government sent two armies west in the summers of 1793 and 1794. One was to subdue the rebellion near Pittsburgh, where frontier settlers mocked the authority of the federal government in what amounted to a frontier independence movement. Erecting liberty poles and marching through their towns swigging whiskey, the rebels refused to pay an excise tax on their liquid currency. The other army, Anthony Wayne's Legion of the United States, marched to destroy Kekionga and with it Indian militancy in the Ohio Valley. The fields were so vast that the Miami world appeared "one continued village for a number of miles." To conquer the "grand emporium of the hostile Indians of the West," Wayne fashioned a new army. Full of veterans from the Revolutionary War, Wayne's force would give no quarter and kill anyone who resisted their march. American diplomats hoped that military action would help to announce the arrival of the United States into the Ohio Valley. They hoped that this would dissuade "all peoples of any notions they might have about resisting or ignoring the grand plans outlined in the legislation of the 1780s," as Andrew Cayton has argued.[50] Wayne found his fight when a battle erupted in August 1794 near Fort Miami at Fallen Timbers (present-day Toledo, Ohio), where the Indians suffered a serious reversal by Wayne's army.

The American victory signified an important turning point for the Indians of the Wabash-Maumee Valley. Destruction to countless crop fields throughout the region and the permanent presence of Wayne's legion forced Indians to reconsider their options. Harmar's, St. Clair's, and Wayne's expeditions had also devastated Miami agriculture, forcing the various Indian communities into a greater dependency upon British and American goods. In 1791, American troops destroyed acres of cultivated Miami lands near Ouiatenon and Kekionga. Under orders from Secretary of War Knox, Brigadier General Charles Scott attacked the Wea towns west of Kekionga, destroying Ouiatenon and various Kickapoo villages as well. His subordinates destroyed Kethtipecanunk [Tippecanoe], an important settlement north of Ouiatenon, but found it completely rebuilt by the Kickapoos upon their return two months later.[51] Nonetheless, prolonged warfare throughout the early 1790s wreaked havoc on Indian subsistence strategies, which made them more receptive to treaty negotiations where trade goods and food were offered in exchange for land cessions.

The subsequent Treaty of Greenville in 1795 marked an important moment for the fracturing of the Miami borderland. The treaty council at Greenville provided new opportunities for Shawnee, Lenape, Potawatomi, and Kickapoo Indians to collaborate with the Americans on an equal level to the Miamis by agreeing to Anthony Wayne's terms. This was a dangerous first step, for until 1795, the Miamis had been able to influence if not control most Natives living in their communities. Little Turtle fought back in council, demanding that the lands "enjoyed by [his] forefathers [from] time immemorial" not be subject to arbitrary boundaries and the desires of outsiders. Astonished by Wayne's proposed boundary lines that included large parts of Miami interests in Ohio and their lands around Kekionga, Little Turtle reminded the American general that his "forefather [had] kindled the first fire at Detroit" which then extended to "the head waters of Scioto, from then to its mouth; from thence, down the Ohio, to the mouth of the Wabash, and from thence to Chicago."[52]

Although Little Turtle recognized that Potawatomi and other Indians such as the Kickapoos lived within this region, he concluded that they resided within the "Miami nation," lands that the Great Spirit gave his forefather "a long time ago, and charged him not to sell . . . but to preserve . . . for posterity." More than to defend his ancestral lands and to promote his power as a Miami leader, Little Turtle sought to combat Wayne's proposed boundary lines and to prevent other Indian communities from partaking in the council. In fact, Little Turtle's admonishing of Wayne demonstrated his comprehension of Miami sovereignty. He said that the "lands on the Wabash, and in *this* country, belong to me and my people. I now take the opportunity to inform my brothers of the United States, and others present, that . . . these lands were disposed of without our knowledge or consent." He declared that the Miamis "have pointed out to you [the Americans] their country."[53]

Little Turtle's comments are significant. Not only did he challenge the right of non-Miami Indians to partake in the council, but he referred to the Miamis as a nation, as a singular entity. While he was not speaking of a nation similar to the American nation-state, his words evoked a history of Miami power and influence in the region. In effect, Little Turtle was identifying a Miami borderland, a place where Miami peoples had controlled trade, settlement patterns, and at times even violence. Yet his language also spoke to the fracturing of the borderland as Little Turtle condemned those Indians who had laid claim to the Miami homeland and those who were preventing the Indians from speaking with "one voice."[54] Such recognition was important given that the Miamis would now seek alternative routes to maintain power, at first looking toward an alliance with their fellow Indians, but then then finding ways to incorporate and even manipulate Euroamericans.

Days later, Little Turtle shifted course and informed the council that the treaty was "an affair to which no *one* among us can give an answer." Indians needed to "unite in opinion, and express it unanimously." Little Turtle shifted his approach by speaking of all Indians as one group, yet earlier he had chastised his fellow Indians for not recognizing Miami preeminence. This likely reflected Little Turtle's growing and conflicted influence both as a Miami but also a representative of Indian interests. Ascendant during this period of military success, Miami leader Little Turtle used his encounters with Harmar and St. Clair to broaden his influence among the Indians of the region. He claimed control over the Indian force that defeated St. Clair despite a prolonged challenge from the Lenape leader Buckangehelas, whom some Indians preferred. Eventually, Buckangehelas admitted that Little Turtle was, according to one missionary, the "youngest and most active man" and that Buckangehelas preferred Little Turtle "to himself." Such an admittance was not simply a recognition of Miami influence in the region but also a reflection of Little Turtle's growing authority. According to Samuel Drake, Little Turtle continued to expand his influence after St. Clair's defeat by visiting Montreal "for the purpose of raising all the Indian force he could to go out again in the spring against the whites."[55] Yet by 1795 and the debate over the Treaty of Greenville, it was obvious that Little Turtle no longer enjoyed the same degree of influence among non-Miami Indians. The Miamis had once made decisions with impunity. Now that was impossible.

Little Turtle's resignation to the treaty capped a decade-long process in which American forces waged destructive missions throughout Miami territory. The Indians signed away a large piece of land that constituted present-day Ohio and sixteen much smaller cessions of land that were just as important. Kekionga ceased to exist as the seat of the Miami polity by the late 1790s. Anthony Wayne constructed a fort at Kekionga and named it in his own honor; his forces constructed a road along the north edge of the Maumee River to its source at Kekionga so that the Americans could easily supply the fort and defend any Indian counterattack. Fort Wayne displaced the various Indian communities that had settled the area, forcing them to abandon more than five hundred acres of cleared cropland. The Miamis abandoned their villages at Kekionga for other settlements along the Wabash and Mississinewa Rivers, splitting into several disparate communities that could subsist more easily. Thereafter, the Miamis would no longer dictate the terms of trade as the Americans asserted their right to furnish licenses and regulate offenders.[56]

Despite losing Kekionga and Vincennes to the Americans, the Miamis maintained the central corridor along the Wabash, through Ouiatenon, and south toward the Ohio. The treaty also recognized those lands as being outside "the protection of the United States," a small consolation for the Miamis, whose homeland was now officially outlined by a treaty.[57] Thereafter, most Indian communities depended upon American goods at Fort Wayne; the forces under Harmar, St. Clair, and Wayne had destroyed large stores and vast fields of Miami corn and disrupted trade that reverberated for years. The post-1795 period forced the Miamis both to consider their growing dependency on the Americans and to deal with their decentralized organization that had proven beneficial over the previous fifty years. In addition, post-treaty dynamics convinced many Indians to consider treaty negotiations, rather than trade relationships, as a means for survival.

The loss of Kekionga did not unify the Miamis. Le Gris, Jean Baptiste Richardville, White Loon, and Little Turtle had signed the Treaty of Greenville on behalf of the Miamis; Metocina and the Owl, who spoke for Pacanne, did not sign. The divisions apparent among the Miamis were also present among other Indian groups. The Treaty of Greenville had spurred great disagreement within many Indian communities. In an ironic twist, the St. Joseph Potawatomies, who had objected so strenuously to their western brethren's alliance with the Americans, signed the Treaty of Greenville. Thus, they benefited from annuity payments even though they did not have a right to make decisions about the fate of the ceded territory. In fact, the Potawatomies constituted more than 25 percent of those who signed the treaty. This outraged the Miamis, for they did not recognize the historical legitimacy of the Potawatomies as residents of the valley. Although some groups utilized the violence caused by American military incursions into the region to their benefit, others removed west in hopes that they could maintain their autonomy. The majority of the Kickapoos, unlike the Shawnees, Lenape, Miamis, and Potawatomies who remained in the region, moved farther west and south. A few Kickapoo lingered behind, and some even returned in the early 1800s to sample Tenskwatawa's nativist teachings and to attack the remaining Illinois Indians.[58]

The Shawnees had a violent history with the Americans and understood better than most that resistance might prove disastrous. Black Hoof's Shawnees hoped to settle permanent agricultural villages near the Miami River by opening diplomatic relations with the Americans in Washington DC. These negotiations fueled a growing animosity between Black Hoof's Shawnees at Wapakoneta and those Shawnees in Missouri and the small group of Kispoktha, Thawegila, and Piqua Shawnees who had followed Tenskwatawa and his brother Tecumseh to western Ohio.[59] Some Shawnees such as Cornstalk advocated accommodation and negotiation, while others like Blue Jacket believed that militancy was the Shawnees' only option. These same ideological camps remained within the Shawnee polity well into the nineteenth century and would shape the ways in which the Miamis positioned themselves socially and politically.

By 1800, treaty negotiations were the means through which many Indian communities found security. Greater competition for resources and American expansion after 1795 only exacerbated the ideological divisions between Native groups. Indians could no longer play European powers off each other, nor could they influence trade as they once had. Moreover, treaty negotiations and annuity payments increasingly replaced trade, providing Indians with new opportunities to access goods. Since many had been displaced from their traditional homelands, they had little to lose. The Miamis watched in disgust as the Potawatomies, Kickapoos, and others illegitimately signed away Miami lands. William Henry Harrison, the future governor of Indiana Territory, would facilitate many of the councils between the United States and various Indian communities within the Wabash-Maumee Valley. Harrison took advantage of shifting inter- and intratribal relations as the Miami borderland began to weaken. Native communities hoped to access trade goods and annuities from the Americans, but they often did so by ceding land outside of their authority. Harrison capitalized on this situation and gained acre after acre of land in the name of the United States. Several Indian groups agreed to sell land, which legitimized a process the governor would use repeatedly. Harrison allowed Indian communities to sign treaties even when he knew they had no claims to the area. Their desire to gain annuity payments provided the governor with a convenient tool to force resistant Indians to the negotiating table.

Few Indians were as complicit in this process as the Potawatomies. They succeeded first during the Vincennes-tract conference in September 1802, which they used to protect their northern settlements. Henry Dearborn, the secretary of war, had cautioned Harrison a year earlier to "sound the Piankiashaws [sic] and Kickapoos on the subject of their sale [of the Vincennes land] to the company [Illinois and Wabash Company] in the year 1795" in order to determine the validity of the sale. He did not direct Harrison to negotiate with the Potawatomies because their "claims to any of that region were nebulous." The Potawatomies and Harrison disregarded Dearborn's instructions. The Potawatomi leader Five Medals, aided by fellow pro-American leaders, ceded nearly 1.6 million acres to the United States. This treaty at Fort Wayne in June 1803 upset other groups such as the Miamis who felt that the Potawatomies lacked the right to participate in Wabash-Maumee politics. The Potawatomies had filled the void left by the Piankashaw Indians, who had departed from Vincennes in the mid-1780s to escape the violence that had become endemic to the town.[60] As violence spread throughout the region, remaining small communities of the Illinois Confederacy such as the Kaskaskians found themselves the easy victim of Indian raids by the Potawatomies. The Potawatomies played into Harrison's hands when their threatening presence forced the Kaskaskians to sign a treaty ceding almost 8 million acres in present-day Illinois in order to gain the protection of the American government.[61]

Harrison's ability to play the Indians against each other advanced the American agenda only insofar as it weakened the Miamis. There were a variety of factors outside the control of the American government that threatened to unravel every move that Harrison made. Not only did Secretary of War Henry Dearborn worry about Harrison's aggressive attempts to take lands away from the Indians, but Thomas Jefferson sent Harrison a secret letter warning him that "the crisis is pressing." Jefferson, like many other Americans of his day, feared that France might return to the region and rally their Indian allies to attack the western American settlements. Jefferson warned that "the occupation of New Orleans, hourly expected, by the French, is already felt like a light breeze by the Indians." A renewal of the French-Indian alliance might ignite violence detrimental to the young republic. In Jefferson's mind, controlling the Ohio Valley Indian peoples was an important turning point in "finally [consolidating] our whole country into one nation only." His dream of consolidating the area into one nation was far more a product of Jefferson's republican fantasies, as the Indians, not simply the French, remained the biggest threat. Harrison worried that Pacanne, having recently returned from the Illinois country, and the Owl would destroy any efforts to gain lands from the Indians, going so far as to say that the Owl "had it in his power to thwart or obstruct any of the disigns [sic] of the government." Harrison was well aware that "nine tenths of [the Miamis] acknowledge Pacanne," the Owl, and Richardville as "their chiefs."[62]

When John Adams officially signed Indiana Territory into law in early May 1800 and made Harrison governor, he had no idea just how important that territory was to the French and Miamis and just how willing they would be to fight for it. As if pushed by the ghosts of his ancestors, Pacanne returned to the Wabash-Maumee Valley shortly before Harrison's arrival.[63] What he witnessed likely elicited nothing less than sheer terror. Kekionga was gone. The Americans had commandeered Vincennes. And Little Turtle had situated himself as the leader of the Miami people through a relationship with the hated Americans. Even worse, the Americans were governed by a Virginian! Although only a decade had passed, Pacanne's world—and with it the Miamis' world—had shattered, leaving behind a contested space where the Miamis no longer commanded complete authority. Americans coveted Miami lands and were willing to negotiate but only by pitting various Indian communities against each other; with the help of Indian collaborators, whites turned the once vibrant Miami borderland into a contested space where no one group could impose its will on another.

The fracturing of Miami lands, though, did not mean that the American conquest of the Miami homeland was inevitable or that the Americans were in control. In fact, it is important to remember that Harrison's plans, much like Jefferson's dreams for the nation, were real only on paper. Instead, the Miamis found ways to challenge the American colonial endeavor and place themselves at the center of regional diplomacy despite the loss of power that they had once enjoyed. In that sense, they recognized that they were no longer dominant but could still continue to interfere if not shape relationships between Native and non-Native communities in the region, much as they always had. Even the Americans wondered what was to become of Indiana. They controlled only Vincennes and Fort Wayne but were otherwise surrounded by the Miamis, French traders and their families, refugee Indians, and nativist Indians who also hoped to win control of the region. Furthermore, there were stark divisions among the American settlers moving west over the shape that the territory—and with it, the nation—should take. What resulted was not a contest of nations or tribes or races, but a fight between communities and the ideas and cultures they held dear.

The Miamis were at the core of this contest. However imperceptible they were as diplomats or accommodating their actions appeared to be, the Miamis had not simply survived the eighteenth century. In fact, for much of the eighteenth century, the Miamis had been ascendant and had not suffered any large-scale displacement from their ancestral lands. Thanks to Memeskia, Pacanne, the Owl, Little Turtle, and countless Miami women, the Miamis continued pushing decentralized relationships that allowed for the incorporation of outsiders and the expansion of trade. And when the Americans and nativist Indians sought to extend their national movements into the Miami homeland during the nineteenth century, the legacy of the Miami borderland and the local relationships central to its construction would prove to be far more powerful and influential than anyone could have imagined.

Twelve years after Pacanne returned to the upper Wabash Valley, Little Turtle was dead, the United States and Great Britain were engaged in open warfare in the Great Lakes, and Tenskwatawa (the Shawnee Prophet) had established a nativist Indian settlement in the heart of Miami territory. Little Turtle, his son-in-law William Wells, and a host of their French brethren had made every effort during the previous four years to frustrate any sort of understanding between the Shawnee Prophet and the Americans, convincing the latter that the Prophet only wanted war. Yet despite recent frontier violence, Tenskwatawa led many of his followers to Fort Wayne to talk peace in the summer of 1812. Standing on the same hallowed ground where Kekionga had once existed, Tenskwatawa asked federal officials if he could meet with Governor Harrison. As Indian agent at Fort Wayne, Benjamin Stickney recognized that any overture of peace by the Indians—Indians many whites suspected of being allies to the British—might be subterfuge.

Like many frontiersmen, Stickney dismissed this request as mere "flattery." Undaunted, the Prophet held out "a large belt of [white] Wampum with a small spot of purple wampum in the centre" and gave a great speech about the necessity for peace between the three nations. The spot of purple represented Prophetstown with one "end of the belt extended to Vincennes, and the other to Fort Wayne." Tenskwatawa may have been responding to Harrison's declaration that he had "forgiven the Prophet, and Tecumseh, and [that] the hatchet is buried."[1] Several months earlier, the Americans and the Prophet's followers had met in battle at Tippecanoe, a fight still very much alive in the minds of the participants. Tenskwatawa spoke of a national trinity, a peace between the Americans, the nativists, and the Miamis. If sincere, such a plan could put a stop to endemic violence by creating separate spheres of influence.

The Prophet's suggestion of a national trinity did not necessarily reflect a naïve view that such a division of powers was possible, but rather a recognition that the Miamis were key to any discussion of sovereignty in the region. The probability of a trinity was small given that centralized political authority and cultural uniformity simply did not exist in the Wabash-Maumee Valley. Although William Henry Harrison, the Shawnee Prophet, and, to a lesser degree, Little Turtle and Pacanne hoped to unify their peoples through a more centralized system of control in the period after 1806, none had the power to combat local and community interests undermining such unity. Conceptualizing a national trinity was one thing, but creating it was something else entirely. Even as the balance of power shifted toward the Americans by 1812, Indian communities continued to protect their local interests rather than unite against non-Indian intrusion. The local nature of life in the valley was so entrenched that the residents of Vincennes and Prophetstown would see their attempts to centralize their cultural and political power collapse as communal and ethnic groups defined the boundaries of organization.

Why do we need to understand the divisions and multiethnic nature of these communities? Doing so allows us to reconsider what Stephen Aron has labeled the "power politics of territorial hegemony" in order to reconfigure our understanding of the western Ohio Valley as at once the Miami homeland, Indiana Territory, and nativist confederacy. Scholars have identified several ideologies playing out in the post-1795 Ohio Valley, but they do so primarily within the context of American nationalism. Indians are cast as nativist or accommodationist; white settlers are identified with one of two dominant political ideologies—Jeffersonian republicanism or Hamiltonian federalism. More recently, scholars have used race and religion to frame the relationship between frontier settlers and Indians but continue to dismiss the significance of ethnicity. Although American political ideologies were undoubtedly in play on the frontier, as were nativist ideals, no one set of political or cultural beliefs trumped the rest. As a result, every ethnic group became an agent of autonomy as long as it maintained some influence over the larger intellectual debate about boundaries, violence, or economies.[2] Lack of unity forced various Indian communities and Euroamerican factions to vocalize and eventually construct a static identity. By articulating physical borders and rehearsing their own histories, these peoples began a border-making process. As local interests persisted, these communities sought cross-cultural and cross-racial alliances that fueled much of race-based rhetoric, in particular the dialogue surrounding the Prophet and his town. From 1795 to 1809, communities of French, Miamis, Americans, and other Indians continued to fight for their own needs, refusing to subvert their local and ethnic interests to larger racial and national agendas.

Dissecting the idea of the national trinity allows us to trace nascent political and cultural boundaries as they formed within Native and non-Native communities. It was the varied efforts to promote these nascent boundaries that caused the violence at Tippecanoe in 1811. In effect, the Wabash-Maumee Valley was the anti-trinity, a place where national unity was elusive save for the moments when violence appeared to bring people together. And although the idea of national (and even racial) unity framed the actions of the nativists and Americans, other key historical actors among the Miami and French communities stood ready to defend themselves on a community level. In fact, while the American rhetoric of the 1800s described the Miamis as a uniform and cohesive nation, this perception was largely mistaken. Two of the key Miami leaders of this period, Pacanne and Little Turtle, certainly fought over who would speak for the Miamis, in particular when it came to diplomacy with the Americans, but their actions and relationships with the Americans should not be read as an acceptance of American sovereignty. In fact, underneath the umbrella of American rhetoric were decades-old patterns of the Miamis trying to incorporate but limit intrusive outsiders.

American policies coupled with the Prophet's nativist dictates quickly undercut the trading system that allowed both the French and Miamis to thrive. At the same time, divisions among nativists and Americans added to an already complicated multicultural and multidimensional frontier. Ethnopolities of the Wabash-Maumee Valley identified different and often opposing paths to national unity and ethnic renewal, which undermined the likelihood of national unity. The cross-cultural relations that defined the Miami and French worlds became the contested physical and intellectual space between the republican and nativist colonial domains. When Miamis, Americans, and others tried to impose their cultural agendas on others, they prevented unity across national and racial boundaries by participating in often personal and petty disputes. Therefore, it is not enough that we simply consider the interactions between the three "imperial" or "national" powers; we must also examine the things that tore at each ethnic group. The contest for space and ethnic identity in the Wabash-Maumee Valley was not an imperial or national contest, but a fight between communities for sovereignty.

Understanding the reciprocal relationship between nation forma-tion and ethnogenesis—the relationship between self-identification and outside identification—is key in this regard.[3] As leaders vied to control public social space by defining the terms of national identity, they faced resistance from the people they hoped to galvanize who were engaged in their own process of self-identification. These contentious debates fueled a much larger discussion about the existence of ethnic identities within an already contentious public social space dominated by the dispute between the Prophet and Harrison. These political, ethnic, and some-times racialized identities were all part of a larger contest to secure phys-ical control over these imagined spaces. Although illusory, these debates over self and sovereignty are important in that they help us understand the larger and more significant ethnic disputes that shook these com-munities and fueled regional violence, which in turn became central to the construction of real instead of imagined boundaries.

Pacanne and Little Turtle

The collapse of their borderland in 1795, asserted the Miami leader Little Turtle, made the Miamis like "poor hunted deer, scattered abroad without a house or home." Little Turtle worried that unless someone helped them, "no trace" of their communities would remain. He also remembered that before the wars of the 1790s, the Miamis "were united and peaceable," no doubt a reflection of the sovereignty the Miami once enjoyed in the Wabash-Maumee Valley. But now Kekionga was gone, and the Miamis' hospitality was used against them by former allies who served as willing participants in Harrison's efforts to gain title to Indian lands. Little Turtle fumed at Harrison's efforts to manipulate the Indi-ans, arguing that no one could cede lands "without the consent of the Miamis."[4]

From Little Turtle's perspective, the Miamis maintained sovereignty over the land despite welcoming groups such as the Potawatomies and Lenapes into the region. Harrison belittled Little Turtle's authority, declaring that "nine tenths of that tribe who acknowledge Richardville & Peccan for their Chiefs . . . utterly abhor . . . the Turtle." Harrison also realized that the Miamis were increasingly desperate; he used their weakened position to his benefit when he convened a treaty council at

Fort Wayne in 1803. In negotiations, the Americans recognized the Lenapes' right to cede land along the White River. Outraged, the Miamis protested the legitimacy conferred on outsiders. According to Harrison, the Miamis had never wanted "to convey an exclusive right" to the lands. Vocal objections from the Miamis forced Harrison to alter course and amend the treaty two years later. Harrison had not expected such "persevering obstinacy" to thwart his plans.[5]

On the surface, such arguments appear to be little more than disagreements between Indians and whites, but in reality, Little Turtle was engaged in something much more complicated—a contest to gain greater influence and recognition among the Miamis. In some ways, the relationship between Little Turtle and Pacanne mirrored the fight between the pro-French and pro-British Miami communities of the 1740s that resulted in Memeskia winning hundreds of Miamis to Pickawillany. Both Little Turtle and Pacanne were fighting for greater influence among their people, not necessarily to destroy the other. Harrison's comments about Pacanne rang true; it was Pacanne, and not Little Turtle, who was poised to speak for the Miami people, which is probably why Little Turtle sought a stronger relationship with the Americans while Pacanne maintained his relations with the British.

To that end, Pacanne's ally, the Owl, made a concerted effort to stop the Miamis from collaborating with the Americans. One period writer stated that after returning to the region from the Illinois country in 1800, the Owl was "busily employed in dissuading the Indians from meeting" with the Americans. Pacanne saw no need for the Miamis to treat at Fort Wayne in 1803. This writer noted that the "Miamis had been before represented by the Turtle and Richardville, although three fourths of them, with the Eel river Indians, were still kept back by the intrigues of the Owl."[6] Pacanne and the Owl were actively engaged in trying to isolate Little Turtle and his son-in-law William Wells. For instance, although Pacanne and the Owl told Harrison that they would participate in the 1803 treaty council, they did not arrive until shortly after the council ended.

Instead, Pacanne's Miamis met secretly with a group of Lenapes and convinced them to recognize Pacanne's community as the only group who had authority to recognize the lands between the White and Ohio Rivers as then belonging to the Lenapes. After the Lenapes agreed, the two groups cemented the pact with a wampum belt. While Little Turtle used the Americans to empower his community, Pacanne used the Lenapes in a similar way. Harrison commented that Pacanne and the

Owl wanted to strengthen their party by "gaining over the Delawares an object which engaged the Turtle's attention" as well. Such actions were only normal for the Miamis, but Harrison was livid at such a display of disrespect. Pacanne's distaste for Harrison was likely rooted in his disgust for Clark's Virginians and the violence they had caused at Vincennes. Pacanne likely saw no real difference between Clark and Harrison (and therefore no reason to respect the governor) as they were both Virginians and enemies to the British. Harrison lectured Pacanne's followers at length that their behavior "embarrassed their affairs," but in reality it was Harrison who was humiliated for he was unable to control the Miamis. In an attempt to question Little Turtle's influence, and likely to prevent any real alliance with the Americans, the Owl visited Vincennes weeks later to declare his friendship with the United States, hoping that Harrison would favor Pacanne's group if they were as cooperative as Little Turtle's, or at least to convince Harrison that a relationship with Pacanne and the Owl was more valuable. According to one source from the period, the Owl "had it in his power to thwart or obstruct any of the designs of the government."[7] Pacanne wanted to limit Little Turtle's influence, but not become him. In his work on factionalism among the Miamis, Rob Mann has argued that the competition between Little Turtle and Pacanne was in reality a fight between Little Turtle's pro-assimilationist policy and Pacanne traditionalist ideals.

Yet this dispute had begun long before the Americans' arrival. Framing Pacanne's behavior within his personal past makes his motives and values easier to recognize.[8] Mann dates Pacanne's strong resistance toward Little Turtle as both the product of British overtures to renew trade in 1807 and the fallout from the 1809 Treaty of Fort Wayne. Pacanne's positioning and support of the British started much earlier.[9] He had a history of challenging those who sought to gain influence over Kekionga, the long portage, as well as the Miami polity, and he routinely sought to maintain Miami interests tied to his community's trade relations. Little Turtle threatened to destroy the decades-old relationship between Pacanne's community and the British at a time when that relationship was crucial. By taking advantage of the 1803 negotiations at Fort Wayne, Pacanne seized an opportunity to trump an adversary, or at least to remind Harrison that it was Pacanne who would make such important diplomatic decisions. Pacanne's fight with Little Turtle and his persistent efforts to protect what he identified as Miami interests would continue for many more years and have profound effects on how the Americans thought about Indians.

Competition continued between Pacanne and Little Turtle as they sought to protect their versions of Miami sovereignty, yet their actions also enabled Harrison's expansionist policies. The Miamis traditionally found ways to welcome outsiders into their communities in order to strengthen their influence in trade and diplomacy. In their attempt to assert themselves, Pacanne and Little Turtle seized upon this tradition. When Francis Vigo and John Gibson asked the Indians to convene at Vincennes in August 1805, Little Turtle waffled and tried to delay. He continued to seethe at Harrison's behavior at treaty councils in 1803 and 1804, when Little Turtle and Wells had threatened war over the illegal cession of lands to the Americans by the Lenapes and Piankashaws. Little Turtle's reticence was Pacanne's opportunity. Pacanne claimed "the Turtle had no right" to delay the Indians from visiting Vincennes and made it known that he "wanted to go on to Vincennes . . . and would go at any time." He had on several occasions in the past. Pacanne used this chance not only to undermine Little Turtle's authority to dictate Miami behaviors but to deny that the Lenapes had an exclusive right to the country between the Ohio and White Rivers. Despite Harrison begging the Lenapes to force the Miamis to acknowledge the treaty, the "Lenapes finally gave up the contest" because Pacanne and the Owl could not be swayed.[10] Pacanne also made himself appear more favorable to the Americans, an important gesture given Little Turtle's caginess.

Overwhelmed by the Miamis' resistance, Harrison sought compromise and declared the Miamis, Eel River Miamis and Weas, "who consider themselves as one nation . . . joint owners of all the country on the Wabash and its waters." The treaty also stipulated that the United States would not "purchase any part of the said country without the consent of each of the said tribes." Such a treaty proved empowering for two important reasons: the Miamis successfully modified the 1803 and 1804 treaties to recognize their own sovereignty; and the Owl, Richardville, Lapoussier, and Pacanne successfully challenged Little Turtle's influence with the Americans. However, to do this, the Miamis ceded nearly 2 million more acres of "some of the finest land in the Western Country," including a large swath of land near Kekionga.[11] The competition between Little Turtle and Pacanne was not simply a contest for influence among the Miamis but also a struggle to dictate Miami values and identity. The treaty recognized Miami sovereignty in the region, but it also cemented the divide between Pacanne and Little Turtle.

For his part, Little Turtle continued to court new allies, in particular the Quakers, who had offered to help the Indians improve their farming techniques. He hoped to win supporters for his particular community and made no effort to include Pacanne or other Miami leaders. It was a delicate game. Little Turtle ordered the Quaker missionaries to settle thirty-two miles southwest from Fort Wayne at a place called the Boat Yard on the footprint of a Lenape town. The twenty-five acres of cleared land would be the perfect spot. Such a small farm far from Little Turtle's village would not prove overly invasive, and it would secure a stronger relationship with American missionaries and with it the American government. His motives were twofold. He was deeply involved in a cultural contest with Pacanne, who was far more popular among the Miamis; the Quaker missionaries provided a convenient ally. Secondly, Little Turtle did not see a stark difference between Indians and whites and in fact believed that the difference in color between the two peoples was only a product of the sun, "the father of colours."[12] In that context, Little Turtle did not hesitate to dress in American attire when visiting Philadelphia and then change to his traditional clothing when he returned home.

Similar to Pacanne's behavior when he ventured into Spanish territory, Little Turtle pacified the Americans by employing their cultural norms. Little Turtle deftly adopted the identities of his allies to forge bonds. He was an Indian leader who was willing to become both literally and figuratively the people whom he hoped to incorporate. Such behavior was necessary at a time when what C. F. Volney described as "intestine feuds and anarchy" were raging among the Indians and when Little Turtle continually confronted the ire of Pacanne and his supporters. Harrison recognized the value in maintaining Little Turtle's allegiance, and he allocated more money for Little Turtle's personal benefit, even instructing William Wells to buy a slave for the Miami leader.[13]

Little Turtle's efforts to incorporate the Americans proved too much to bear for the other Miamis, for Little Turtle's efforts appeared to make the Miamis subservient to interlopers. While Pacanne was willing to acknowledge the power of outsiders on a limited basis, Little Turtle was willing to visit their cities and to dress like them. Instead of forcing the Americans to adapt to Miami interests, Little Turtle did the opposite. It is not surprising, then, that Pacanne refused to allow Little Turtle to parcel out Miami interests to non-Miamis. Pacanne had a history of opposing outsiders who tried to use their connections with the Miami people for personal profit.

In Pacanne's eyes, Little Turtle embodied the destructive decisions that had pushed the Miamis to the point of losing Kekionga. Pacanne was the rightful leader. He had been the leader of the Miami cultural capital at Kekionga. His family had controlled the portage for decades before its destruction. Yet after Pacanne departed for the Illinois country in the late 1780s, Little Turtle had undermined Miami interests by making concessions to the Americans under Anthony Wayne in 1795. Pacanne could not even think of Little Turtle without remembering that Little Turtle's leadership had resulted in the physical destruction and displacement of Miamis. To cooperate with Little Turtle in order to protect what remained of the Miami domain would have made little sense. In time, the disagreements between Little Turtle and Pacanne proved fertile ground for rumors about the Shawnee Prophet to take root because the Americans were unable to see the disagreements as an internal affair among the Miamis. Instead, the Americans interpreted such debates as a by-product of the Prophet's teachings.

The Intruder

Pacanne's resistance to outside threats grew when rumors began circulating of a Shawnee prophet who was leading a revitalization effort in the Ohio country. Tenskwatawa's mission to reform Shawnee society began in the spring of 1805, when he experienced a vision so profound that he gave up alcohol and decided to help his fellow Shawnees divorce themselves from the destructive forces of Euroamerican culture. Within a year, he established a settlement for this purpose at Greenville, Ohio, three miles from Anthony Wayne's Fort Greenville. Alcohol was banned, as were interracial marriages, polygamy, and the domestication of livestock. The Shawnees constructed nearly sixty lodges around a long and imposing council house that sat atop a hill. Dawn and dusk were met with equal drama, according to Al Cave, as "the faithful offered prayers to the Great Spirit . . . in a ceremony described by white visitors as both solemn and dramatic."[14]

Tenskwatawa hoped that the settlement at Greenville would become a cultural center where all Shawnees across North America would gather in unity. Although often overlooked by scholars, the Prophet's original settlement was to be, as described by Al Cave, "the new center of Shawnee life" and a place where refugee Shawnees could gather together. While most historians mention the Prophet's first community at Greenville, Ohio, they typically frame it as the first stage of the Prophet's pan-Indian nativism instead of a settlement devoted to Shawnee renewal. The Prophet and his town would eventually evolve into a haven for all Indians who hoped to stop the polluting influence of Euroamerican culture, but this lofty goal took time to develop as the Prophet's goals changed. Yet examinations of the extent to which the Prophet's methods remained Shawnee in substance despite his efforts to incorporate non-Shawnee Indians have remain limited in larger part because Prophetstown has always been seen as pan-Indian in ideology.[15]

The evolution of Prophetstown from a Shawnee to pan-Indian village occurred as Tenskwatawa mounted witch-hunts against Indian leaders who aided the Americans or who failed to abide by the Prophet's dictates. Some claimed that the Prophet and his followers had gone "religiously mad," but others saw promise in his leadership and flocked to Greenville to hear him. Given the relative distance between many of the Shawnee communities, Tenskwatawa's community at Greenville served as a gathering place for people who had been displaced. Greenville's reach extended to the Potawatomies, Lenapes, Ottawas, Ojibwas, Sacs, and Wyandots. To a certain extent, Greenville only continued a tradition of diverse Indian gatherings in the region.[16] Yet disagreement among Indians prevented Tenskwatawa from establishing a unified Indian community just as it had disrupted meetings at the Glaize in earlier years.

Among the Shawnee people, disagreement was frequent. While the Prophet hoped to construct a permanent physical and cultural barrier between the Shawnees and Euroamericans, Black Hoof's Shawnees rejected his message. Black Hoof, like Little Turtle, remained wary of continued militancy against the Americans. Instead, he advocated adapting to American social mores in order to prevent full-scale annihilation of the Shawnees. Desperate to protect Shawnee culture, Black Hoof believed that associating with the Prophet would spell disaster. Because he was a highly influential leader, Black Hoof's resistance was especially difficult for Tenskwatawa and Tecumseh to bear. Without support from Black Hoof, Greenville became more of a symbolic settlement for displaced and frustrated Indian communities throughout the Ohio Valley rather than a cultural capital for the Shawnee people. Tenskwatawa probably hoped that his fellow Shawnees would see the remarkable influence he had upon other Indian communities; perhaps then they would join him in Ohio. This did not happen, though, and Greenville remained a heterogeneous Indian settlement rather than a Shawnee center.

The relationship between the Prophet and Black Hoof was more than a reaction to American intrusions into the region. Framing Shawnee actions within the context of American nationalism can do only so much to explain Native motives. Individual Shawnee villages had long been in competition for influence among the many Shawnee bands.

As one historian noted, "Black Hoof was a member of the Maykujays (traditionally the least prestigious of the Shawnee divisions)" and had long been overshadowed by other Shawnee leaders. Like Little Turtle, Black Hoof had proven himself in war and become an esteemed village chief, but his continued ascendency as a leader after 1795 bothered many people. Tecumseh saw Black Hoof as an overambitious leader who neglected Shawnee custom in challenging his fellow Shawnees.[17] Black Hoof's growing influence rankled other Shawnee leaders—especially the two brothers—who refused to recognize his power as legitimate. Scholars typically read divisions between Shawnee communities—and Black Hoof's support of the Americans—as a reflection of American intervention and influence among the Shawnees. The rationale follows that as the Shawnees were displaced through violence, small fractures within the Shawnee polity grew into much larger divisions. In reality, animosities that existed between Shawnee settlements demonstrate that Shawnee life and identity was localized during this period and that Shawnees were not necessarily attracted to the idea of a singular Shawnee nation, much like the Miamis.

Black Hoof's behavior does not indicate that he accepted the inevitability of American expansion; on the contrary, his actions show that there was an ongoing contest for power among the Shawnees. One scholar notes that Indian leaders such as Black Hoof used their relationships with the Americans "to increase the power of their villages." The persistence of localized identities likely reinforced what Stephen Warren describes as Black Hoof's and Tenskwatawa's "single-minded obsession with coercive, and centralized authority" over their villages.[18] In that sense, Black Hoof and Tenskwatawa were quite similar in their actions after 1795. Both sought to empower their respective Shawnee communities and were willing to incorporate non-Indians to that end. Their differences rested in their methods for constructing power and influence after 1808. Black Hoof saw the Americans as willing allies whose friendship would protect his Shawnee community; Tenskwatawa rejected Americans in order to make his people safe. Tenskwatawa's frustrations (and his evolution as a leader) were a reaction both to the imposing power of the American nation and to the divisions within his own Shawnee community.

Despite Tenskwatawa's failure to unite Shawnee peoples at Greenville, other Indians remained convinced that the Prophet exercised too much influence. Little Turtle's son-in-law William Wells continued to pressure the Prophet to leave the region. Wells was not alone; French traders also warned Harrison that the Prophet planned to murder any Indian "whom he suspects of an attachment to the United States." They told Harrison that the Indians at Greenville were gathering for war against the Americans. However, Wells and the Euroamericans had little power to force Tenskwatawa's removal from Ohio. Despite assuring the Americans that he was not unduly sympathetic to the Miamis, Wells hoped to protect Little Turtle's party. Wells and Little Turtle had grown increasingly wary of the Prophet's confrontational statements and feared he might start a war. Like the French traders, Wells spoke of the Prophet in dramatic terms, saying that through him "the Great Spirit will in a few years destroy every white man in America."[19] Tenskwatawa's rhetoric rankled Wells because it challenged Little Turtle's leadership in the valley. The Prophet defied Miami authority by claiming that no single Indian polity had the right to sell lands.

As an Indian agent who had intimate ties to the Miamis, William Wells hoped to control post-Greenville diplomacy to benefit his father-in-law, Little Turtle. Some historians have framed Wells's actions in relation to his desire to protect American expansionism, but this neglects the cultural and familial ties he had to the Miamis. Taken captive by the Miamis at age twelve, Wells forged strong relationships with the Miami Indians and eventually married Little Turtle's daughter while reestablishing connections with his Euroamerican family in Kentucky. Little Turtle knew Wells's value as a go-between. Harrison recognized this too, for he made Wells the Indian agent at Fort Wayne. Devoted to Little Turtle and fearful that the Prophet might overshadow his father-in-law, Wells manipulated information and material goods to protect the interests of Little Turtle. He purposely overspent his allowance as factor of the Fort Wayne Indian agency in order to distribute goods and garner support for Little Turtle. Moreover, Wells used his exaggerated descriptions of the Prophet to sway Harrison's opinion.

In August 1807, Wells detailed the Prophet's militancy and the many Indians who flocked to his community, implying that more than a dozen different Indian communities were in support of the Prophet. In describing a secret meeting between Miami leaders, Richardville, Pacanne, and the Owl, Wells described the rogue Miami leaders as supporters of the Prophet. Wells detailed a situation in which Pacanne and the Owl were secretly organizing the Indians of the Kickapoo towns where "13 different nations will be represented." Such a gathering was especially threatening given that, according to Wells, the Shawnee Prophet promised that "the Great Spirit will in a few years destroy every white man in America" and that the British were "at the bottom of all this business" as they were plotting for war against the United States.[20]

But Pacanne would not have so readily handed over his influence to a Shawnee intruder. Caught between the pro-American Little Turtle and the nativist Tenskwatawa, Pacanne sought a middle ground just as he had with the 1804 treaty. He hoped to find a place where the Miamis could unify to protect their interests at a time when outside threats continued to gather momentum. Wells's intent seems clear. He wanted Harrison to see the Prophet and Pacanne as collaborators who would continue to oppose American advances. Wells's efforts to force the Prophet out of Miami affairs appeared to backfire. An Indian agent at Fort Wayne questioned Wells's loyalty to the government's assimilation plans, and Tenskwatawa echoed this sentiment when he told Harrison not to listen to the "advice of bad birds."[21] This is not to suggest that Wells was the only deceitful party. Nevertheless, it is clear that Wells could not separate himself from his Miami roots, and that attachment worked to his benefit. Wells's rhetoric about the Prophet convinced many Indians and Euroamericans that Tenskwatawa meant them harm.

In early 1808, the Prophet, his brother Tecumseh, and a host of followers trudged west through the woods bordering the Miami and Maumee Rivers. They were on their way to a settlement near the confluence of the Wabash and Tippecanoe Rivers. Weary of the hostility from his fellow Shawnees and from Euroamericans, the Prophet had decided to move west, where he could find many Indians who had thus far been isolated from whites. The Prophet's migration represented more than a piece of the Shawnee diaspora; it was also a shift in Wabash-Maumee Valley politics that would influence the structure of the Prophet's town.

In the summer of 1807, Main Poc visited the Prophet at Greenville, where he heard Tenskwatawa and Tecumseh decry interracial marriages, liquor, witchcraft, and American goods. The three men forged a close friendship through their shared rejection of American ways.[22] Main Poc exercised great influence among Potawatomi Indians communities as a spiritual leader; people relied on his ability to heal disease, locate animals for the hunt, and to see the future, but many also sought his support because he rejected the growing American intervention in the region after 1795. Main Poc hoped to protect Potawatomi interests by forcing the Americans out of their new settlements at Vincennes and St. Louis. This angered the Americans and Miami Indians, who feared Main Poc's growing influence among the Kickapoos and Sacs and Foxes because it primed the area for open war.

Given that Main Poc was a relative outsider to the valley, his invitation to the Prophet constituted an insult to the Miamis and other long-term inhabitants of the region. The Prophet's presence at Tippecanoe placed him in an important position to influence Indians deep in the interior of Miami territory. Main Poc's collaboration with the Prophet irked William Wells, for the Indian agent had hoped that Main Poc, "the pivot on which the minds of all the western Indians turned," would aid him in banishing the Prophet.[23] Such a comment is surprising given that scholars have largely ignore Main Poc and catalogued the actions of the Shawnee Prophet with near obsessiveness. To that end, Wells tried to bribe the Potawatomi leader with more than eight hundred dollars' worth of goods. Main Poc bested Wells, enjoying free food and provisions while organizing an attack on Potawatomi enemies in direct opposition to Harrison's wish that Indians refrain from fighting. Main Poc remained independent from American and Miami control, which represented another threat to Little Turtle and Pacanne.

Tenskwatawa settled in the heart of Miami country without considering the extent to which their communities' politics might upset the established economic, political, and social relationships in the area. The Miamis could no longer associate with the Americans without first proving their loyalty, and the French watched trade decline throughout the area around Ouiatenon and Prophetstown due to the Prophet's demands that his followers shun non-Indian goods. More important, memories of Potawatomi attacks on Piankashaw and Wea Indians convinced many people that the attacks would resume with the appearance of Main Poc and the Prophet.[24] But the local geopolitics of the Wabash-Maumee Valley mattered little to Tenskwatawa or Main Poc, for the two men valued Tippecanoe for its location between large settlements of Indians along the Great Lakes and the Mississippi and Ohio Valleys. In addition, any settlement at Tippecanoe was just a two days' canoe trip from Vincennes and less than four days from Fort Malden, a British hub south of present-day Detroit. River travel enabled swift communication and allowed warriors from various Ohio Valley communities to gather at Malden whenever necessary.

Prophetstown, for all intents and purposes, replaced the once vibrant Indian center at Kekionga: it reoriented Indian migration to the Tippecanoe rather than the Wabash-Maumee portage and displaced the Miami-speaking residents of Tippecanoe. While Miamis had been able to associate with the Prophet's Greenville settlement without undermining their interests, they could not do so at Prophetstown, for that would indirectly acknowledge the Prophet's influence in the heart of Miami territory. The likelihood of the Miamis ever recognizing Tenskwatawa's and Tecumseh's pan-Indian confederacy diminished greatly when the outsiders constructed their capital in the center of the remaining Miami homeland.[25]

At the root of the animosity between the Prophet and the Miamis lay a fundamental difference in their understandings of what it meant to be sovereign. Tenskwatawa demanded that Indians unify under *his* leadership, focusing on shared Indianness rather than unique cultural histories. Such a belief was the product of Tenskwatawa's nativist ideals, but it was also uniquely Shawnee. Unlike the Miamis, Shawnee creation stories reflected an itinerant identity and a malleable sense of place due to their constant displacement and migration. The Shawnees learned to maintain their "distinctiveness through beliefs and practices that were not linked to place and that could be sustained in a wide variety of geographic contexts." The Shawnees' diasporic history involved frequent moves in order to access trade and to solidify diplomatic relationships. By the early 1800s, one could find Shawnee communities from Ohio to Missouri. The Miamis, by consensus, had protected their settlements and interests by controlling an important trade portage between the Wabash and Maumee Rivers and by accommodating outsiders in order to access their trade goods. Thus, they perfected a system that forced outsiders to adjust their interests and migrate to Miami country, which enabled the Miamis to remain relatively sedentary. The Shawnees could remain culturally Shawnee even if their mission at Prophetstown failed and they were forced to move. The Miamis could not do the same without risking a terrible social crisis.[26] C. C. Trowbridge confirmed the value the Miamis placed on the region around Tippecanoe when he interviewed the Miamis in the 1820s. The Miamis' story reflected the cultural importance of areas such as Kekionga, Ouiatenon, and Vincennes. In talking to Trowbridge, the Miamis emphasized geographic markers, specifically their historical connections to Ouiatenon, the Vermillion River, and Vincennes. For some Indians, conception of place was in many ways portable, while the Miamis did not consider outmigration to the same extent as the Shawnees.

Simply put, the national trinity had little traction when village and ethnic identities predominated. Various Indian and non-Indian settlements tried to protect the local relationships they had fostered throughout the eighteenth century while two new towns (Vincennes and Prophetstown) vied for cultural hegemony in the region. Kathleen DuVal has masterfully detailed the ways in which Indians of the trans-Mississippi West fought to control their "sovereign identities," yet the same discussion is absent in discussions of Indians in the Wabash-Maumee Valley who ignored the more nationalistic precepts espoused by men such as the Prophet to protect their ethnic values.[27]

Vincennes

In some cases, whites acted in ways that were nearly indistinguishable from their Indian adversaries and neighbors. Like Indian country, Vincennes was a contested place and lacked sufficient cohesiveness and unity necessary for the people to function effectively as one community and nation. When Governor William Henry Harrison negotiated land-cession treaties with the various Wabash Indian communities, he also imagined the western boundary of the United States and the confines of Vincennes. In doing so, he fueled a passionate dispute over the cultural identity of the town: would it be American, French, or Indian? Euroamerican settlers felt so strongly about the answer to this question that they willingly attacked each other in the streets to get what they wanted. Harrison's attempts at consolidation should not lead us to think that American movement into the region signaled a position of strength that made dependent and marginalized figures of Indian peoples. Instead, factionalism within the white community undermined efforts by the Americans to assert one single policy and agenda. Andrew Cayton concludes that the Wabash Valley had cast off its multicultural cloak by this period and that "whites and Indians saw themselves as unique and were unwilling to sacrifice the core beliefs of their society."[28] At times, the very opposite occurred. Neither whites nor Indians stood shoulder-to-shoulder in defending their interests. Americans did hope to refashion Vincennes into an American town, but they became fiercely divided over the identity that their community should take. Much like residents of the Prophet's settlement, the inhabitants of Vincennes shared common space but fought to protect their cultural and political identities at the expense of their town. And as they vocalized their displeasure with each other, they created an atmosphere of violence that nearly ruined the territory.

How did the American town of Vincennes come to be? Shortly after the destruction of Kekionga, Congress carved the state of Ohio out of the Northwest Territory, renaming the remaining area Indiana Territory with Vincennes as its capital. Federal officials laid out a plan for expansion in the Land Ordinance of 1785 and hoped that the burgeoning American population would settle the vast territory, eventually fragmenting those lands into new states. Territorial governments offered social and economic opportunities for men desperate to find steady income, social distinction, cheap land, and stability during a time when American society experienced large-scale demographic growth, an evolving political structure, a fickle market, and religious revivalism. These changes revolutionized American society by reorienting social, political, and economic relationships during the late 1700s and early 1800s. Although opportunities gave people more chances to succeed in the growing market society, they also created many more chances for failure. As Americans tried to survive in the western territories, they forged new identities as they struggled to create physical spaces they saw as familiar and safe.

Most settlers realized their well-being was fundamentally connected to physical security, an issue determined by local decisions and circumstances rather than national dictates. Safety often depended upon a delicate balance of trade and goodwill between the various European, Indian, and American peoples in the area. The potential for violence and even death was ever-present. It took only one person—for instance, Daniel Sullivan—to act without regard to the well-being of Vincennes and unwittingly incite a frontier war. Sullivan was notorious for his hatred toward the Miamis: he was often seen about town carrying his collection of Indian scalps, and he once killed a sick Indian in retribution for an unrelated Indian raid and then dragged the dead body about town. Many Anglo settlers had experienced some sort of Indian-related violence at some point in their recent past or imported family stories that served to shape their understanding of safety. Vincennes in the early 1800s crystallized out of the dynamic interplay between this frontier violence, revolutionary nationalism, and the legacy of failed European colonialism and the localized world that resulted. This is why the question of slavery loomed so large in Vincennes: a national law such as the Northwest Ordinance mattered very little when no one party or community held sway and where the federal government had little to no enforcement power.[29]

Complicating matters, what the Americans called Indiana Territory was in fact the Miami homeland, and in the minds of some, culturally New France. The Americans could not enforce their laws without destabilizing the area because their ability to exert any sort of control in the region surrounding Vincennes depended upon peoples who had been living there for much longer. The atmosphere of the town bordered on anarchy. Shortly after he arrived in the early 1800s, the territorial printer Elihu Stout described several intoxicated Indians lying in the mud next to their dead brethren and decomposing horse and pig carcasses. C. F. Volney, a visitor to Vincennes around the same time, described the Indians as "almost naked, tanned by the sun and air, shining with grease and soot; head[s] uncovered; hair course [*sic*], black and straight; face[s] smeared with red, blue, and black paint, in patches of all forms and sizes." These Indians visited Vincennes because they had a historical connection to the area and had family members in the French community, many of whom were traders. Although both Indians and non-Indians needed to trade to survive, economic relationships often ignited violence in the streets when disagreements broke out over the sale (and abuse) of alcohol. Volney described the violence he witnessed as common, noting that "it was rare for a day to pass without a deadly quarrel, by which ten men [lost] their lives yearly."[30] Though alcohol was a factor in the violence, it was not always the underlying cause. Diverse interests and diverse peoples came into regular contact with each other, which forced the sectarian nature of the Wabash-Maumee Valley to overflow into the streets of Vincennes. Here, various peoples (Indian and non-Indian alike) fought over their interests and defended their presence in the region.

Yet within this mess, Indians and French traders thrived. And many hoped to continue to do so at the expense of the American infiltrators who wanted to extend their republic west. One of the few things on which the American residents agreed was that Vincennes was a distinct French town in terms of the economy, land ownership, and culture. And the Americans hated them for it. The French survived by trading regularly with the local Indians while also farming communal lands. They resisted adopting American values requiring the farming of private property and large-scale participation in the market economy because it would have placed undue pressure on them and their Indian neighbors. Many French chose to defend their autonomy and way of life in the face of greater political and economic marginalization by the Americans. As a result, the Americans in Vincennes viewed the French with distaste and contempt, as though they were de facto Indians.

Although the arrival of the Americans in the late 1770s transformed relationships throughout the area, the French maintained their unique village identity that many saw as distinctly European. Vincennes was at once an American and French town. Even the physical differences between French and American buildings reflected this dual identity.

Most structures were French-made and lacked the more "civilized" features visible in American homes. To the Swiss immigrant John Badollet, the French "did not . . . conceive the importance of timber" and covered their houses, stables, and barns like a European village "with bark, which destroys more timber than can well be calculated." Badollet decried the peoples' "uncouth combination of French and Indian manners." While industrious Americans worked hard to develop the land, the French lived "in a great state of poverty, hauling their firewood from a distance of three or four miles, raising a little corn in the neighborhood," seemingly content with few comforts. One could stand in the commons of Vincennes and see, as Badollet described, "trees strewed over & covering the ground, just as if a west Indian hurricane had exerted its destructive fury on the land, & the whole appearing like a barren waste." Americans would not stand for such "nonsense."[31]

Physical descriptions of Vincennes reflected the distaste that Americans had for the French. Jonathan Jennings—the first governor of the state of Indiana—watched dozens of Frenchmen plowing their fields with visible distaste, for the French held land in common rather than dividing it into individual plots. Although the French men plowed the fields, quite unlike Indian women, Jennings saw shared property as "very ridiculous," if not Indian. Such prejudice played an important part in Anglo settlers' dispossession of the French in Vincennes. Jennings's observation, moreover, demonstrates that Anglo settlers had forgotten their own history of holding land in common and had begun to generalize all commonly held lands—even if they were French lands—as "Indian" and backward. Lieutenant Larrabee was only moderately kinder in his assessment. He enjoyed dancing with the "Fair Sect" at the French balls periodically held in town but noted that the French had corrupted the character of Vincennes through their regular trade with Indians. Although the French offered great hospitality, Volney described their "idleness and ignorance" in domestic affairs and the market as exceeded only by that of the Indians, whom many Americans saw as lazy and unproductive.[32]

Vincennes earned a reputation for violence in part because of the trading houses and taverns operated by the French. The chance to see French relatives and friends and trade for goods (particularly alcohol) attracted an assortment of Indians into the town. The Americans cried out against such rowdy gathering because they feared that drunkenness and violence would threaten their livelihoods, as well as the sanctity of their Anglo spaces. Governor Harrison wrote of the disorder that Indians brought to the town: "intoxicated to the number of thirty or forty at once, when they commit the greatest disorders, drawing their knives, and stabbing every one they meet . . . breaking open the houses of citizens; killing their cattle and hogs, and breaking down their fences."[33] Harrison tried to quell violence by regulating liquor through new laws that governed the sale of liquor to Indians. As violence declined, the Americans began to establish mercantile and hospitality businesses alongside their French counterparts.

For William Henry Harrison, Vincennes represented an opportunity for a displaced Virginian to add to his family's prestige by serving as the territorial governor and superintendent of Indian affairs. His father, Benjamin, had signed the Declaration of Independence, and his brother had served in Congress. His father's death in 1791, however, left Harrison without enough money to continue studying medicine at the University of Pennsylvania. He entered the military, serving as Anthony Wayne's aide-de-camp during his campaign against the Indian confederation. After Wayne's victory at Fallen Timbers, Harrison served as the Northwest Territory's delegate to Congress and occupied Arthur St. Clair's post as governor during his absences. In March 1800, John Adams appointed Harrison as governor of Indiana Territory, a post he held from 1800 until 1812.

Harrison was well versed in the territorial politics of the era and understood that it was his job as governor to establish American hegemony in the Wabash-Maumee Valley. This involved remaking the physical image of the town while also extending American sovereignty by negotiating treaties with the various Indian communities. But it also required that Harrison convince his fellow Americans that his policies were beneficial. This was a tiring and intense process for a man who probably suffered through his governorship as the people he hoped to lead routinely questioned his policies and regularly petitioned Congress to replace him. In addition, Harrison found himself having to negotiate with various divided Indian communities who were often unwilling to work with each other. Harrison saw no end to their combativeness, and he began to despise them for it. As a result, he had to reconsider his Indian policies—and even earlier treaties like those of 1802 and 1803—at every treaty ground in order to appease the Indians. During Harrison's tenure, then, governance relied on a set of continually evolving relationships rather than immutable policies and laws. The territory was remaking him as much as he hoped to make it.

Each Indian community had a different relationship with the Americans—some were peaceful while others were violent. Harrison's attempt to use expansion as a ladder to political office, while understandable, proved remarkably difficult and frustrating. Given the factionalized and multi-ethnic nature of the region, he was faced with the impossible task of satisfying a diverse array of peoples who often held conflicting views. When he was not defending himself to his superiors, he was often trapped in heated negotiations with Indians, caught between the needs of local factions and his national duties as a territorial governor.[34] Increasingly, he found himself more focused on local factional politics because he rightly feared that certain cliques might convince the federal government to replace him. Harrison's government functioned well largely because it consisted of like-minded men beholden to the governor, but the governor's policies created factional strife within Vincennes that undermined his governance. Men such as John Badollet, although initially a supporter of Harrison, quickly found themselves disgusted by governor's territorial politics, eventually breaking with him entirely.

If Harrison had looked beyond the alcohol-fueled brawls, he would have realized early on that the French were a necessary presence. Not only did they serve an important role in developing trade throughout the valley, but they used their familial and historical connections to maintain peace in the region by serving as diplomatic go-betweens. Even though they did not hold influential posts in the territorial government, they did determine in large measure the safety of the region and, with that, the success of the American settlement.[35] Furthermore, the task of distinguishing between an American "Self" and the non-American "Other" within the territorial polity became all the more difficult when Americans were forced to rely on French outsiders. Such identities were not as rigid and concrete as historians have suggested. And once the Americans invited French traders to aid their efforts at expansion, the Americans no longer enjoyed a monopoly on the movement of information and money through the region. By letting the French into the process, the Americans taught them how the territorial system worked, which was essential if the French were to manipulate regional circumstances to their advantage.

By participating in various treaty negotiations, the French traders meant to protect the evolving trade network, which in turn allowed them to protect their own economic interests. These complex relationships, and Harrison's dependency on the French traders and interpreters, were evident in Harrison's descriptions of treaty councils. After the Indian signatories and interpreters came to an agreement, Harrison paid the French traders, who would then distribute (and profit from) the goods

Indians "purchased" from their trade houses. In addition, in order to "prevent jealousy" from undermining the council, Harrison paid the interpreters amounts "greater than usual" for the "indulgence[s]" necessary to appease Indian leaders. But French efforts to use treaty councils to facilitate trade and profit should not be confused with friendship. The French remembered the violence ushered in by Clark's victory in February 1779 and Sullivan's murderous rampage through the streets of Vincennes. Trade declined precipitously during the early American period, causing great suffering among the French residents, who depended upon it for their livelihood. The French also recalled when the Americans intentionally burned their trading houses at Tippecanoe in 1791; American military commanders believed that the French had protected the Indians and collaborated with the British. Threatened by disaffected Indians and ethnocentric Americans, the French had to use any means necessary to protect their interests. When Americans flooded the region, they simply bullied their way into the preexisting economy and eventually displaced the French. In response, the French continued to use their connections with the Indians to forge some semblance of normalcy in a rapidly changing environment. As one scholar has noted, French traders "who were able to persuade their Indian clients and relatives to cede lands . . . stood to profit."[36] By gaining land from the Indians and money from the Americans and by distributing annuity goods, the French hoped to use the Americans and Indians to protect their network of trade routes, mercantile houses, taverns, and agricultural lands. Harrison's dependency on the French was necessary, given that American power was weak. The only military force in the region was the volunteer American militia, and the small towns scattered throughout the region lacked proper defense.

The potential military threat posed by the French convinced Harrison and his officials to tread lightly with Indian land cessions. Lenape Indians warned Harrison that he must "prohibit all your traders along the Mississippi from selling arms and ammunition" to the Osages because they "frequently come to those French traders, and beg for such articles, whereby they have been enabled to do more mischief." Although the French only hoped to trade, it was a quick and likely deadly step to war if the French so desired. Federal officials recognized as much when they instructed Harrison to be cautious when negotiating with the Indians of the Wabash-Maumee Valley. Although the 1795 Treaty of Greenville ceded a tract of land including Vincennes to the Americans, Henry Dearborn instructed Harrison to ascertain and define the exact boundaries with the Wabash Indians.[37] Dearborn worried that the Indians who appeared "uneasy" might react violently if the surveyors marked the wrong lands, but he also knew that the Treaty of Greenville had not forced the Indians to leave the ceded areas.

Despite Harrison's belief in the indisputable nature of the treaty's provisions in regard to the Vincennes tract, he also said that "none of the Piankashaw chiefs (by which tribe all the former sales in this country were made) attended the Treaty of Greenville, and the Wea chiefs, who are said to have represented them, are all dead." To a certain extent, Harrison recognized the fraudulent nature of the treaty and the possibility of war if the Indians continued to oppose it. In Harrison's mind, the Indians did not quite recognize their collective power, but it was "the French [who] could induce them to [war]." Rather than incite confrontation, he suggested not "taking the whole" of the tract guaranteed in the treaty and instead sought to negotiate with the Indians for the remainder, an important reminder that earlier treaties were more imagined than real.[38] Harrison felt that continued diplomacy would result in the same land cessions stipulated in the treaty while also maintaining peace, but he knew that this would not be possible without French support. Even with the aid of traders Joseph Barron, his brother-in-law Michel Brouillet, and Toussaint Dubois, the Miamis continued to resist the land cessions outlined by the Treaty of Greenville. By late summer of 1802, it became obvious that another council was necessary to solidify the Vincennes tract boundaries.

Harrison's frustration in treaty councils that summer compelled him to seek extralegal means to delineate the boundaries of the recent land cession. According to Harrison, the Wabash Indians originally gave the tract to the French, who then sold it to an American speculation company before the Revolutionary War. Harrison argued that these transactions voided French and Indian claims to the area and made the land the rightful property of the United States. In doing so, he ignored a congressional decision that had rejected the legitimacy of speculative land sales.

While Harrison used the old French claims to define the boundaries of Vincennes, the Americans sought to alter the physical nature of Vincennes itself. The French were well aware of townspeople like Jennings who snubbed their noses at communal farming, but few could ignore men like Harrison, Stout, and Badollet, who suggested selling off communal lands in order to expand the local American school, aptly named the Jefferson Academy.[39] Distaste for French cultural traditions was one thing, but such a major alteration to the French character of the town was intolerable. Many French residents felt that the territorial government wanted to eradicate any semblance of their society, and they grew increasingly angry at Harrison for seeking their aid with the Indians while also supporting policies that undermined their economic stability.

Resisting the American policies was a challenge for the French once their taxes began to increase. The new tax burden forced several French families to move out of the area; others feared ruin, for the Americans would seize their lands if they defaulted on their tax payments. Unhappy with burdensome taxes and unresponsive public officials, the French demanded that Elihu Stout print resolutions on their behalf in his paper, the *Western Sun*. They expressed their "deep regret and chagrin" toward the elected officials for whom they had voted, men who had failed "to realize the promises and assurances which [the French] too credulously relied upon." If the taxes and unsympathetic representatives were not enough, once the French were in arrears, the Americans began auctioning off their property. Confusing tax laws were amplified by a language barrier that prevented most French residents from understanding the laws in the first place. These developments added to the increasingly bitter feelings most French residents had toward the Americans, guaranteeing that the pluralistic community of Vincennes remained segregated.[40] To make matters worse, most Frenchmen blamed American intervention for Indian violence. In fact, most French routinely socialized with their Indian friends and family members. Few French could find a silver lining in the American policies that forced them to either abandon their homes or their traditions in order to survive in Indiana Territory. Their choices were much like those of the nearby Indians—adapt or move.

Negotiating land cessions for the territorial government allowed the French to maintain existing economic and social relationships with the Wabash Indians. Their influence among the various Wabash Indian nations, not to mention the Indians camped in the immediate vicinity, made the French useful to the Americans. By facilitating land cessions, French traders and interpreters controlled annuity payments and goods sent by the United States government to the Indians. It was common for the French traders to siphon off goods to trade at a later time, to charge the federal government for items they never delivered to the Indians, and to preserve traditional social relationships through the distribution of gifts. Since they were essential to the diplomatic process, the French interpreters and merchants maintained a certain degree of autonomy in the region because the Indians simply refused to negotiate without the French. The American officials did not understand the geographical layout of the lands, nor did they recognize the important differences between the various Indian communities living along the Wabash. American ignorance of Indian affairs in the Wabash region meant that the French would remain important for territorial affairs. In fact, even Harrison struggled to understand French, the language of diplomacy, and relied on an interpreter when available.[41] Harrison knew that he could not protect Vincennes without appeasing and relying upon the French.

By 1807, it was increasingly apparent that the French had not fully assimilated into American society. In fact, the Americans in some ways had adapted to French norms of trade and social living. The central area of the town remained French property, underdeveloped in the eyes of the Americans, and most French still did not speak or even understand English. This bothered the governor, who privately expressed his deep ethnocentrism by questioning French loyalty to American interests. In 1807, when disputes over maritime rights increased hostilities between the Americans and the British, Harrison asked the French to make their opinion clear. Harrison needed to gauge French sentiment, for the Americans would be at a disadvantage if their neighbors allowed the Indians to side with the British. Although the French expressed their loyalty to the Americans, they also questioned why such a loyalty oath was necessary. Their resolutions reflected deep-seated anger over years of displacement. In their minds, Harrison needed to abandon his political rhetoric and focus on the facts. Rather than simply accede to Harrison's demands, the French used the situation to question the governor's doubts and to state bluntly that their "conduct" in Vincennes had always been peaceful. Eric Hinderaker suggests that Congress in this era mitigated disagreements between Americans and the French by affording rights and privileges to both groups.[42] Yet it is important to consider the ways in which the territorial system created stark divisions between the French and Americans. Interconnected with Indians in a diverse system of regional trade, the French refused to abandon their way of life.

Given that their community had been forged in an era of colonialism, the French often played political forces against each other to their benefit. Although the Americans recognized such duplicity, they could do very little to prevent it. Hyacinthe Lasselle, one of the most respected French traders in the region and benefactor to many of the French living in Vincennes, did not hesitate to play American and Indian interests against each other. Americans misinterpreted Lasselle's economic ventures as a form of loyalty to the United States when in fact he was simply protecting his own interests. Most Americans believed that the French traders were pro-American because they negotiated for the United States in important treaty councils. But some of these traders, like those in Lasselle's family, had a history of switching sides. In 1794, Lasselle's uncle Antoine was nearly executed for being a British spy. Similarly, his brother Francois was accused of war crimes during the War of 1812. One historian concluded that "it is hard not to notice a certain self-serving persistence in French attitudes" in Vincennes. Michel Brouillet, longtime resident of Vincennes, married a Miami woman with whom he had a son, Jean Baptiste Brouillet. Furthermore, Michel's father had held commissions as both a British and American officer.[43] This sort of maneuvering between nations and imperial interests was certainly a hallmark of Miami society, and it became more pronounced among the French after the end of the Seven Years' War.

Several other traders and interpreters had intimate and material connections with the local Indians, in particular the Miamis. Many if not most of the French traders and interpreters who facilitated American diplomatic measures during this period married and had children with Miami women. Even Harrison recognized the ulterior motives of the French interpreters when he told William Eustis that "nine tenths of them prefer the interests of the Indians to that of their employers." This was more than the French wanting to trade with Indians. Miami women also played a key role in attracting the French men into their communities through sexual relationships. Marriage, companionship, or simply sexual intercourse with coureurs de bois allowed Native women to build, as Richard White has argued, "a bridge to the middle ground," and these relationships could facilitate trade and diplomatic relationships between Indians and the French.[44] Despite the short-lived nature of these relationships, they no doubt affirmed French connections to Native communities that Harrison's policies could not undo. Harrison's inability to gauge French motives and the social and sexual nature of trade allowed the French to use Americans and Indians to maintain some degree of independence.

The challenges Harrison faced were twofold: not only did he depend upon several diplomatic intermediaries who were less than trustworthy, but he also failed to recognize just how much his fellow Americans would oppose many of his policies. Furthermore, Harrison's plot to acquire Indian lands did not go as planned. Frontier residents could not read about ceded Indian lands in the *Western Sun* without wondering how the United States would develop as a nation. How would it be

governed? How would the lands add to the identity of the young republic? As settlers began considering the larger ideological significance of
political activities, two American factions began debating the development of the territory in relation to the use of slaves. Many people had
moved west to avoid change within their communities, but even if settlers escaped whatever albatrosses might hang about their necks, they
were often unable to escape the larger national dialogues wrought by the
Revolution.

The Land Ordinance of 1785 and Northwest Ordinance of 1787 codi-
fied Revolutionary ideals into the system of territorial expansion. These
laws mandated that each new territory could only replicate laws already
in force in the states rather than create their own. Furthermore, each territory had to follow the exact same process for constructing a territorial
government and making application for statehood. National leaders such
as Jefferson believed that this process would maintain equality between
the states while also making sure that each new territory created itself
within the existing framework of republican laws. Yet as settlers moved
west, they crashed headlong into republican traditions that seemed at
odds with changing times. Slavery would be their Rubicon.

According to the Northwest Ordinance, slaves were not allowed north
of the Ohio River; to many settlers, this seemed an arbitrary and even
shortsighted law given the increasing need for bonded labor. Frustration
with Indians also caused frontier communities to question the Founders' plans. Jefferson's civilization program privileged Indians over poor
whites by helping Indians to adopt Anglo systems of farming and husbandry despite the fact that many white settlers struggled without aid.
As a result, settlers began to question the laws of the young republic and
to wonder if they were in fact detrimental.

Although these dialogues employed nationalistic rhetoric, discussions
themselves were often local in substance. The territorial government at
Vincennes governed more than five thousand white people in an area
covering two hundred thousand square miles. Indiana's territorial government employed fewer than twenty men in 1800, most of whom lived
within the confines of Vincennes. The territorial government was not a
policing force or even an enforcer of policy—it simply lacked the power
to assume such roles. In many cases, settlers simply ignored the federal
and territorial laws without any repercussions. Thus, the territorial government was not a bureaucratizing force, but a vehicle through which
Indiana residents became American. In other words, the town was the
structural framework through which they would define and implement

their ideology of nation. And in Vincennes, the structure of territorial government reflected a particular kind of national ideology. In their effort to transform frontier space into a territory, they constructed a new American identity rather than transplanting an existing one.

In this sense, the territorial government was a community unto itself, separate from the larger territory where political leaders could exert a great deal of influence. Whether by marshalling the territorial militia, passing new laws, or negotiating pacts and treaties with nearby Indian communities, the relatively few men in territorial office could shape the daily life of territorial residents in real and significant ways. The making of Vincennes (and Indiana Territory itself) held within it what Eric Hinderaker describes as an "extraordinary capacity to reap the benefits of its citizens' energies." But there were ramifications for such grand potential.[45] In the ever-evolving western territories, one's security rested fundamentally on an ability to maintain peaceful relationships with nearby Indian communities and to earn a living by farming, trading, or speculating in land. It was impossible for frontier Americans to build their nation-state without considering the local European and Indian populations, not to mention the divisions within their own communities. Furthermore, few people had political voice—it was not until 1809 that all white males could vote in the territory—and men had little impetus to participate in national dialogues. The debate over slavery, though, was an important exception, for men realized that their ability to create and maintain successful farms was at stake. Similarly, the opponents of slavery knew that introducing human bondage to the frontier might affect the freedom of all who lived there.

By 1805, slavery had become the most divisive issue in Vincennes. Several influential men objected strenuously to the legalization of slavery and sought to replace Harrison in order to protect their territory from its polluting effects. Men who initially supported Harrison found themselves disgusted by the governor's sponsorship of slavery. John Badollet, for example, rankled at Harrison's attempts to legalize slavery in the region. Born in Geneva, Switzerland, in 1758, Badollet immigrated to Georges Creek, Pennsylvania, by the fall of 1786 to join his close friend Albert Gallatin. Badollet eventually moved to Vincennes with his wife in 1804. Gallatin, secretary of the treasury for Thomas Jefferson, had appointed Badollet as registrar for the land office in Vincennes. Within a year of his arrival in town, Badollet voiced his displeasure with Harrison's attempts to negate the sixth article of the Northwest Ordinance; Badollet wrote that "the introduction of Slavery into this territory continues to be the Hobby horse of the influential men here. . . . The members of the legislature [men appointed by Harrison] have signed a petition to Congress praying for some reasonable modifications to the ordinance, but this favorite topic of slavery, will I trust meet with a general disapprobation in Congress." Badollet decried Harrisonian legislators for their desire "to entail on their Country a permanent evil."[46]

Badollet's role in the office of register necessitated that he speak to almost every new inhabitant of the town; as a result, he came to the conclusion that most citizens rejected slavery, even those from southern states such as North and South Carolina and Kentucky. Badollet quite possibly remembered the oppressive power exercised by the federal government during the Whiskey Rebellion, when he attended the negotiations between the federal government and rebels. Having observed pervasive poverty and complete "human wretchedness" along the Pennsylvania frontier, Badollet could not fathom why the federal government marched soldiers into the region to enforce a tax upon people who were already experiencing great suffering.[47] In his mind, the federal government abused its authority when it used force to impose the law, much like Harrison was doing in his support of slavery.

Slavery persisted in the region after 1800 in part because the French and Indian residents had traditionally owned slaves but also because territorial governors such as Arthur St. Clair and William Henry Harrison did not and could not enforce slavery's prohibition. Slavery, although contrary to article six of the Northwest Ordinance, remained in the area well after the War of 1812 because the territorial and federal political system did not have the power to arrest its spread. Harrison and his supporters believed that the ban on slavery had an adverse effect on the territory; in 1802 they sent a petition to Congress that claimed that the ban on slavery led many people to leave Indiana for Spanish settlements farther west. Settlement meant eventual statehood, but in a more immediate sense, emigration to Indiana Territory would lead to increased revenues—much of which would go to fund the government at Vincennes.

Divergent perspectives about slavery reflected economic developments in the territory. Most Americans owned individual farms outside of Vincennes while the French continued to farm their communal holdings in town. Small manufacturers also popped up throughout the southern half of the territory; by 1810, 33 gristmills, 14 sawmills, 28 distilleries, 1,256 looms, 1,850 spinning wheels, and 18 tanneries produced nearly $160,000 worth of manufactured goods. Small-scale

Table 1. Non-native population statistics

Census for Indiana Territory	1800	1810
Whites	4,577	23,890
Slaves	135	237
Free blacks	163	393
Total population for Indiana Territory	4,875	24,520

Sources: Data adapted from Pamela J. Bennett, ed., "Indiana Territory," Indiana Historian, March 1999, 1–16; Indiana Territory; 1800 U.S. Census, population schedule. Digital Images. June 10, 2015. www.historykat.com/US/census/1800/second-census-united-states-indiana-territory-1800.html.

manufacturing and farming clearly dominated the economic landscape. Most American residents opposed the legalization of slavery in the territory because it would provide incentive for individuals to buy vast tracts of land while also undercutting the need for hired help, thereby replacing free labor with slaves. Labor was a precious commodity during this period. Those who supported slavery tended to own a great deal of land and likely wished to work it with unfree labor. They hoped that slaves and large-scale agriculture would increase their profits. Others worried that they might not be able to afford land if a planter culture took root. In a letter to Attorney General John Breckenridge, Thomas Davis pleaded, "For God's sake don't let Congress introduce Slavery among us." Others like him begged Congress to appoint a governor "who in Sentiment is opposed to Slavery."[48]

Slave experiences in Vincennes did not reflect the antislavery rhetoric printed in the Western Sun. Because Vincennes was a society with slaves rather than a slave society, it lacked the restrictive codes present in the southern states; while the legal record reflects this, the public rhetoric regarding slavery does not. Euroamericans cleverly circumvented the Northwest Ordinance's ban on slavery by freeing their slaves and then forcing them to agree to ninety-nine-year indentures. The judicial record of Vincennes reflects an African American community that enjoyed relative social and legal freedoms compared to their brethren farther south. When some slaves in Vincennes lodged complaints against Euroamerican residents for "ill usage & cruel treatment," the court responded in their favor. Slaves and free African Americans gathered freely with each other and walked throughout the town without passes or supervision; even when imprisoned, slaves could count on the European American community to protect their rights.[49] Yet despite African American mobility, the antislavery men in Vincennes made it seem as if slaveholding practices in the Carolinas and Georgia represented those in Indiana Territory.

The disconnect between the reality and rhetoric reflected the extent to which political factions would ratchet up their language in order to marginalize their political enemies. The rhetoric also demonstrates the ways in which those settlers who opposed the governor extended the cultural and economic boundaries of the South north of the Ohio River in order to engage their adversaries.[50] With boundaries ill-formed, such rhetoric about the potential shape the territory might take could mobilize settlers to action. While the groups initially sought to influence Congress through petitions and by electing a territorial representative responsive to their desires, they eventually decided to settle the issue themselves.

In 1805, Harrison circumvented the Northwest Ordinance by passing an indenture law that would permanently bind former slaves to their owners for up to ninety-nine years. Harrison firmly believed that the federal government had no right to determine the legality of slavery. To him, the Constitution left the question of slavery to the states. By circumventing the Northwest Ordinance, Harrison firmly believed that he was protecting the constitutional liberties of settlers in the territories. If slaves refused to sign their indenture, they would be sold into slavery for life with no hope of freedom. A growing number of Indianans were not pleased. A committee of the territorial legislature declared that the indenture law contradicted the spirit and intention of the Northwest Ordinance because it forced African Americans to spend their entire lives as indentured servants. Such a law not only forced them into "involuntary servitude but downright slavery." George Washington Johnston, the chairman of a committee handling petitions on the subject, called the act a "retrograde step into barbarism."[51] Yet despite the uproar over the law, the proslavery Legislative Council refused to repeal it.

That the pro-Harrison legislature found it necessary to pass such an act speaks volumes about the power of the antislavery factions in Indiana. Thanks to their efforts, Congress had condemned the efforts of those who sought to overturn the sixth article of the Northwest Ordinance. Yet the factions were not as clearly defined as it may appear. Some were antislavery, some were anti-Harrison, and some were both. In the fall of 1808, the anti-Harrisonian divisionists from the Illinois counties joined with the anti-Harrison antislavery men in the eastern counties and petitioned the U.S. House of Representatives. The so-called divisionists wanted to carve a new western territory from Indiana in order to make the new government more responsive to settlers in Illinois country. Despite being proslavery, the divisionists opposed Harrison because he opposed division of the territory. General Washington Johnston's report demanded "that the territorial statue of 1807 legalizing the introduction of negroes and mulattoes should be forthwith repealed." Others opposed to slavery also submitted a petition to Congress, but Congress tabled both the petition and the report.[52] For men like Badollet, these efforts seemed increasingly fruitless, especially after Harrison won reappointment to his post as governor.

Like Badollet in his letters to Treasury Secretary Albert Gallatin, loyal Harrisonians Jesse B. Thomas and Sam Gwathmey looked beyond Congress to petition Vice President George Clinton for support. Their petition played both sides of the issue, claiming that the spread of slavery (legalizing it in Indiana Territory) would be the first step to emancipation.[53] Petitioning the branches of the federal government was only the first act of the debate. Although people throughout the territory argued about slavery, it took a peculiar course within Vincennes.

Disagreements about slavery culminated in a contentious debate in Elihu Stout's newspaper, the *Western Sun*, where a political circus about slavery erupted into charges of treason and violence. The upcoming vote for territorial delegate to the U.S. Congress in 1809 forced several hopeful politicians to state their case for election. They soon found themselves trapped in a calumny-ridden dialogue about slavery. Elihu Stout welcomed the chance to facilitate the dispute. Residents used the power of the press to draw attention to their political positions and argued bitterly about the foundations of Jeffersonian republicanism and the future of Indiana Territory. This long debate defined and identified territorial politicians based on their feelings about slavery. They were, as recent scholars of republicanism contend, confronting an ideological dilemma: "how to maintain the moral force of republicanism without strengthening values antithetical to the expansion of the American economy."[54] For these men, understanding the Jeffersonian tradition was necessary if they were going to lay claim to a purified tradition of civic consciousness essential for the public good. The changing dynamics within Vincennes were much like Harrison's own political career, which reflected the fact that local circumstances and factionalism had the power to redirect and shape national dialogues.

Badollet and other residents soon coalesced into two large factions defined by their stance on slavery. The factions consisted of well-educated men born throughout the United States and Europe who had a firm understanding of republican ideology and the political atmosphere in Washington DC. Benjamin Parke, Thomas Randolph, Elihu Stout, and William Henry Harrison were proslavery and hoped to overturn article six of the Northwest Ordinance or at least pass a law restricting its application in the territory. Parke served as the attorney general to the territory from 1804 to 1808, a position held thereafter by Thomas Randolph, a first cousin to Thomas Jefferson. Stout had immigrated to the territory from Kentucky to serve as the territorial printer. These men represented Harrison's core group of supporters and defended the governor's stance on slavery as well as his policies toward the Wabash Indians. They hoped to force the Indians out of the territory by purchasing their lands and then open up the area to slaveholders in order to spur settlement.

Other residents of Vincennes opposed many of the Harrisonians' policies, especially slavery. They believed that slavery would undermine Euroamerican labor and prevent the settlement of the territory, and they disagreed with Harrison's Indian policy because it seemed to punish the Indians for defending their property. Besides Badollet, the most influential of these anti-Harrisonians were Nathaniel Ewing, Dr. Elias McNamee, Judge John Johnson, William McIntosh, and Jonathan Jennings. All of these men met each other while working for the territorial government. Ewing was the receiver of public monies, McNamee a doctor in town, Johnson a territorial judge, and Jennings worked with Stout before he became the territorial representative in Congress. McIntosh had moved to the territory after fighting with the British during the Revolutionary War, serving as the territorial treasurer until 1804. These men, though from divergent backgrounds, were unified in their opposition to Harrison's proslavery policies. They welcomed an opportunity to discuss slavery when the factions began mobilizing for the territorial elections.

A combative debate over slavery's influence on Indiana territorial affairs broke out in the *Western Sun* in early 1808. Although the debate initially focused on slavery, the rhetoric quickly switched to much deeper issues such as republicanism, religion, and patriotism. In many ways, the newspaper was a frontier version of Warner's "cultural matrix" where settler factions redefined the terms "republican," "slavery," and "Jefferson" to fit their ideological agendas. The Harrisonians and anti-Harrisonians published lengthy articles about the American Revolution and the ways in which their politics embodied the ideals of the newly independent republic. The factions framed their articles around the views of President

Jefferson in order to connect themselves to a republican tradition they believed should be guiding territorial politics. Yet, in their debate over Jefferson, they constructed two competing views of the man. If, according to Warner, the "community of readership is a corporate body . . . and this imaginary community . . . is the elemental form of the nation," then the political factions used the *Western Sun* to define two separate paths to sovereignty, two conceptions of the nation.[55] And, most important of all, slavery became the language through which people discussed the boundaries of the commonwealth.

Most of the men involved in the dispute wanted their faction to win the territorial representative's lone seat in Congress. They hoped that publishing their side of the debate in Stout's paper would tip the balance, for winning office would allow them to implement an intellectual agenda that would shape territorial and national life. Such efforts were not uncommon. As one scholar notes: "When public opinion is fixed, [James] Madison taught, it must be obeyed by the government. When not settled, it may be influenced by those in government."[56] Although the congressional representative would not have voting power, he would be in a position to persuade national leaders in terms of territorial policy. The high emotions created by the debate and the republican pretense meant that participants had to assume pseudonyms.

In February 1808, a man writing under the pseudonym "Slim Simon" challenged Dr. Elias McNamee and George Washington Johnston's suggestion that slavery would reduce the price of labor and undercut the poor, allowing slaveholders to monopolize the market and undermine American religious values. Simon claimed that a class of laboring poor did not exist in the area because residents of the area were "too proud and independent to be day labourers." Slaves were like spinning machines and printing presses—they were tools necessary for the advancement of industry and the creation of a competitive and open market. Simon argued that God had ordained slavery by favoring slave owners Abraham, Isaac, and Jacob. Simon vowed to "unmask" these men so that the public could "behold [them] in all [their] naked deformity."[57] The imagery is powerful. The proslavery Harrisonians believed that their enemies were without clothes, that their political bodies were bare and unmade.

Such rhetoric represents factions who were increasingly tying cultural values to territorial identities. Although slaveholders' daily actions mattered more, the factions increasingly focused on the larger ideas that framed American republicanism. Both parties professed to be true Republicans and also republicans, upholding the religious and national promise inherent in the American Revolution while also emphasizing their disinterested nature toward politics. Both sides also utilized the term "Federalist" as a way to attack their opponents. The different interpretation, and even manipulation, of the meaning of republicanism and the American Revolution played a central role in the debate over slavery. In fact, one of the Harrisonians mocked the anti-Harrisonian understanding of republicanism and suggested that "a special messenger be sent to the tombs of the departed patriots and heroes of '76, to inform them of the discovery of the meaning of the terms Federalist and Republican." McNamee struck back. He claimed that Jefferson and Madison owned slaves out of necessity because they lived in a region "where slaves are almost the only laboring hands." According to McNamee, republicanism and slavery were incompatible because human happiness could only be attained in a society without despotism or slavery. Those who believed otherwise were not real republicans and needed to construct their societies far from Indiana. Slim Simon reminded McNamee that "the republican Congress of 1804 authorized the introduction of slavers in the Orleans and Louisiana territories." General Washington Johnston believed that slavery would "tarnish the fame of our growing country, hitherto held up as the asylum of freedom!!" The anti-Harrisonians saw Jefferson's slave holding as a necessary evil, while the Harrisonians saw it as reinforcing the notion that slavery was legal and just. Both group saw their interpretation as truly republican. Both refashioned a man into the identity and values that would best reflect their territorial visions.[58]

Weeks later, Badollet asked readers to consider the long-term implications of slavery. If slave families were sent north, their population would grow as it had in the South; this would place Indiana "in the same perilous situation, whereinto the southern states have been forced, and which excites so much sympathy for them amongst us." It was not just a debate about the legality of slavery in a territory, which many interpreted as a short-term issue given the inevitability of statehood, but also a debate about the shape Indiana would take as a slave *state*. Allowing slavery "would present to the world the scandalous spectacle of a people asserting in one page, what they deny in the next, declaring in almost the same breath, that *all* men are born free, and yet that a number of men are born *slaves*."[59] Badollet aptly framed the debate within Indiana's eventual statehood in order to force voters to think about Indiana's role within the larger republic. Did frontier settlers really want to become a slave state and an extension of the emerging Cotton South?

The results of the election for territorial representative were less than ideal. The anti-Harrisonian Jonathan Jennings beat Thomas Randolph by just 26 votes, a slim margin in a region ready to explode.[60] With fewer than 1,000 votes to count, Jennings had 428 votes to Randolph's 402. The close election whet the appetites of the Harrisonians, who craved influence in Washington City and convinced them that their enemies had stolen the election. They refused to recognize the victory and began to marshal their forces to nullify it. The factions could not accept that their enemies might have their own claim to Revolutionary republicanism that they held dear. The same held true for both groups' views of slavery.

Irate at the election results, Harrison sought out the ringleaders. He approached Badollet after discovering that he had circulated an antislavery petition throughout the territorial counties. Their heated discussion dampened what had been a friendly relationship. Harrison saw the petition as a personal attack and savaged Badollet in a letter to Albert Gallatin. Harrison demanded that Badollet apologize, but Badollet remained silent. According to Harrison, "a distant & cold politeness succeeded to [their] former intimacy." The governor's anger toward Badollet was only tempered by his suspicion that McIntosh had masterminded the petition. Furthermore, Harrison gave credence to President Jefferson's idea that McIntosh was really the leader of the French faction. The French had overwhelmingly backed Jennings, and not Harrison's friend Thomas Randolph. In Harrison's eyes, it was McIntosh who manipulated Badollet because "there was not a man on earth more easily duped." And in an effort to protect and likely manipulate Badollet, Harrison wrote to Gallatin that he had "prevented a petition being sent from this county signed as I am sure it would be by at least four fifths of the citizens for the removal both of the Register [Badollet] & Receiver [Ewing]." Harrison was equally angry with Gallatin, reminding him that he could make trouble despite being far from Washington. Harrison's friend John Randolph was soon to visit Gallatin for an explanation about rumors that Ewing had circulated to the effect that "Mr. J. Randolph was known to be entirely under British influence."[61]

Harrison's motives were clear. By mentioning all that he had heard from Ewing and the Randolph family, he was telling Gallatin to stop interfering with politics in Vincennes. Gallatin responded within a month, defending Badollet and saying that he had never made any comment about John Randolph. In his anger, Gallatin failed to sign the terse letter. By the fall of 1809, Badollet was no longer simply a Swiss immigrant who held territorial appointment. He had become fully invested in the territorial republican debate and stood as an antislavery advocate devoted to challenging Harrison's politics. To Harrison, Badollet was now an enemy. To Badollet, Harrison was a "moral cameleon" who had "greatly impeded" the settlement of the territory and "filled it [with] intrigue and discord."[62] This was not simply an argument about slavery or territorial governance, but an argument about the interests that would control the United States. With each word—or even with each lie—each side hoped that their influence in the Northwest would grow.

An important pattern is apparent in the slavery debate and the election. The parties started a process in which they divorced important issues (slavery and Jefferson's politics) from territorial realities in order to fashion persuasive arguments that would reinforce their ideological positions. Rather than discuss the actual experiences of slaves in the territory in relation to its proposed development, the factions chose instead to focus on the institution of slavery and its national implications. But as Indian affairs and the threat posed by Prophetstown loomed on the horizon, white frontiersmen compartmentalized these issues, divorcing Indian affairs from territorial truths with deadly repercussions.

With rampant infighting seemingly infecting every community throughout the Miami frontier, the racial and national unity envisioned in the Prophet's national trinity remained impossible. The Prophet's suggestion that the Miamis, Americans, and nativists divide the region into spheres of influence for the sake of coexistence ignored the deeply competitive and divisive nature of life in each community. If a national trinity were to succeed, inhabitants of the region would have to agree upon the physical boundaries of their "nation," and more importantly, members of each community would have to agree upon an ideological and cultural identity. While defining physical boundaries might be possible in the short term, the conflicting ethnic and cultural debates within each community prevented uniformity of action. French traders and interpreters maintained their own cultural and economic space within American diplomatic prerogatives. Pacanne continued challenging Little Turtle's growing influence as a Miami leader, and Badollet refused to see Harrison as an American. Although each community and faction undoubtedly wanted power and to control their boundaries, the disputes went much deeper, to the very core of what it meant to be Indian and American. And as the region destabilized after 1809, these polarized communities would find new opportunities to silence their enemies all the while pushing the western Ohio Valley toward war.

3 /   Prophetstown for Their Own Purposes

In the spring of 1805, Tenskwatawa slipped into a deep trance. In several visions, the Great Spirit revealed a plan that would allow Indians to renew their culture. These became the basis for Tenskwatawa's community at Prophetstown. The Prophet believed that all of his followers were "determined to practice what [he had] communicated to them, that [had] come immediately from the Great Spirit through [him]." The Prophet also declared that Indians needed to unite politically and militarily in order to resist the destructive forces of Euroamerican culture. The pan-Indian alliance the Prophet and his brother envisioned would require Indians to segregate themselves from Euroamericans in almost all facets of life. Such an alliance would lead to the revitalization of Native American communal life.[1] The Prophet and his brother Tecumseh believed that Indians throughout North America needed to consider themselves as one; otherwise, solitary native communities would find themselves at the mercy of a white onslaught.

The pair's historical fame belies the reality of the situation they faced. The brothers failed to prevent American encroachment into the Ohio River Valley because factions of the French, Miamis, and Americans exaggerated, manipulated, and misunderstood the Prophet's nativist message. They did so to advance their own agendas, which ultimately led to the weakening of the pan-Indian experiment at Prophetstown and to the surge in subsequent frontier violence. Yet as Prophetstown suffered internally and externally under the weight of ethnic factionalism, a singular sense of the town as a hotbed of Indian militancy developed throughout the region. By restraining and manipulating what Anglos and Indians thought about Prophetstown, French traders and Miami Indians created a framework for gathering and distributing knowledge about the Prophet and his town.[2]

As Indians and whites used Prophetstown to attack one another, ethnic factionalism created an atmosphere of fear and violence along the frontier that culminated at the Battle of Tippecanoe in 1811. French and Miami agendas eclipsed racial unions. Self-interest and multi-ethnic alliances, rather than race, were at the root of frontier violence and trumped increasingly rigid racial boundaries. In many cases, factionalism increased as different ethnic groups spread lies about each other. The frequency of French-Indian alliances (and the influence of mixed-heritage people) is instructive in this regard. If we put aside the tropes of "race" and "nation" and focus on historical actors, small communities, and the lies they told, we can better explain the divisiveness and violence among and between both non-Natives and Indians in the Ohio River Valley. When the Miamis and French lied about Prophetstown, they gave what David Brion Davis calls "symbolic expression to the deepest . . . needs of a people, and thus the truth of a most revealing kind." Thus, the Miamis and French used falsehoods as a way of defining themselves. Although some scholars have used cross-cultural lying to understand what Gregory Dowd calls the "common concerns" of Native and Euroamerican peoples, the lies spread by the inhabitants of the Wabash-Maumee Valley tell much deeper stories about inter- and intra-ethnic disputes, and the extent to which Prophetstown was central to the growth of ideas, boundaries, and borders.[3]

Not all lies about Prophetstown were equal. The Miamis and French were not simply confused or spreading information they had misunderstood. They had many neighbors and conversed regularly with people in Vincennes and Prophetstown, which meant that they were well-positioned to understand the size and intentions of the inhabitants in both communities. The French and Miamis were skilled at cross-cultural diplomacy and trade, which positioned them to understand the intentions and desires of Native and non-Native settlers and to manipulate information to their advantage. The Miamis and French were interethnic liars. While the Americans lied as well, their lies were the creation of French and Miami misintelligence. Internal disputes among the Americans (such as the debate over slavery) made unreliable information sometimes attractive and also provided the Americans with opportunities to exaggerate perceived truths about Prophetstown. In this sense, the Americans were guilty of exaggerating lies but not necessarily of creating them. The historical record contains an abundance of material on Prophetstown, but we cannot truly understand the reality of the place until we reconsider the motives that drove the people who lived there.

Tenskwatawa's mission was fraught with challenges given the diverse and multi-ethnic nature of Ohio Valley Indian communities. Of the Miamis, Kickapoos, Potawatomies, and Lenapes already in the area, most favored local interests over identifying with a singular tribal entity. Instead of heeding the Prophet's call for unity, Indian people remained divided. Miami influence in the region complicated the situation even further. Though they had never functioned as a unified "tribe," the Miamis offered staunch resistance to any Indian group that tried to challenge their hegemony in the region—thus the Prophet's daunting task. Now Tenskwatawa would have to communicate with each Indian group at the village level in order to incorporate them into his community *and* confront the Miami/French network of trade and political influence that developed over the previous century. The Americans' presence in the region complicated the situation even more. In July 1800, they had commandeered the French town of Vincennes, located 160 miles south of Prophetstown, and made it the capital of Indiana Territory. William Henry Harrison, governor of the territory, pursued American expansion into these western lands by extinguishing Indian title through a series of treaties. As the contest for land and influence grew during the early 1800s, leaders such as Harrison, Miami leaders Little Turtle and William Wells, and the French focused on the Prophet and Prophetstown as the root of regional instability.[4]

Prophetstown

Characterizations of Prophetstown's militancy rested on the assumption that the Prophet and his brother would succeed in their efforts to unify Indians under their nativist banner. But Prophetstown's success depended as much on the willingness of the Indians to abide by the Prophet's teachings as it did on Tenskwatawa's leadership. There is little doubt that hundreds of Indians traveled to Prophetstown and stayed there for months or years at a time. Prophetstown was much more than simply a Shawnee town, though. It was a place where a variety of different Indian communities—Kickapoos, Potawatomies, Ho-Chunks, Miamis, Shawnees, and many others—visited, settled, and, in some cases, died. The town evolved as each of these different groups came and went, for some groups came to hear the Prophet and his brother speak, and others to trade, socialize, and spy. Furthermore, not all Indians arrived or left as nativists. The core group of Indians consistently present at Prophetstown were Ho-Chunks, Kickapoos, Potawatomies, and to a lesser extent, the Prophet's faction of Shawnees. And while each group represented a potential convert, they also represented a potential threat. Many continued to trade with Euroamericans, and more important, they ignored the Prophet's teachings in favor of their own traditions.

Despite these problems, the Prophet and his followers constructed a vibrant and fluid town. At its height, the Indian residents cultivated between one hundred and two hundred acres of corn in order to feed the seasonal migrations of indigenous visitors, in addition to tending a small herd of domesticated cattle despite the Prophet's demand that Indians stop practicing animal husbandry in the Euroamerican fashion. A few lodges were visible near the crops that lined the river, but the center of the town was atop a hill from the river's edge near the meeting house and storage facilities.

Prophetstown's leader attempted to engender other changes as well, centralizing his own authority and solidifying gendered boundaries. While Prophetstown was new as a physical place, it was also new in terms of its organization and functionality. The Prophet's efforts to centralize his authority had immediate benefits for the town. He was able to organize the town according to his vision and encountered limited vocal opposition to his wishes. Indians who supported his nativist vision were able to challenge their traditional leaders, who may have not been as reform oriented. Given the severe disruptions caused by prolonged violence and the alcohol trade, opportunities to challenge more traditional leaders in order to alleviate such stresses were welcomed. But at the same time, his actions had serious consequences. The Prophet and his brother sought to extinguish the power of the village leaders, through whom, Tecumseh said, "all mischief is done." These were the men who sold native land to Americans with impunity. The Prophet took steps to undermine the clan leaders and their hereditary privilege, leaving younger men in charge. These men were often far less experienced in the art of diplomacy and thus typically more prone to violence. As Stephen Warren has argued, the Prophet demanded that his followers "unite . . . around reforms rather than kinship ties."[5] In doing so, he also lost many influential allies who might have helped him control the younger warriors.

As the Prophet undermined the authority of established Indian leaders and replaced it with his own, he also asserted greater patriarchal authority over his followers. Prophetstown was not simply nativist—it was gendered in ways that increasingly mirrored the male-dominated nature of American society. While women in many Native communities typically played a central role in cultivating the land, Tenskwatawa led many of his followers to work daily in the immense field that was, according to John Badollet and Nathaniel Ewing, "beautifully fenced in" by the Indians. Given the significance that agriculture—in particular corn—played in regional trade with the French and British, the Prophet may have asserted his control over women and agriculture as a symbolic gesture to communicate his nativist principles. Corn would no longer be a commodity traded between Indians and Euroamericans. Such trade would only threaten his nativist mission. Moreover, the Prophet certainly recognized the role that women played in the growth of the market in European goods. Not only were they central to the agricultural commodities that fueled regional trade, but it was Native women who married French traders and invited them to live in Indian communities. Women therefore represented two of the most important reasons Indians were suffering spiritual collapse; they were key to trade in bringing non-Native goods into the Native world, but they were also marrying white traders. It stands to reason that when the Prophet denounced interaction with Europeans, he might have cast a very suspicious and angry eye at Native women. Tenskwatawa chipped away at women's power in other ways; he disbanded the Shawnee women's council that had traditionally affirmed decisions to go to war.[6] In asserting control over women, he was doing more than expressing his patriarchal authority and limiting the capacity others had to limit his use of violence. His behavior toward women was a reflection of his understanding that Native women had played a central role in the interethnic and interracial connections he saw as destructive to Native peoples.

Although centralizing authority allowed the Prophet to exert more influence among his followers, such power was only effective if Prophetstown's residents accepted it. Moreover, the practical necessities of supporting several hundred Indians put Tenskwatawa's entire experiment in danger. In the late summer of 1808, the Shawnee brothers were forced to seek assistance because they had not harvested enough food to support their followers. (Their situation was so dire that William Henry Harrison offered them assistance in order to alleviate their suffering.)[7] Tenskwatawa was not able to purge Prophetstown from the destructive influence of European trade, nor was he able to force every Indian community to abandon their ethnic identities for his reformist agenda. In fact, European traders set up their trade shops quite near if not inside Prophetstown, and many Nativist converts continued to domesticate animals and abuse alcohol. Though the Prophet had denounced Native dependency on whites, he realized that hunger could drive people away. Ideology, no matter how powerful, could not compete with basic needs.[8]

If Indians chose to ignore his teachings or to attack their traditional enemies, Tenskwatawa could do very little about it. John Tanner, a long-time resident among various Indian communities north of the Miami homeland, expressed as much in his contemporary narrative of the era. Having spent thirty years among Indians, namely the Ojibwe, Tanner was in a position to judge the effectiveness of the Prophet's teachings. He saw little proof that the Prophet had much lasting influence, writing: "For two or three years drunkenness was much less frequent than formerly, war was less thought of, and the entire aspect of affairs among them was somewhat changed by the influence of one man. But gradually the impression was obliterated, medicine bags, flints, and steels, were resumed, dogs were raised, women and children beaten as before, and the Shawnee Prophet was despised."[9]

Indians had different motivations for residing at Prophetstown. Miamis, Potawatomies, and Kickapoos had connections with the physical land that were decades old. Some Potowatomies settled along the Wabash because of the region's spiritual significance; they called the area north along the St. Joseph's River *Sahg-wah-se-pe* (Mystery River). Other lakes and waterways in the valley, such as Manitou Lake, had significance which pre-dated Prophetstown. The Weas valued the area because it played an important part in Miami-speaking Indians' migration story, particularly their movement down the Wabash River. Wea leader Lapoussier acknowledged the area's spiritual importance to the Wea when he remarked that the Great Spirit had put Prophetstown "on the choicest spot of ground." The Kickapoos' connection to the region was less spiritual but nonetheless enduring. In the late 1780s, an American identified several Kickapoo towns and sugar camps along the Wabash River near the mouth of the Tippecanoe. Moreover, a Kickapoo village of nearly 160 cabins welcomed the Prophet when the Shawnee arrived in 1808. Associating with the Prophet was as much a sign of an individual Indian community's protecting its interests as it was a product of Indians' unifying behind the Prophet's ideological mission. Dissecting the difference proved challenging for Tenskwatawa.[10]

Adding to the Prophet's frustrations was the fact that his own brother Tecumseh appeared to be working against him. Tecumseh accepted

French traders and gunsmiths at Prophetstown because they provided tools necessary for uniting various Indian communities that were more concerned with maintaining the viability of their communities than strictly following the Prophet's teachings. Such associations undermined the Prophet's nativist vision. More importantly, the split between Tecumseh and his brother caused dissension at Prophetstown. In recounting their experiences with the Shawnee brothers, the Kickapoos approached the memory of Tecumseh with reverence, saying that "his intentions were good." At the same time, they believed that he was "led astray from time to time by his brother the Prophet." According to the historian C. C. Trowbridge, the Kickapoos called him *Paamaunawaashikau*, or "sounding tongue," because he talked on and on and was apt to create stories "to suit the credulity of his heaven."[11] That is, his rhetoric did not lead to immediate and practical benefits and in some cases, it created public disagreements that undermined Tenskwatawa's efforts to unify his community.

Open dissension became evident when outsiders appeared in the town. An Indian agent named Joseph Barron reported in August 1810 that the "Kickapoos & other Indians" were unhappy with the Prophet because they feared that his actions would lead them into violent conflict with the Americans. Barron witnessed a confrontation involving the Potawatomi leader Winemak, the Prophet, and a group of Kickapoos who were furious at the death of three of their kinsmen. Although Winemak told Barron that the three Kickapoos "had been buried in as many days," Tenskwatawa accused the Potawatomies of lying about the happenings at Prophetstown; he insisted that no one had died in the town. The deaths presented a challenge to the Prophet's medicine because Tenskwatawa had promised "that no man should die in his town." Furthermore, the fact that such a public disagreement took place in front of Barron, an outsider whom the Indians knew to be in Harrison's employ (and married to a Miami-speaking woman), signified the deep fractures and dissent undermining the Prophet's efforts. Yet Barron's presence was brought on by one of the many challenges that the Prophet faced, communication. Tenskwatawa needed Barron to assist in translating Winemak's comments. According to Harrison, after listening to Barron, "the Prophet observed that the Potawatomies had lied" and that no Kickapoos had died. Language barriers even between Indians of common Algonquin stock and open disagreements laid bare the factionalism and challenges facing Tenskwatawa at Prophetstown. Such dissent fueled violence between members of the Prophetstown community. In one instance, the Prophet's loyal Ho-Chunk supporters killed some of the Kickapoos and Sacs, and the Kickapoos vowed to avenge the deaths. Even Harrison commented that there were "causes of jealousy between the prophet's followers" that he hoped would further the divisions at Prophetstown.[12]

"Prophetic" Identities

William Wells hated the Prophet long before Tenskwatawa settled Prophetstown. Wells was not only the son-in-law of Miami leader Little Turtle—as U.S. Indian agent to the Miami, he served a key role in regional diplomacy. Wells was suspicious of the Shawnee leader from the moment he drove other Indians, as Wells described, "religiously mad." Long before he moved to Indiana Territory, the Prophet so alarmed William Wells that he wrote to Governor Harrison that the "Prophet should be removed" from Greenville, Ohio, because he had caused such excitement among the Indians there. Given the factional politics between Little Turtle and Pacanne, Wells recognized that Tenskwatawa (even in Ohio) could siphon Indians from the Fort Wayne region and possibly undermine Little Turtle's authority. Wells's position as Fort Wayne Indian agent allowed him to influence Harrison; by acting as a negotiator between non-Native and indigenous peoples, Wells was able to manipulate Tenskwatawa's comments about Indians and Euroamericans. When Tenskwatawa moved to Indiana Territory in 1808, Wells told Harrison that the Shawnee leader "should be the first object of our resentment." Wells even suggested that Harrison "starve all those" who followed the Prophet.[13]

Wells was far more concerned with the needs of his small band of Eel River Miamis than he was in promoting the needs of the United States.[14] As a go-between, Wells was in an incredibly powerful position to empower the agenda of his father-in-law, Little Turtle. He hoped to represent all of the Miamis in council but also to be the one Indian leader through whom the Americans negotiated land cessions and annuity payments in the Wabash-Maumee Valley. In turn, Little Turtle would strengthen his small community of Miamis by distributing annuity goods to the various Indian communities throughout the region. By doing so, the Miamis would maintain a certain level of hegemony over Indians in the region. In doing so, Little Turtle would destroy more respected Miami leaders like Pacanne and Jean Baptiste Richardville in regional affairs. Pacanne's family had long controlled the eight-mile portage connecting the Wabash and Maumee Rivers, and he and his nephew Richardville had benefited greatly through their trading relationship with the British. Little Turtle and Wells were desperately trying to solidify their relationship with the French and Americans to oppose the Pacanne-Richardville-British alliance. Like Little Turtle, Wells recognized that the Prophet could easily thwart their goal of supremacy over the Pacanne-Richardville clan if he successfully attracted Indians away from Little Turtle and to Prophetstown. The pair provoked and antagonized the Shawnee leader regularly, hoping to drive him from the area.

As the Prophet would do many times, he leapt to defend his name. Tenskwatawa made it clear to Harrison that he wanted to "live in peace and friendship" with the Americans. The Prophet emphasized that his community shared similar interests with the Americans. They were farmers who possessed a deep spiritual faith. Tenskwatawa also claimed that the Euroamericans and Indians shared a racial heritage since both Americans and Indians came from the same creator, even though the two differed "a little in coulour." Tenskwatawa's hope (at least in public) was to coexist with the Americans. Harrison echoed these sentiments when he responded that the Prophet's "religious opinions [will] never be the cause of dissention and difference between us."[15] Of course, while the Prophet emphasized religious connections, he tempered his call for the segregation of Indians and Americans to avoid disrupting diplomacy. In reality, he very much hoped to segregate Indian peoples from Euroamericans, but he was careful to speak of Native-white unity while he strengthened the position of his town. Doing otherwise would have denied him access to important trade goods and sources of information at a critical juncture in his plans.

But Wells did not believe one word that the Prophet said. Like many of his kin, Wells feared that Tenskwatawa's militant politics would upset regional stability and displace the Miamis. Having lost their cultural capital at Kekionga after the Battle of Fallen Timbers in 1794, the Miamis viewed the newly arrived Indian migrants with suspicion, especially because many of these people had participated in treaty councils that had led to land cessions. The destruction of Kekionga and rise of Prophetstown not only represented a regional power shift by reorienting Indian migration to the Tippecanoe; it also represented a danger to the cultural identity of the Miamis, who had used Kekionga to enable their hegemony.

The Prophet's move from Ohio to Indiana Territory in 1808 was but one more assault on the Miamis' diminishing hegemony in the region. Although Miamis had visited Tenskwatawa's settlement in Ohio, they refrained from doing so when the Prophet moved along the Wabash because his community at Prophetstown was in the heart of Miami territory and therefore a threat to Miami interests. In addition, by 1808, the Kickapoos and Americans had displaced the Miamis from their settlements along the Vermillion River and at Vincennes. The Miamis feared that the Prophet would soon do the same to them. The Kickapoos and Potawatomies legitimized their presence in the region by signing land-cession treaties rather than operating within the boundaries established by the Miamis.[16] Miamis had once emphasized geographical markers in speaking of their identity, but now the foundations of Miami community were divorced from the earth as lands were bought and sold as if they were furs. The Miamis despised the Prophet's intrusion into the complex political affairs of the region because his teachings and efforts to centralize power threatened relationships between Indians and non-Indians. In turn, he challenged traditional Miami diplomacy. The Miamis had used the British, the French, and Indians to construct and defend their hegemony in the valley during the previous decades. Now they feared that the Prophet's rhetoric would ruin the relationships with non-Indians that the Miamis had worked so hard to construct.

At the root of the animosity between the Prophet and the Miamis lay a fundamental difference in their understandings of what it meant to be sovereign. Tenskwatawa demanded that Indians unify under *his* leadership and focused on shared Indianness rather than unique cultural histories. Such a belief was the product of Tenskwatawa's nativist ideals, but it was also uniquely Shawnee. Unlike those of the Miamis, Shawnee creation stories reflected an itinerant identity and a malleable sense of place due to their constant displacement and migration. According to Stephen Warren, the Shawnees learned to maintain their "distinctiveness through beliefs and practices that were not linked to place and that could be sustained in a wide variety of geographic contexts." The Shawnees' diasporic history involved frequent moves in order to access trade and to solidify diplomatic relationships, and by the early 1800s, one could find Shawnee communities from Ohio to Missouri. The Miamis, by consensus, protected their settlements and interests by controlling an important trade portage between the Wabash and Maumee Rivers and by accommodating outsiders in exchange for access their trade goods. Thus, the Miamis perfected a system that forced outsiders to adjust their interests and migrate to Miami country, which enabled the Miamis to remain relatively sedentary.[17] If forced to relocate, the Miamis would be risking a terrible social crisis. However, the Shawnees could remain culturally Shawnee even if their mission at Prophetstown failed and they were forced to move.

Gender roles also played an important part in the nature of Indian identity. While the Prophet centralized patriarchal authority at Prophetstown by undermining the Shawnee women's council and by taking greater control over agriculture, the Miamis did much the opposite. The Miamis continued to function in a decentralized manner despite the contest for influence between Pacanne and Little Turtle. They continued to grow corn in individual communities, which allowed for Miami and other Native women to maintain their role in agriculture, which, for the Miami especially, was central to trade. It was Miami women who married French traders, and it was Miami women who used their new connections in trade to exert greater influence over their communities. When the Miamis worried about Prophetstown, they did not do so simply because the Prophet threatened trade and the disruption of the Miami world, but because the Prophet's teachings represented something inherently un-Miami both in terms of attachment to place and gendered identities.

Tenskwatawa's challenges at Prophetstown were twofold. He had to deal with Wells and a host of other people who opposed his community in addition to controlling the town itself. From the very beginning, the Potawatomi leader Main Poc continued a brisk trade in alcohol contrary to the wishes of the Prophet, who forbade both trade with Americans and the use of alcohol. Although Main Poc forged a relationship with the Prophet at Greenville and Tippecanoe, he was not necessarily a nativist. Main Poc objected to the idea that Indians should refrain from trading with Euroamericans and prioritize community interests above local ones; if he abandoned his assault on the Potawatomies' Osage enemies, he risked losing his religious power.[18] Main Poc's personal identity was bound up in temporal and spiritual concerns; he was possibly a member of the wabeno cult that allowed participants to purge enemy spirits from their bodies through frenetic dancing. Members believed that spirits were exorcised through the burning of the dancer's flesh.[19] Main Poc and Tenskwatawa shared a similar distaste for Euroamericans, but Main Poc's participation in the wabeno cult challenged Tenskwatawa's own religious dedication to the Master of Life and opposition to such dances. Both men sought purification from outside forces, but the wabeno cult was far more individualistic in method, and often physically destructive, which many blamed for the loss of self-control among its members.

From 1808 to 1812, Main Poc challenged the Shawnee brothers' demands for intertribal cooperation by attacking American communities in southern Illinois and Osage villages in western Illinois. These assaults had an unforeseen effect—they convinced many Americans that the Prophet meant to do them harm. Americans interpreted Main Poc's raids as evidence of the Prophet's influence instead of a challenge to it. Americans saw Main Poc's militancy in stark contrast to other nearby Potawatomi leaders like Winemak and Five Medals who cooperated with the Americans. Given the growing influence from Prophetstown, many Euroamericans felt that it was only a matter of time before Main Poc turned his attention to the whites in the same manner he had to the Osages.[20]

Main Poc's reasoning for settling in the area was cultural as much as political. For one thing, the Potawatomies considered the region near the St. Joseph's River sacred. Main Poc's group of Potawatomies had invited the Shawnee brothers to the region to bolster his efforts to protect himself from the Americans.[21] Inviting more outsiders into the area was especially important in a region dominated by the Miamis. By convincing other marginalized Indians to come into the region, Main Poc effectively leveled the playing field between his community and that of his opponents. He forged an alliance with the Prophet to gain provisions and support for his efforts, but he was unwilling to subsume Potawatomi interests for the Prophet's benefit.

Like Main Poc, William Wells remained devoted to his community's interests. His actions were the product of a desire to protect American expansionism, and also a result of his cultural and familial ties to the Miamis. Wells took advantage of his diplomatic position to fill Harrison's ear with rumors, rumors that would empower his agenda. In the spring of 1809, he warned Harrison that many Ojibwa, Ottawa, and Potawatomi Indians had fled Prophetstown because Tenskwatawa, as Wells said, "told them to receive the Tomahawk . . . and destroy all the white people at Vincennes." Yet Wells reassured Harrison that he did not believe that the Prophet meant whites any harm. Wells's conflicting advice hid deep-seated emotions about the Prophet's community; his letters to Harrison, while ostensibly impartial, were meant to sow doubt and insecurity and to maintain Wells's position as an information source.[22]

In letters to Harrison, Wells juxtaposed observations of a Shawnee leader who "only wanted power" with descriptions of starving Indians who had abandoned Prophetstown. When Wells distributed rations to those who had left the settlement, he told the governor that humanity had compelled him to do so. But Wells's real motive—keeping Indians away from Prophetstown—served instead to check Tenskwatawa's growing popularity and to empower Wells's Miami polity. Wells's efforts to defend his influence applied to his fellow Miamis as well. At one point prior to Tenskwatawa's resettlement in Indiana Territory, he informed Harrison that Lapoussier—fellow Miami and adversary to Little Turtle—should be suspected of aiding the Prophet.[23]

Harrison was in a difficult situation with Wells. Despite reconnecting with his family six years after his capture by the Miamis, Wells remained with the Miamis. Having married a Wea woman with whom he had a child, a subsequently married Little Turtle's daughter, Wells's overtures of loyalty to the United States were noticeably self-serving. Even though Harrison wrote to the secretary of war about Wells's duplicity and "disposition for intrigue," he continued to rely on the Indian agent to distribute annuity payments to Indians. Harrison firmly believed that Wells's qualifications as Indian agent "could not be found in any other individual." Wells could function within Miami and American societies seamlessly, and his qualities as an interpreter and diplomat could not be surpassed. Nevertheless, Harrison feared that if he did not continue to employ Wells, "every measure of the Government will be opposed & thwarted by himself & [Little Turtle]."[24] Damned either way, Harrison retained Wells.

French traders compounded Tenskwatawa's frustrations by echoing Wells's accusations, for it was in the best interests of the French to act out against Prophetstown. Ever since the Sieur de Vincennes had established a post on the Ouabache in 1732, the French had sought to maintain a lucrative trading network with their Indian neighbors and relatives. Now the Prophet's policies threatened to end this trade and leave the French with few economic opportunities in the region. He banned the cession of lands by any Indian who lacked unanimous consent among the various Indian tribes; furthermore, he restricted trade between Indians and Euroamericans, making it nearly impossible. Moreover, the French worried that they themselves would become a target of American territorial expansion.

Despite these hindrances, American frontier diplomacy provided the French with the opportunity they needed to maintain regional influence. Although the Treaty of Greenville forced Native peoples to cede much of Ohio to the United States in 1795, most of the lands in Indiana Territory remained untouched. As directed by President Thomas Jefferson, Harrison worked diligently to expand American land claims by getting

Indians to cede their lands. However, most Indians simply refused to negotiate without the French. American officials, quite unlike the French, did not understand the cultural boundaries or ethnic differences that demarcated Indian communities. As a result, Governor Harrison's expansionist policies meant that he relied on people whose loyalties were often difficult to determine. Harrison owed much of his success to the careful manipulations of the French and Miamis rather than simply his own ability to pit Indian communities against one another.[25]

French motives for aiding the Americans were more complicated than have been traditionally understood; scholars have tended to focus on the immediate needs of the French rather than their long-term goals. One historian concludes that there was "a certain self-serving persistence in French attitudes" in Vincennes, a point shown by the experiences of Michel Brouillet. Brouillet's father held commissions as both a British and American officer and routinely used imperial powers to the advantage of the French community. Brouillet's first wife was a Miami woman, and their son, Jean Baptiste Brouillet, became a Miami leader. Although Brouillet eventually married a French woman, he maintained connections with his former wife and métis son in order to further his contacts with traders. Harrison recognized the ulterior motives of the French interpreters when he wrote to Secretary of War William Eustis that "nine tenths of them prefer the interests of the Indians to that of their employers."[26] Yet Harrison failed to recognize how much the French shaped regional diplomacy to their advantage along with his perception of Prophetstown.

When reports surfaced in 1809 that the Prophet had failed to unify local Indian communities, the French made sure to speak of his settlement as a menace. In their own series of lies and half-truths, the French spread false intelligence about Prophetstown. That spring, two Indian traders reported that the Indians associated with the Prophet had left Prophetstown after the mysterious murder of an Indian woman. Harrison considered reversing an earlier decision to call out two companies of the militia, but he wanted to hear "something decisive" from Governor Meriwether Lewis in the Illinois Territory, who sometimes shared intelligence with Harrison. Two French traders, Peter Lafontaine and Toussaint Dubois, told Harrison that the Prophet had nearly five hundred supporters "within the distance of 40 or 50 miles of his Village." Such an estimate ignored long-standing factionalism as the groups of Miamis and Potawatomis who lived within twenty-five miles of Prophetstown had little or no connection with the settlement. Winemak, a Potawatomi leader who lived nearby, spoke out against Prophetstown but was eventually ostracized from visiting. Another Potawatomi, Five Medals, warned that having the Prophet so near to his villages would undoubtedly upset regional stability. Yet Lafontaine told Harrison that the Prophet "determined to commence hostilities" in order to "'sweep all the white people from the Wabash and White River' and then attack the Miamis." Such phrases were repeated time and again, always pointing toward Vincennes and its white denizens. Considering that Lafontaine moved from Detroit to trade among the Miamis and had even married a Miami woman, the intelligence he provided seems suspiciously self-serving.[27]

Despite intelligence that showed Prophetstown to be in disarray, French traders remained adamant that the rumors of factionalism along the Tippecanoe River were only an elaborate ruse designed to hide the town's true militancy. In order to test the power of the Prophet, some Ojibwas and Ottawas had killed an Indian in Prophetstown, hoping to discredit Tenskwatawa's warning that the Great Spirit would punish any violent behavior. Toussaint Dubois, an interpreter with strong connections to the Miamis, used this murder and the story of Prophetstown's decline to his advantage. He revealed that the Ottawas and Ojibwas had not defected from Prophetstown after the murder had taken place. Dubois argued that some of the Prophet's followers had actually committed the murder in order to "carry on the deception" that Tenskwatawa was losing control over his people. The homicide would keep people "from taking the alarm" at the force that Tenskwatawa gathered. Yet according to other observers, "it was not the common impression . . . that [the Prophet's] doctrines had any tendency to unite [the Indians at Prophetstown]."[28] As with Lafontaine and Brouillet, Dubois's motives for exaggerating the situation at Prophetstown were likely a product of his French interests.

Rather than admit that the ethnic landscape of the Ohio Valley was immensely complicated, the French presented Anglo-Americans with essentialist and monolithic descriptions of Native people. Such rhetoric complemented a frontier culture that was increasingly polarized between American expansion and pan-Indianism. Ironically, Harrison's job was to temper this polarization in order to gain more land cessions for individual Indian communities. By keeping Indians divided, Harrison had a better chance at pinning them against each other in order to win land cessions. Harrison's personal beliefs about the inherent differences between whites and Indians rarely made it into diplomatic discussions. He could not risk reinforcing the Prophet's calls for Indians to unify and instead kept his racism private, even once dismissing Little Turtle's "violent opposition" to a few treaties as a product of his "consciousness of the superiority of his talents over the rest of his race and colour." Harrison did dismiss Michelle Brouillet for providing faulty intelligence, yet on the whole, Brouillet's commentary, like that of Wells, reinforced Harrison's suspicions that the Prophet and his settlement were focused on destroying whites. In fact, despite firing Brouillet for grossly exaggerating the Prophet's force, Harrison would employ him again in 1811 to gather intelligence on Prophetstown. Overt bias by the French traders was nothing new. Harrison had actually dismissed Brouillet as interpreter from the 1803 Fort Wayne treaty for "drunkenness, keeping bad company, and neglect of his duty." The interpreters' estimate of the number of combatants at Prophetstown amplified its militant character in Harrison's mind, as well as the mind of the secretary of war, to whom Harrison forwarded his reports. Population estimates were immensely important given that Vincennes had fewer than one thousand residents. As a result, Harrison continued to train the militia despite being convinced that the Prophet would "not dare attack."[29] Such behavior not only reflected Harrison's state of mind but played an important part in reinforcing a belief among local inhabitants that there was indeed something to fear.

Furthermore, although go-betweens such as William Wells, Little Turtle, and the French traders threatened American hegemony, Harrison relied on them because he could not admit that they had been leading him astray, not to mention that he had no other options. Harrison wrote to Dearborn that he was truly convinced that the Prophet "intended hostilities" and "wicked designs." As a result, Harrison mobilized his resources to understand just how much other Native communities had joined the Prophet by ordering John Johnston, Wells's eventual replacement as Indian agent at Fort Wayne, to send a delegation "from all the friendly tribes" to Prophetstown.[30] Doing so placed Johnston right in the hands of the French and Miamis, who were more than willing to shape the intelligence that Harrison received.

Tenskwatawa's actions also demonstrate just how much Little Turtle and William Wells had influenced the Americans. Tenskwatawa reacted strongly to the accusations that an increasingly unstable Prophetstown seethed with violence. He recognized that building a vibrant community at Prophetstown was as much about controlling the perceptions of his town as it was about securing the loyalty of Indian converts. In May 1809, he traveled to Fort Wayne to beg Johnston to recognize Little

Turtle's "private and personal motives" for protecting his small community of Miami followers. The Prophet discussed the charges against him, saying that Wells and Little Turtle "were the authors of the reports that went out against him." After questioning a number of local Indians, Johnston could not "find that there existed any grounds for the alarm." Instead, Johnston concluded that Wells caused "the alarm . . . to bring Governor Harrison into the measure by calling out the militia." Johnston decided that Tenskwatawa was right. He already disliked Wells, whom Secretary of War Henry Dearborn recently dismissed for abusing his power as Indian agent. Wells had been caught cheating Native people and keeping the profits from illegal whiskey sales for himself. While the historian R. David Edmunds argues that the Prophet was "able to beguile the inexperienced Johnston" and hide his true intentions, the Prophet's motives were not that sinister. He simply did not exert enough control over his followers to create the type of violence the Americans feared. Wells's motives appear equally underhanded, given his history of abusing power, coupled with his father-in-law's (Little Turtle) fear of being displaced by the Prophet. But Harrison played right into Wells's hand when he called out the militia, which reinforced the growing public alarm over Prophetstown.[31]

The Prophet found it increasingly difficult to counteract Harrison's suspicions, especially when other factions of Shawnees contradicted his message. Rather than accept Johnston's assessment of Prophetstown, the governor sent two spies to see if the Prophet had been truthful. They witnessed what Harrison described as anti-American activity. In early June 1809, Tenskwatawa and several of his supporters visited Vincennes, hoping to defend their actions, but Harrison remained convinced that the Prophet enjoyed a special hatred for the Americans. After all, the Shawnee leader Black Hoof, who lived in Ohio, had recently expressed his fondness for and friendship with Wells. The factionalism among the Shawnees undermined Tenskwatawa's complaints, for it revealed that some Shawnees did support Wells and, indirectly, American policies on the frontier. Harrison believed that the Shawnee leader would eventually abandon his mission once he saw the whites who swarmed to Indiana Territory. In turn, Harrison hoped that the increased pressures brought on the Prophet would convince other Indian communities to cede more lands to the Americans.[32]

Harrison began organizing a council in Fort Wayne to that very end. In the summer of 1809, factions of Lenape, Miami, Eel River, and Potawatomi Indians gathered at Fort Wayne to negotiate a major treaty.

Little Turtle's Miamis supported the treaty but were strongly rebuffed by Pacanne's group, which refused to cede any more lands. In fact, "parties of young men of the Miami Tribe were constantly arriving [sic] loaded with goods from the British Agents at Malden" instead of collaborating with the Americans.[33] Their travels to Malden made clear the divisions that pulled at the Miami polity and also proved their attempts to reaffirm historical relationships with the British. The Miami factions signed the treaty because they realized that they could not allow Little Turtle to use the treaty to define himself as the Miamis' sole representative. Similarly, Pacanne, an adversary of Little Turtle and his son-in-law William Wells, signed the treaty in order to affirm his identity as a prominent leader and to defend the Wabash-Maumee portage.

Pacanne's efforts to legitimize himself were also part of a longer process to marginalize Little Turtle from Miami society. Although Miami women were prevented from participating in treaty negotiations by the Americans, they could nonetheless threaten rogue Miami leaders through other means. Years before the Treaty of Fort Wayne, Little Turtle had discovered his first cow killed by unknown parties. Women from Pacanne's community—or at least women who opposed Little Turtle's relationship with the Americans—likely killed Little Turtle's cow as a warning that he had strayed too far from Miami principles. Such an instance had occurred years earlier when Miami women from Pacanne's community at Kekionga killed Alexis Maisonville's cow. Maisonville had been a key ally to Tacumwah's (Pacanne's sister) ex-husband Richardville, who had tried to wrest Kekionga from Miami control.[34] Little Turtle represented a similar threat to Miami values.

Yet Pacanne's efforts to protect Miami interests resembled the Prophet's actions all too closely. Rather than turn his support toward the Prophet, however, Pacanne traveled to Malden in order to reestablish relationships with the British. Since Malden was the same place that the Prophet and his brother purchased trade goods and ammunition, increasing numbers of Americans erroneously believed that Pacanne's actions reflected his support of Prophetstown and Tenskwatawa's nativist agenda.[35] Yet Tenskwatawa hoped to use the trade goods to protect all Indians by unifying them in a pan-Indian confederacy and Pacanne wanted to renew Miami power and ethnic identity. The Prophet's vision worried Americans because it demanded the unification of many more thousands of Indians in the name of a common (and anti-American) cause. But for Americans, seeking the support of the British and advocating unity among the North American Indian community meant the same thing.

American negotiators misunderstood Pacanne's frustration over the Treaty of Fort Wayne, for the land cession benefited a selected few. Federal authorities assumed that Pacanne favored resistance and even militancy. The devastating effects of the treaty also compelled groups like the Potawatomies and Kickapoos to look toward Prophetstown when they realized that Harrison would no longer recognize them as legitimate power brokers in the region. In the same way, Pacanne's signature on the Treaty of Fort Wayne allowed him to assert his identity as a Miami leader. Nonetheless, most European Americans interpreted the actions of Pacanne's Miamis, the Potawatomies, and the Kickapoos as another example of Tenskwatawa's growing influence over disaffected Indians and not a result of the consequences of the treaty itself.

It was typical for informants (who were often French or Miami) to frame the information they received in racialized rhetoric. Indians were unifying to attack the Americans. One trader reported to Harrison that a prominent Miami leader "had entered into all the views of the Prophet and even that of murdering all those who stand in opposition to his measures." The report also mentioned that an important but unnamed Miami leader had visited the fort at Malden and received gifts in an effort to renew his community's long-standing relationship with the British. Another inducement for the Miamis was the fact that British goods were cheaper than those sold by the French. The disaffected Miami leader, likely Pacanne, used the British to protect his community's interests and did not intend to place himself and his people entirely at the bidding of the Prophet or the Americans.[36]

After all, Pacanne's faction enjoyed a historic relationship with the British, which was key to the influence Pacanne enjoyed at Kekionga. When Henry Hamilton seized Vincennes from the Americans in 1778, Pacanne offered his assistance in order to acquire more British supplies.[37] Two years later, Pacanne helped defeat the Frenchman LaBalme in his attempt to conquer Kekionga. Pacanne did not wish to make his Miami faction subservient to a European power, but he recognized that the British provided the best possible means to maintaining Miami hegemony. Horrified by Little Turtle's attempt to sign away more Miami lands to the Americans, Pacanne's Miamis, while protesting the treaty, refused to subvert their desires to satisfy Tenskwatawa's nativist goals. Few outsiders recognized this. Gregory Dowd and R. David Edmunds have identified this treaty as an important juncture—one at which Tecumseh began to transform his brother's religious revival into a pan-Indian movement. While this is true, the treaty also served as a catalyst that prodded the

Miamis to lash out against Prophetstown and the Americans. Pacanne's reaction and other Indians resistance to sign the treaty created a popular perception in the minds of many non-Natives that the Prophet and his brother were plotting for war.

Given the contentious nature of the Fort Wayne Treaty and the success the Miamis enjoyed in using the treaty to assert their primacy in the region, it is not surprising that non-Miami Indians turned toward Prophetstown. Yet Prophetstown was not nearly as unified as the Americans feared. The Indian groups at Prophetstown were trapped between the Prophet's more rigid ideology, which centered on a singular Indian identity, and their pluralistic traditional ethnic identities. Conflicting interests likely led to the violence between the Prophet's followers during October 1810, when Ho-Chunks murdered some Kickapoos and Sauks. Harrison believed this sort of violence reflected "the declining influence of the Prophet's party," and he hoped that the "jealousy" among the Prophet's followers would "completely dissolve the confederacy he had formed." As usual, a Miami Indian arrived in Vincennes to contradict the story and assure Harrison that the Prophet "absolutely meditated an immediate attack upon [Vincennes]." While one Miami warning Harrison that the Prophet planned to destroy all the white people may not have caused great alarm, the cumulative effect of various Miamis and French traders predicting such an atrocity preyed on Harrison's mind. Clearly unnerved, Harrison admitted to Secretary of War Eustis that he had felt obligated to send intelligence that was "vague and in some respects contradictory." Worse yet, Harrison confessed that he had obtained information from "various sources, not always the most intelligent."[38] Increasingly convinced that the Prophet intended war, Harrison was unable to interpret Indian behavior outside of a racial dichotomy.

Much of Harrison's confusion arose from the internal politics of the Miami homeland. It was easier for the Americans to associate Pacanne with the Prophet than it was for the Americans to understand the complex dispute between Pacanne and Little Turtle. That is, it was easier for Americans to assume that any recalcitrant Indian was militant. In Pacanne's eyes, Little Turtle's efforts threatened traditional Miami culture and regional hegemony by silencing other Miami leaders and communities important to trade and diplomacy. In this sense, Little Turtle's willingness to negotiate with Americans was no different than the Prophet's aims. Little Turtle hurt the Miamis by willingly ceding Miami lands in order to gain annuity payments. The Prophet angered Pacanne by settling on the Miami lands and ignoring their spiritual significance.

Miami communities that agreed with Pacanne believed that Prophetstown posed as big a threat as did the Americans and British. It is not
surprising that different groups of Miamis used each group to protect
their own interests.[39] They associated with the Americans to threaten
Little Turtle, traded with the British in order to maintain a degree of
independence from the Americans, and then provided information to
the Americans to marginalize Prophetstown. There is no doubt that
some Miamis associated with the Prophet, but their motives for doing
so are tied more to maintaining Miami independence and not simply a
product of a nativist impulse. If Pacanne signed a treaty that he abhorred
in order to challenge Little Turtle's authority, then why would other Indians not associate with the Prophet to gain recognition as well?

The Prophet had no way of limiting the extent to which Americans
like Harrison depended upon the Miamis for information. This dependency was especially difficult in the aftermath of the Treaty of Fort
Wayne, when Indians were increasingly concerned with the course of
diplomacy. The reaction from the Miamis was nothing short of remarkable. Gros Bled, a Piankashaw (Miami-speaking) leader, visited Harrison personally and asked to move west of the Mississippi because he had
"heard amongst the Indians nothing but the News of War." Gros Bled
told Harrison that the Prophet planned a "Massacre in the Town" and
"boasted that he would follow the footsteps of the *Great Pontiac.*" Gros
Bled's story had the power to intimidate on its own, but in Harrison's
mind it was—coupled with Michel Brouillet's exaggerated estimate that
Prophetstown's combatant population was near three thousand people—
just another example of the Prophet's militancy. Brouillet's assessment,
like Gros Bled's tale, reflected efforts to rid the region of a problematic
Indian leader through fear and rumor rather than legitimate threats.
Brouillet's confession proved as much. In recanting the estimate, he
numbered the warriors at 650.[40]

Weeks later, residents of Indiana Territory picked up their copies of
the *Western Sun* and read Elihu Stout's rich description of Brouillet's
encounter with Tenskwatawa. The trader was "made to deny that he was
an American," and a man transporting a salt shipment north along the
Wabash had been shaken "violently by the hair" because he looked like
an American. Most important, Stout's articles stated that Brouillet and
Dubois were "to be relied upon," that the "Miamis had agreed to attend
the Prophet's council," and that the French had been warned to leave the
town before the slaughter started. Stout was giving credence to Harrison's reliance on lousy intelligence. Stout continued publishing editorials

that reminded the Vincennes residents that "the Prophet had been preparing for war for a long time."[41]

A Constructed Militancy

The amount of misinformation surrounding the actions of the Miamis demonstrates the extent to which the Americans recognized their influence. Harrison, his Indian agents, and even the Prophet routinely tried to understand the intentions of the Miamis. Yet the information was so contradictory that Harrison was left to make decisions based on his own fears and biases. What started as infighting among the Miamis could quickly evolve into a conspiracy inside the white community at Vincennes. Harrison and many Americans believed that the fate of the territory depended upon the loyalty of the Miamis; they were more numerous and enjoyed great influence among the nearby Indian communities. But Harrison and his agents failed to recognize the degree to which American policies and Prophetstown's nativism had caused the Miamis to divide. Americans mistakenly concluded that the Miamis who opposed Little Turtle in turn supported the Prophet. This amplified negative perceptions that the Prophet had won many Miami converts. In council, the Miami leader Pacanne condemned the Fort Wayne Treaty and the belligerent Americans who forced the Miamis to cede lands. Pacanne remained adamant that his people "would not agree to the treaty, that it must be broke, that for their part they would not receive any part of the annuity." John Johnston believed that the Miamis were a "band of the Prophet's followers" because "every sentiment they uttered was in unison with those of the Prophet." Yet in another instance, Johnston noted the Mississinewa Miamis' "reluctance" to meet with the Americans. Johnston feared "that there was mischief going on among them," and he tried in vain to "remove the existing bad impressions" they had of the Americans. An assistant Indian agent claimed that the "Miamis and Putawatamies [sic] [were] to attack Fort Wayne." Even Harrison told Secretary of War Eustis that one of the Miami leaders, "a very artfull [sic] and sensible fellow, who (as a principal chief told Colo. Vigo) had entered into all of the views of the Prophet, and even that of murdering all those who should stand in opposition to his measures." Shortly thereafter, Harrison claimed that the problems among the Miamis were part of a larger scheme that "originated with William McIntosh who lives at [Vincennes], and that Wells was the instrument made use of to effect it." White people must be responsible, Harrison believed, because they were the only ones capable of filling the Indians' "naturally jealous minds with suspicions of the justice and integrity of our views towards them."[42] Without reliable intelligence, Harrison quickly found information that was less credible.

Tensions flared in the fall of 1810, when Pacanne decided to visit British headquarters near Detroit with thirty of his men after refusing to accept annuity payments. Shortly before his departure to Detroit, Pacanne demanded that the Treaty of Fort Wayne be negated because the Indians had only signed it under the threat of war. Johnston averred that Pacanne's Miamis had been "corrupted by the Prophet's Council." His conclusions about the Prophet's "contagion" echoed Harrison's. Neither recognized the extent to which some Miamis had separated themselves from both the Prophet and the Americans. In fact, earlier that June, Johnston had said that he "cherish[ed] the Mississinewa chiefs," which included Pacanne, and claimed that Little Turtle was "contemptible" and "beyond description."[43] More surprising was Johnston's conclusion that the Prophet had won over Pacanne. The exact opposite had occurred. If anything, the Prophet would have wanted Pacanne to remain in the valley, for the Miami leader's presence would exacerbate problems. Yet Pacanne rejected a relationship with the Prophet just as he had rejected the Americans.

Americans did not want to distinguish Miami factionalism from Prophetstown militancy. They were simply too fearful of what a pan-Indian confederacy might mean for their safety on the frontier. The Miami leader the Owl reminded Johnston that "all the mischief that is going among" the Miamis "has sprung from Wells & the [Little] Turtle," but such declarations mattered little to the Americans, who had grown obsessed with Prophetstown. Harrison disregarded the Owl's warning because the governor believed that "the Miamis have been so frightened by the threats of the Prophet" that they would likely deny the recent land cession and join Prophetstown. Harrison suspected that the Prophet was winning the fight for the Miamis, which would be "of infinite prejudice to the United States."[44] Americans believed that the Prophet was the root of the problem and that Pacanne was only acting in accordance with Tenskwatawa's wishes. By stopping the Shawnee brothers, Harrison hoped to force the Miami factions to accept American terms.

In October 1810, French spies once again warned Harrison that the Prophet had gathered an imposing force, intelligence Harrison identified as "entirely a fabrication." Harrison had discovered that the Prophet had fewer than one hundred ardent supporters. Moreover, the large contingent of Potawatomies near Prophetstown continued to reject Tenskwatawa's authority, so much so that they wanted to fight Tenskwatawa rather than the Americans. Despite evidence of dissension and instability at Prophetstown, Harrison demanded that a fort be built north of town and that soldiers be at the ready.[45]

News from the Illinois country only complemented Harrison's suspicions that the Prophet was indeed plotting for war. Who handled that news was just as important. Despite their proven unreliability, Wells was back at Fort Wayne as an Indian agent, and Brouillet had returned to Prophetstown. Both were once again pleading their case to Harrison that the Prophet intended to attack Vincennes. Brouillet informed Harrison that "secret meetings" were taking place at Prophetstown between Tenskwatawa and Indians "not friendly to the United States." Brouillet described an even deeper conspiracy in which the "Prophet [had] constant intercourse with some Person or Persons in or about Vincennes" who was helping the Shawnee leader plan a ruthless slaughter of the Americans. Brouillet's intelligence was unreliable, and the Americans noticed as much when they forced him to swear to the veracity of the intelligence that he provided. Harrison would replace Brouillet months later because he was "too well known to be in the service of the Government to do much good." Harrison did not do himself any favors; he replaced Brouillet with Jean Baptiste LaPlante, a man who could speak "no English and who have always been engaged in the Indian trade." Harrison believed that LaPlante was "entirely worthy of confidence" and loyal to the United States, even though "very few of them [were] so."[46]

Replacing Brouillet did very little to the information crossing Harrison's desk. After reports surfaced in the spring of 1811 that a small band of Main Poc's Potawatomies had murdered several white settlers in the Illinois country, Wells targeted and then visited Prophetstown to investigate. Although Wells concluded that while the Shawnee brothers had no direct connection with the violence, he believed that Tenskwatawa and Tecumseh were guilty nonetheless because the murderers were under their influence. Shortly thereafter, several of the Potawatomi leaders also visited Fort Wayne to inform "Captain Wells that they had put themselves under the protection of Main Poc," whom everyone knew to be the "great war chief of the tribe" and a member of Prophetstown.[47] But Main Poc's actions did not represent a broader scheme of violence originating from Prophetstown. In fact, Main Poc's behavior was symptomatic of the problems Tenskwatawa faced. No matter his efforts, the

Prophet could not maintain control over those people outsiders liked to call his followers.

For his part, Harrison did not know what to think. The Prophet was either a master at deceit or unable to control his followers. And in such a precarious situation, he continued to employ Brouillet—despite having relieved him months earlier because he failed to "procure correct intelligence"—as a means to police the frontier. Surprisingly, he ordered Brouillet to ride throughout the territory to visit "the Indian camps" and inform "the whites of what he has learned respecting them." Even Harrison admitted how difficult it could be to distinguish "good" Indians from the "hostile" ones. Given Brouillet's obvious bias, it seems incredible that Harrison put him in a position to influence settlers' perceptions at a time when frontier paranoia had reached its apogee. Relying on Brouillet yet again might seem as though Harrison picked agents who would reinforce a militant perception of the Prophet. More likely, Harrison simply had no other option. The only capable agents who could provide him with information were traders who were trying to protect a colonial world that Harrison hoped to destroy. This was especially important given that Harrison was himself confused by the Prophet's actions. Harrison could not "account for the conduct of the Prophet upon any rational principle— many of the Potawatimies have left him—from the best accounts I can get he has not more than 450 men."[48] Harrison's actions seem confused and at times self-serving. However, like many around him, the governor had fallen victim to the pervasive rumors and faulty intelligence spread by Brouillet, Wells, and a host of others.

Harrison's actions were also symptomatic of the ills plaguing the American territorial experiment. Although laws existed governing territorial trade and diplomacy, the French routinely acted independently of the territorial system. At times, traders such as LaPlante or Brouillet were more than willing to assist Harrison. At other times, they were engaged in trade and made themselves unavailable to Harrison, which is why the governor would rely upon such notoriously unreliable men. The territorial structure depended upon outsiders—whose attachment to the region was much older and entrenched—to speak and negotiate in their stead. Simply put, the Americans suffered from a major weakness, an inability to communicate with those people whom they hoped to displace through land cessions. And as Harrison waffled or debated the intelligence he received, Wells and Brouillet demonized Prophetstown to ensure that the Americans remained opposed to Tenskwatawa's measures. It worked. In a letter to Eustis, Harrison detailed his fear that the Prophet might "immediately throw off the mask and commence the war," reflecting his suspicion that the Prophet secretly hoped for a confrontation.[49] Although Harrison recognized the mask under which the Prophet operated, he failed to fully grasp its complexity. By spreading rumors, lying, and through infighting, the Miamis and the French created a diplomatic mask of sorts that even the Prophet hoped to "throw off."

A complicated web of relationships rooted in the legacy of French and British colonialism limited the extent to which the Prophet could unify the various Indian communities throughout the Wabash-Maumee Valley. In addition, disunity within Prophetstown made it nearly impossible for Tenskwatawa to mount a unified front to challenge Little Turtle, William Wells, and the French traders. How, then, did Miami/Shawnee/ French factionalism lead to Harrison's taking the desperate step of provoking the Battle of Tippecanoe? A large part of the answer had to do with the misinformation and misunderstandings created by the French, Miamis, and Americans compounded by the clashing cultural agendas between the Prophet and the Miamis. From the moment the Prophet arrived, Little Turtle and William Wells moved to destroy him. The Miamis rankled at this Shawnee outsider, for his call to Indian unity would only take away from the Miamis' decades-long efforts to assert themselves in the Wabash Valley. With every movement the Prophet made, the Miamis were there to challenge him and to accuse him of plotting to destroy the American settlements. The French played their part as well. Increasingly fearful that the Prophet might cut them off completely from the regional trade, the French demonized Tenskwatawa by using their roles as interpreters and diplomats to manipulate the intelligence about Prophetstown that flowed into Harrison's office and influencing the public rhetoric through Stout's *Western Sun*. As a result, they successfully created an image of Prophetstown as a militant community and direct threat to American settlements.

Intra-Indian relationships were as important to the hostile atmosphere that surrounded Prophetstown. Not only did a fundamental disagreement over the nature of what it meant to be Indian drive a wedge between the Shawnees and the Miamis, but the factionalism within the Miami ethno-polity also shaped impressions of the Prophet. Although sometimes willing to work with the Americans, who (at times) implicitly recognized Miami hegemony, the Miamis refused to collaborate with the Prophet. From the Miami perspective, joining with the Prophet meant no longer trading with the French or British, losing control over the lands they held sacred, and declaring the fundamental facets of Miami ethnicity to be null and void. Moreover, the fact that the Miamis were not unified as a single political entity created an atmosphere of confusion and competition that itself shaped perceptions of Prophetstown. When Pacanne and other Miami leaders challenged the dictatorial nature of Little Turtle's leadership by refusing to negotiate at the Fort Wayne treaty grounds and by trading with the British instead of Little Turtle's American allies, he unwittingly provided the French and other Miami factions with new opportunities to assert themselves.

The events that consumed Prophetstown and Vincennes in 1808–11 were not confined simply to the actions of important leaders such as Harrison and the Prophet or to racial groups like "whites" and "Indians." Individual decisions and factionalism allowed Miami, French, Shawnee, and American communities and even individuals to alter the course of American and nativist movements through rumor and outright lies. Such a world was possible in an environment framed by what Pekka Hämäläinen and Samuel Truett have labeled "conditional terrain," where a "tangled web of imperial, national, and cultural journeys" provided these opportunities.[50] As we examine the roots of frontier violence and the polarization of racial relationships with the Ohio River Valley, we must consider the extent to which intra-ethnic factionalism shaped negative perceptions of Indians, which in turn shaped a sense of shared victimization that whites felt along the frontier. Euroamericans came to demonize Prophetstown because of the violence unleashed by the War of 1812, and they eventually categorized Indians as trapped within immutable biological categories. Yet they often did so based upon fears and violence generated by a complex set of intra- and interethnic relationships. The unifying effects of warfare and shared victimization shaped the racial identities along the frontier, but the roots of warfare, violence, and the resulting victimization are not as clear-cut as some historians have argued. The Prophet and his followers hoped to stop the encroachment of non-Native settlers, but the extent of indigenous political unity needs to be reevaluated. While primary sources may detail *fears* of Prophetstown, those fears are not necessarily representative of the Prophet's actions, the town itself, or its inhabitants. Instead, these fears are a reflection of historical actors whose motives remain highly questionable.

Euroamerican fears were as much about personal experiences with both Indian and non-Native neighbors as about the cultural and racial dichotomies that typically frame studies of the frontier. Scholars argue that fears among American frontier communities remain "unclear." In the case of Prophetstown, though, the causes of American fears are evident. Racial unity for both Indians and whites threatened the ethnic identity of the Miami and French. The Miamis and French manipulated others' perceptions of Prophetstown in order to inflame Americans' fears, hatreds, and anxieties. They resisted racialization because doing so would have taken away a key ally at a time when the Miami world was increasingly threatened. When those feelings boiled over, they took the form of physical violence that was aimed at the Prophet and his so-called followers. The resulting violence at Tippecanoe actually protected the Miamis and French because it diverted attention from them. To a certain extent, it protected their borders. But the violence unleashed at Tippecanoe would not have happened had the residents of Vincennes not factionalized as well and used the Prophet as a means to attack and marginalize their enemies. Collectively, the Miamis, French traders, and Americans were creating a frontier world that could think of itself only in terms of Prophetstown and the threat of violence it represented.[51]

4 / Vincennes, the Politics of Slavery, and the Indian "Threat"

Given the turbulent history of the region, it makes sense that Americans would connect a strange new Indian community to violence.[1] There were hundreds of Miami, Kickapoo, Lenape, and Potawatomi Indians in the region who might become willing converts to the Prophet's teachings. To make matters worse, Vincennes sat directly downriver from Prophetstown, meaning that unexpected Indian visits occurred despite the distance between the two towns. Although the river gave Tenskwatawa and Tecumseh the ability to attack Vincennes whenever they wished, they were not necessarily convinced that war was the only option to halt the American advance. Much of their anger stemmed from the Treaty of Greenville, which ceded large portions of Indian lands to the United States. Tenskwatawa and Tecumseh, although quite angry at the Americans, believed that rogue Indian leaders were responsible for signing the document. If they could be controlled and Indians united in opposition to land-cession treaties, no further land cessions would take place. Diplomacy could work if Indians could be controlled centrally.

Just as factions and rivalries threw Indian communities into disarray, tensions threw the Americans of the Ohio River Valley into alarm. Even though few slaves resided in Indiana Territory, the institution of slavery already cast a pall over a burgeoning republic. The slavery debate was only an index of the disputes that would command the attention of all Americans in Vincennes after 1809. Although one scholar has recently suggested that Indian affairs was one of "the least controversial aspects" of Harrison's governance, in fact it was *the* controversy in Vincennes from 1809 to 1812.[2]

Unable to find a compromise to the slavery question and frustrated over unproductive negotiations with the Miamis, the Americans fought each other for control of territorial politics. Factionalism in Vincennes focused on Harrison's policies and, in particular, his handling of Indian affairs. In order to maintain their hold on territorial affairs, Harrison and his supporters found various and often violence-inducing ways to characterize their antislavery adversaries as Indian sympathizers.

Harrison's vision of a slaveholding frontier had tremendous potential to shape the development of Indiana Territory. Although gaining new lands for the still young republic seemed to reinforce grandiose ideas of an American empire, expansion also made the issue of slavery an issue of paramount importance if the nation was to survive. Debates about the legality of slavery plagued the frontier communities in Indiana Territory at the same time that Harrison emerged victorious from several treaty negotiations with the nearby Indians. It was not simply that he was taking lands from Indians. He was taking lands that could eventually be worked by slaves. His opponents found this particularly worrisome because the introduction of slavery had the potential to grant Harrison increased political power. This was especially troubling for settlers who saw Harrison's policies as "repugnant to Republicanism" because it undermined the ability frontier settlers had in attaining land, which many saw as a cornerstone to their newly won independence. White families (and the people whom they owned) would flock to the territory if slavery took root there. A well-populated territory could make a successful bid for statehood, which in turn meant that Harrison could position himself on a national stage. Others feared that if slavery was allowed to take hold in the Ohio River Valley, land might become too expensive, forcing white residents to move elsewhere. Thus, the extension of slavery could determine the fate of the United States. Ignored and angry, the governor's opponents petitioned Congress and wrote letters to federal officials. One Indiana resident begged U.S. Attorney General John Breckenridge, "For God's sake don't let Congress introduce slavery among us."[3] Despite their protests, leading antislavery advocates in Indiana found that their pleas fell on deaf ears. Jefferson's administration was far too busy with international affairs and dragging the young republic out of debt. As a result, the president and other federal leaders relied on Harrison to control the territorial experiment farther west. He was much like the Prophet, a man who hoped to centralize settlers around his vision for the region.

Harrison enjoyed an immense amount of influence as governor of the territory. When Jefferson reappointed him governor in 1803, Jefferson

and Congress also empowered the young Virginian with license to negotiate land-cession treaties with any Indian community north of the Ohio
River.[4] Moreover, when Jefferson was to select five men to serve in the
territorial legislature's upper house, the Legislative Council, he left the
decision to Harrison.[5] The ability to control the Council was key in that it
gave Harrison great influence over territorial legislation. Harrison's ability to shape Indian affairs and territorial policy placed him in a unique
and powerful position to shape the territorial government around his
values. Given such power, Harrison was often unwilling to negotiate or
even discuss territorial dilemmas.

Debates about the legality of slavery plagued frontier communities
in Indiana Territory at the same time that the Prophet started his crusade to unite disparate Indian peoples. Eventually these processes would
coalesce into a polarizing debate about Prophetstown due in large part
to the lies and exaggerations that neighbors spread about one another.
Harrisonians identified their adversaries with Prophetstown in order to
keep them from political power and to make them social outcasts. They
insinuated and told outright lies that white citizens from Vincennes were
spreading rumors among the various Indian communities that the treaty
negotiations were pointless because Harrison was soon to be replaced.
Yet the Harrisonians' attempts to silence their enemies only made
those opponents more powerful and amplified perceptions of a militant
Prophetstown. By using Prophetstown as an ideological weapon, Vincennes leaders and residents intensified native-white antagonisms that
increased the likelihood of frontier violence.[6]

Before the Prophet settled in Indiana Territory, many of the territorial officials participated in a spirited, sometimes calumnious, but never
violent debate over the legality of slavery in the territory. When events at
Prophetstown focused fears of an Indian attack after 1808, few territorial
leaders believed that penning lengthy diatribes in the newspaper would
protect frontier settlements. Territorial leaders sensed a need for immediate action to thwart an Indian war, but they were unwilling to compromise with their enemies, and thus continued to amplify their rhetoric.
Debates about slavery, Indian affairs, and Harrison's growing power
shaped frontier identities. Americans were willing to attack and marginalize each other even if that led to their death. In a world where death on
the frontier was a real possibility, whites created a volatile atmosphere of
fear and violence and even the risk of death to control territorial development. It also demonstrates how willing they were to undermine the
territorial laws in order to get what they wanted.

Fear of an Indian massacre was forever present in many frontier communities. One scholar notes that settlers "had already served childhood apprenticeships as potential victims," which shaped and amplified their perceptions of Indians as adults. The ability to spread rumors and lies about Indians held real power given the ever-present fear of Indian an Indian attack. As a result, the culture of lying in Vincennes was especially dangerous given the power that rumor and paranoia had in priming frontier residents to lash out against Indians as well as one another. Given the rumors and increased fear among Anglo settlers, Harrison's power to negotiate treaties with the local Indian communities provided him with the power to influence the public's perceptions of Indians. Fear was more than just a political tool; it was a key part of how men and women viewed their community, which meant that rumors of an Indian war spreading within the town's political debates often quickly became the substance of family conversations. Women and children, then, although silenced in terms of political voice, certainly reinforced if not amplified fears of possible Indian depredations simply by discussing the reports Stout included in his newspaper or in warning their children not to play too far from home for fear of a possible kidnapping.[7]

Reports of Indian massacres and war surfaced almost weekly in the territory's lone newspaper, the *Western Sun*. Harrison welcomed Elihu Stout, the *Sun*'s editor, into his confidence, who then printed the governor's reports in the newspaper. Although Native-white violence never spread to Vincennes itself, Stout's annotations heightened fears that it could.[8] Stout's commentaries made frontier settlers more susceptible to alarmism because the talks of Indian militancy were connected to threats upon settler families, which invited Americans nationwide into the frontier violence.[9]

While historians have analyzed the contentious relationship that developed between Harrison and the Shawnee brothers during the early 1800s, they have ignored that bloodshed between Indians and Euroamericans was a product of the factionalism *within* Vincennes. The political culture of the town shaped the ways in which territorial officials (all based in Vincennes) interpreted information about Indians and Prophetstown. Leaders in Vincennes were quite different from the average territorial settler. Like Badollet, many of the territorial officers were fairly well educated and had some connection to Revolutionary America. Badollet arrived in Boston in 1780 after finishing his degree in belle-lettres from the College and Academy of Geneva; Harrison's father was a wealthy Virginia aristocrat who had signed the Declaration of Independence; and Thomas Randolph, who would eventually become the territorial attorney general, was first cousin to Thomas Jefferson.[10] These men saw their role in the territory as an extension of the political debates and Revolutionary world into which they were born. In their minds, the fate of the new republic could only rest with them.

These men overlooked one important thing: most frontiersmen were more concerned with the practical benefits of the Revolution than with the ideological debates that followed. After 1795, Americans had greater access to regional markets when the Treaty of San Lorenzo granted them access to the Mississippi River and New Orleans. The Jay Treaty improved relations between the Americans and British and undermined the threat posed by the "Miami Confederacy," a term used by scholars to denote the loose organization of Indian communities that resisted the American army in the Ohio Valley from 1787 to 1794. And last, the American army, fresh off its victory at Fallen Timbers, entrenched itself at Fort Wayne in order to protect the western frontier of the young republic.

Men such as Harrison and Randolph felt it was their destiny to govern the expanding but fragile western territories, and they utilized the power inherent within that system to do so.[11] Local officials both controlled the federal funds and enjoyed a virtual monopoly over territorial affairs. Small landowners could only vote for the rich and powerful. Men with at least fifty acres of land could vote for a representative—white men who owned at least two hundred acres—could serve in the General Assembly. These landowners then nominated members for the Legislative Council to serve in the upper house. The president of the United States determined who would serve in that house after consulting the list of nominees. Moreover, until the territory developed a fully functioning government, the governor had the power to disband the legislature whenever he saw fit and to veto any legislation he disliked.[12] As a result, this system allowed Harrison to wield enormous power. Once he and his supporters controlled Vincennes, they would then have the power not only to shape the Ohio River Valley but also to define what it meant to be American.

Rumors

Springtime in 1809 heightened paranoia among frontier residents as Indians began to move out of their winter camps, hunting and trading with others in the region. Rumors of murder at Prophetstown and Indian depredations in Illinois Territory convinced some residents that violence was spreading east toward the territorial capital. Both Meriwether Lewis

FIGURE 3. A pencil sketch of John Badollet by Charles Alexandre LeSueur, ca. 1800–1846. Courtesy of the Charles Alexandre LeSueur Collection of Words of Art on Paper, Purdue University Libraries.

and William Wells had warned Harrison of a possible war, but rather than sending emissaries to gauge the intentions of the Indians, Harrison jumped at the chance to call out the militia. John Badollet thought this was merely for show—the troops "spent the working season in sloth and idle mockery of military manoeuvres [sic]." It is impossible to know whether Badollet's fear reflected his personal animosity toward Harrison or whether he evaluated the situation fairly. Nonetheless, he and others like him nonetheless understood Harrison's political behavior in relation to Indian affairs. The soldiers' inactivity troubled Badollet and his colleagues, for William Wells told Harrison that the Prophet planned to "distroy [sic] all the White people at Vincennes" and "strike a blow at the White people." Anti-Harrisonians fumed at the governor and his ill-prepared militia, and even Benjamin Parke, a close confidant of Harrison's, worried about the Indians on the Wabash.[13]

Harrison convened a treaty council at Fort Wayne in the fall of 1809, hoping to secure new lands for the republic—lands that Harrison alone deemed necessary for settlement and security. Harrison worried that Chippewas, Ottawas, and Ho-Chunks would soon join the Prophet and attack white communities. He used the treaty council as a way to strengthen nebulous friendships with local Indians and to dissuade Indians from joining forces with the Prophet. Things did not go as planned. Indian leaders scoffed at the proposed annuity payments and refused outright to sell any land.[14]

Indian resistance made Harrison increasingly wary that outside interference and failure on the treaty grounds might lead to his removal. In fact, he wrote Secretary of the Treasury Albert Gallatin to see if the row over the slavery issue and complaints about his leadership had delayed his reappointment as governor. Sixty-eight settlers from Harrison County submitted a petition requesting that Congress deny Harrison's reappointment to the governorship. They cited the fact that he supported slavery; moreover, they insisted that his long term in office was the antithesis of everything for which the republican government stood. Harrison worried less about the substance of the protest and more about the fact that the protest was addressed to Albert Gallatin. After all, Harrison knew about Gallatin's close relationship to Badollet: the two were both from Switzerland and were in regular correspondence. Other members of the anti-Harrisonians continued the assault against the governor. According to Harrison, Nathaniel Ewing circulated "a report amongst the people that the [federal] government has lost all confidence in Harrison" at the same time that he had been told that the newly elected President James Madison had faith in him.[15]

Convinced that his enemies' "unfounded jealousies" over his executive authority drove them to challenge his authority and kindle the "the fury of bloody thirsty savages" against Vincennes, Harrison deftly used his powers as governor to expand American interests and marginalize his political rivals. Blaming his enemies for Indian depredations was an easy way for the governor to undermine any support his rivals had in the territory. John Badollet wrote that when several local Indian communities declined to meet Harrison in the fall of 1809, Harrison blamed "the machinations of certain enemies" in Vincennes in front of the General Assembly. Harrison suspected that his political enemies attempted to ruin the council at Fort Wayne because they had been unable to influence the territorial assembly against him. It would work to Harrison's advantage if people thought his opponents had excited the local Indians in the hope of destabilizing the governor's leadership. Given that the Miamis and French had already primed Harrison to fear the Prophet, it was logical that he would marginalize any enemies he perceived to be challenging his Indian policies. He knew full well that the majority of settlers feared Indians, particularly those at Prophetstown. Exaggerating the Prophet's militancy allowed him to create a certain level of uncertainty and chaos that he could then control. He worked to create an atmosphere in which his leadership was necessary.[16]

Harrison had help. Pervasive fears of Indians turned truth into rumor and rumor into gross exaggerations. The slightest suggestion of Indian thievery could turn into the bloodiest murder. In one instance, Indians stole a number of horses from a farm near Vincennes, but whites, according to Benjamin Stickney, turned the event into "ten persons being killed near Vincennes." One scholar of the American West has demonstrated convincingly that the "license to purvey Indian intelligence was to be had simply by asserting that one "knew" something" and that as a result, "all kinds of people became reporters, often alarming more than informing." Such behavior took on greater significance along the Miami frontier, where Harrison and his supporters confirmed the likelihood of such rumors through their rhetoric about Prophetstown. Although the rhetoric of fear was often tied directly to men arguing territorial and slavery politics, it quickly spread to their wives and children, who had no other option than to prepare for such a threat. In charge of the household, women made decisions to protect their children and even their property that had important political ramifications.[17] By leaving town entirely or by joining other families in the strongest homes, women and their children often made manifest the fear that men imagined. As usual, Harrison would demand leadership in the face of an Indian war in order to legitimize his own authority.

Yet in legitimizing his leadership, Harrison helped to destabilize the community. Factional strife in Vincennes grew in proportion to the threat of an Indian war. The participants became more desperate, turning to physical violence. In one such instance, Dr. Elias McNamee boldly questioned Harrisonian policies in the *Western Sun*. This enraged Thomas Randolph, one of Harrison's confidants, and he challenged the doctor to a duel. McNamee refused, citing his Quaker faith, and he had Randolph temporarily arrested. Once released, Randolph could not be deterred from exacting revenge. He hunted down William McIntosh, one of McNamee's antislavery allies, and in the altercation that followed, McIntosh suffered superficial cuts to his face. Randolph was not so fortunate. McIntosh literally stabbed him in the back, leaving him close to death for several days.[18] The vulgar rhetoric that had characterized the newspaper debate now spilled out into the streets, reflecting the extent to which violence had replaced a balanced and civil discussion.

Physical confrontations coincided with more rumors that the anti-Harrisonians had undermined treaty negotiations with the local Indian communities. Colonel John Small believed that at the recent councils near Fort Wayne, "some abandoned profligate, in the garb of an American, attempted to frustrate entirely the treaty." Small's report reinforced the fear-laden speech that Harrison gave to the General Assembly, and it may have been a ploy to discredit the governor's political enemies. An American supposedly informed the discontented Indians that the president of the United States rejected the 1809 Treaty of Fort Wayne, the same treaty that Tecumseh and Tenskwatawa refused to attend. Even white settlers believed that Harrison had negotiated the treaty only to "retrieve his declining popularity." Other residents hoped to interrogate those tied to the rumors to learn the truth of what had transpired. When questioned about his sources, Small named Elias McNamee, but the doctor denied that he knew anything.[19] The Harrisonians characterized McNamee's denial as yet another anti-Harrisonian trick. The factions chose to use the rumors to attack each other and to speculate rather than work cooperatively to uncover the truth.

Elihu Stout's newspaper added yet another layer to the growing paranoia. He printed the McNamee–Small story in the *Western Sun* while also requesting that residents return petitions to his office in favor of the governor's reappointment. He hoped that his newspaper would cast suspicion on Harrison's enemies and demonstrate that the governor was still widely popular throughout the region. This was not necessarily true. Earlier, settlers in Clark County had asked Congress to appoint "a Governor whose Sentiments are more congenial with those of the people, and with those principles of Liberty." Beyond sharing Harrison's political ideals, Stout owed his job to the governor. The printer feared that antislavery advocates might show their "demoniac [*sic*] crest, and malignant falsehoods . . . in Washington city," much as they had in Vincennes. Stout characterized McNamee as the "drudge" of the anti-Harrisonians and accused him of making a "willful, malicious falsehood." Yet Stout was the one doing the lying. Like his fellow Harrisonians, Stout was well aware that the governor had grown unpopular in the territory. Stout used the newspaper to his advantage, claiming that Harrison's declining popularity was a myth. The governor's supporters, he wrote, "constitute[d] a majority of nine tenths of the Territory."[20] Yet Indiana residents refused to elect Thomas Randolph—a close confidant of the governor—as territorial representative, suggesting that they knew the truth of the matter.

Knowing that his articles might be reprinted in other newspapers throughout the Ohio Valley and along the eastern seaboard, Stout hoped that his characterization of Vincennes would reflect well on the governor. However, Stout's claims ignored the fact that many territorial residents sought to expel Harrison from power. Hundreds of settlers from Knox, Clark, Randolph, St. Clair, and Harrison Counties petitioned Congress for the removal of Harrison in favor of a governor who was "in principal opposed to slavery." In fact, they called the governor's support of slavery "repugnant." They simply did not think that the territory should overturn the Northwest Ordinance, nor did they think slavery would help settle the region quickly. Furthermore, the separation of the Illinois country—largely populated by settlers who were proslavery—from the rest of Indiana Territory in 1809 left Vincennes as the last bastion of Harrisonian policies. Harrison still exercised a great deal of influence in the territory, specifically in Indian affairs, and the anti-Harrisonians believed that replacing Harrison with an antislavery advocate would likely stop the political intrigue and violence. Although the anti-Harrisonians lacked proof to substantiate their claims, they did not hesitate to publicize Harrison's corrupt Indian policies. For his part, Harrison feared that his enemies' complaints delayed his reappointment, which was several months late.[21]

A seemingly innocuous election for territorial representative to Congress in 1809 played an important role in mobilizing the factions. The election of Jonathan Jennings—the son of an abolitionist minister and enemy to Harrison—stoked feared among the Harrisonians despite the fact that Jennings would not have a vote in Congress. The representative's ability to persuade congressmen was just as valuable. Jennings had defeated Thomas Randolph by a slim margin, winning only twenty-four more votes. The Harrisonians realized that they could get Randolph to Washington if they could negate the votes of just one precinct. Fearful that Jennings might succeed in getting Harrison replaced as governor, Randolph traveled to Washington DC to protest the election results. To that end, Harrison and the territorial legislature convinced the territorial election committee to declare unanimously that Harrison lacked the authority to hold the territorial election from which Jennings had emerged victorious. After making his case, Randolph left the federal capital confident that Congress would overturn the election and give him the advantage over Jennings for the next election; however, the House of Representatives refused to do so. Jennings was astonished by the efforts of his "great enemy the Governor" to overturn the election, but it made sense given the changing political atmosphere ushered in by the election of 1809.[22] To Jennings, the Harrisonians would stop at nothing to impose their will in the region.

Although the factions became increasingly obsessed with Harrison's handling of Indian affairs, slavery remained at the center of their disputes. Badollet felt that as long as Harrison was "friendly to the admission of Slavery, this Territory will know no peace. . . . Our next executive ought surely to come from the State of New York or Pennsylvania, no more Virginians." The changing political atmosphere in the territory made this more likely for new legislation curtailed the governor's powers while extending the franchise to more white men. By 1812, a centralized system that favored elite landowners gave way to a local system in which the average territorial resident had more political power. Control of the territory now rested more with its inhabitants than with the governor and the officials back in Washington. These democratic openings would culminate in Harrison's wartime resignation in 1812. Such changes seemingly invited ever-louder attacks against Harrison and his sycophants as they enabled the public to take a greater part in local politics. These changes galvanized Harrison to protect what power he had left. However, even if federal officials wanted to replace Harrison, they could not ignore his success in actively aiding territorial expansion. Harrison had made Jefferson's and Madison's Indian policies a reality.[23] From 1801 to 1809, his successful negotiations with area Indians had resulted in the acquisition of millions of acres of land. These achievements may explain why James Madison reappointed Harrison despite the fact that the evolution of territorial politics had undermined Harrison's traditional, autocratic governing style and soured his relationships with many territorial settlers. Furthermore, the governor still had many influential supporters in the region, including several French traders who helped him maintain his influence with the various Indian communities nearby, a skill that federal leaders saw as key to maintaining regional stability.

Table 2. Evolution of Indiana's territorial government

Stages of territorial government	Elected & appointed officials	Lawmaking body	Suffrage
First stage, May 1800	President Adams appoints and Congress approves territorial governor, secretary, and judges. Territorial governor appoints all local and territorial officials.	The territorial governor and judges make all the laws.	White males age 21 and older owning at least 50 acres of land are eligible to vote.
Second stage, December 1804	President and Congress continue appointing governor, secretary, and judges. White males living in territory can elect members of lower house to territorial legislature. Lower house provides list of 10 men to potentially serve in upper house, from which governor selects 5.	Governor retains power to appoint local and territorial officials. He also has the power to convene or dissolve the territorial legislature; he can also veto any legislative measure.	In 1809, Congress passes legislation for Indiana Territory to elect directly the territorial delegate to Congress. In 1811, U.S. Congress passes legislation extending voting rights to all free white males age 21 years or older who pay county or territorial taxes
Third stage, December 1815	Assembly petitions for statehood in December 1815. Congress passes an Enabling Act. Voters elect the first governor, lieutenant governor, and senators.	Delegates to Indiana's Constitutional Convention complete Indiana's constitution.	Indiana's 1816 constitution allows the vote to every white male citizen of the United States age 21 years or older who has resided in the state for one year.

Source: Adapted from Pamela J. Bennett, ed., "Indiana Territory," *Indiana Historian*, March 1999, 1–16.

"Constructing" Prophetstown

While 1809 proved to be a transitional year in regard to territorial political debates, the spring of 1810 placed Prophetstown front and center in the minds of the settler communities. In a sense, two separate Vincennes existed—one in favor of slavery and against the Indians and the other rejecting slavery and urging diplomacy with Native peoples. Fears about Prophetstown came to trump the slavery debate in the *Western Sun*. Western tribes, including the Sacs, Foxes, and Kickapoos, visited Prophetstown; rumors of Indian gatherings spread throughout the countryside, alarming countless settlers. Gathering the people of Vincennes in a public meeting, Harrison claimed that the Prophet intended to attack the town; he himself would be the first victim. Badollet scoffed at these dramatics, writing that Harrison "painted his fears in lively colours. . . . [I]f it was not for fear of spreading too great an alarm, he would immediately send his family to Kentucky and convert his house unto a fort." He also observed that Harrison's supporters attended the meeting in large numbers, a sure sign that Harrison wanted others to ask *him* to order out the militia.[24] Under the militia acts of 1792, Harrison had the power to call every able-bodied white male citizen into service. While not everyone read Stout's newspaper or heard Harrison's fear-laden pronouncements, they undoubtedly knew someone who served in the militia. Thus, the volunteer force itself became a barometer of the Indian threat. Whenever Harrison mobilized the townsmen, he reminded local settlers that the Prophet and his minions lurked nearby.

Despite Harrison's efforts to whip Vincennes into a frenzy, members of the anti-Harrisonian faction favored sending a diplomatic mission to Prophetstown. In one instance, several anti-Harrisonians met for a short meeting at Badollet's office. All who gathered were opposed to slavery. One of the men gathered there stated that in regard to the militancy of the Prophet, "it appeared to be the general opinion of those present that there was no truth in the report which coincided with my own." According to Judge John Johnson, there was no ulterior motive behind the meeting, and all of the men present recognized and respected Harrison's authority in the matter. Toussaint Dubois, one of the French traders trusted by both Harrison and Badollet, acted on these rumors by suggesting that he visit Prophetstown and inquire about the Tenskwatawa's intentions. All present at the impromptu gathering of anti-Harrisonians believed "that the alarm was unfounded" like the governor's previous warnings. Dubois deferred to Harrison's authority; he would go to Prophetstown only if directed to do so by Harrison.[25]

In the face of such challenges, Harrison openly asserted his right as territorial governor to control diplomacy with Prophetstown by demanding that the participants explain themselves. According to Ewing, Harrison shouted at Dubois in an "angry magisterial and insulting manner" for having fraternized with Badollet's faction. Harrison accused the men of treason and demanded that they abide by his decisions. Ewing said Harrison "exults in the idea that he will make us smart severely for our daring perseverance in opposing his darling and never abandoned plan of Slavery." The anti-Harrisonians pressed their case to Gallatin that the Harrisonians were abusing their power and their neighbors. Ewing was convinced that Harrison was using Indian affairs to defend his governing authority. The Dubois fiasco and Harrison's tirade stood out in particular. The "conspiratorial" meeting was really nothing more than a natural gathering of like-minded townspeople. However, the Harrisonians labeled the meeting as a treasonous affair, "the object of which was to bring the Indians on" Vincennes.[26] Although several public officials supported Dubois's plan, Harrison chose to send a speech to the Prophet. Yet again, Harrison depended on the power of rhetoric rather than on active diplomacy.

The Harrisonians did not stop at condemning the conspirators; according to Badollet, they spread rumors that the antislavery men had helped the Prophet identify "those who were to be sacrificed & those who were to be spared" when the attack did come. Harrison seized on the situation, realizing that it allowed him to do two things at once: he could spread rumors of Indian attack and discredit his enemies. To that end, he convened a grand jury to pass judgment on the secret meeting. But after interrogating three of the would-be conspirators (including Dubois, a man Harrison had once called "one of the most respectable Indian traders in this country"). The jury failed to agree on an indictment. Harrison's "diabolical" plan, in Badollet's eyes, was "at last disappointed." In their quest for the truth about Prophetstown, the anti-Harrisonians recognized their right to question Harrison's policies, despite their enemies' efforts to stifle them. The Harrisonians took a decidedly antirepublican stance in attempting to quash dissenting viewpoints, but their desire to silence vocal enemies outweighed any devotion they might have to Revolutionary principles. Most important, they remained entirely ignorant of the fact that their rhetoric pushed anxious frontier settlers ever closer to a real Indian war. Harrison himself came to believe his own lies about the Prophet's militancy. Elihu Stout also helped the Harrisonians to isolate their enemies by publishing reports on regional Indian affairs and by promoting the governor's message. One article, published in June 1810, traced an interpreter's experiences among the Lenape; the man's story drew attention to the Prophet's hostile measures and made it clear that new converts continued to flock to Prophetstown.[27]

Stout saw a more malicious international influence at play; he suspected a "deep laid scheme of villainy" based in British North America. In addition, he preyed on readers' deepest fears by reminding them to make plans to protect their families. Stout continued to resurrect the specter of Native-white collaboration, claiming that Americans had pushed the Indians not only to refuse the Treaty of Fort Wayne but also to challenge Harrison's right to govern. Stout ended the editorial by suggesting that the "culprits be dragged to the light."[28] Such statements only amplified the rumors and suspicions already shaping perceptions of Prophetstown.

The anti-Harrisonians, intimidated into silence, had no way to contradict falsehoods published by the region's sole newspaper. Nathaniel Ewing found himself increasingly fearful of the Harrisonians after witnessing the governor's tirade; he was so worried that he asked Gallatin for "protection against the persecutions of Governor Harrison." Ewing also worried that Harrison had done too little to fortify the town in the event of a real Indian attack, for the town's active militiamen were concentrated around Grouseland, Harrison's lavish home. Furthermore, Harrison's rhetoric was at odds with the peaceful image that the anti-Harrisonians projected. Ewing respected the Prophet's effort to cultivate corn, raise cattle, fence in boundaries, and share his religious visions. The Prophet did not have any "intention to meddle with the whites," Ewing wrote, and it was Harrison who intended "to make war on them."[29] In the face of a vengeful governor and a frightened town, Ewing believed that he would be attacked by his neighbors if he did not approach federal authorities. The anti-Harrisonians' stance, although ostensibly rooted in slavery, had much more to do with Indians than human bondage. Moreover, their reactions to Harrison served to create a contradictory vision of Prophetstown that left settlers unsure of whom to believe and where to turn.

Harrison did little to stop the transmission of these falsehoods because he had come to view the implementation of his policies as a personal referendum. Having weakened several powerful Indian groups through diplomatic measures, he grew irate at settlers who dared to challenge his authority in a region still suffering from periodic Indian attacks. Harrison could not comprehend why some Americans advocated for the protection of the Indians, a people he felt were inherently predisposed to war. "The mind of a Savage," Harrison argued, was "so constructed that he cannot be at rest,—he cannot be happy unless it is acted upon by some strong stimulus. . . . [I]f he hunts in the winter he must go to war in the summer." As if on cue, the French trader

Joseph Barron poked the fire by reminding Harrison that his neighbors were trying to incite war. Barron said that it was likely the Prophetstown Indians "had been deceived by white people, that [they] had been informed that the citizens were equally divided" over the need for the Treaty of Fort Wayne (1809)." He interpreted opposition as a threat to his governorship rather than simply a reflection of the democratic political process. When confronted, Harrison usually tried to isolate his enemies rather than to negotiate with them. This attitude was evident when the territorial assembly repealed an 1805 act that allowed slaves to be indentured when brought into the territory. While the anti-Harrisonians celebrated, Harrison tried once again to trump his enemies. In a speech to the assembly, Harrison demanded that Americans who had spread "falsehoods amongst the Indians" be punished because they undermined the foundations of government and a peaceful society. Harrison went even further, saying, "There is a constant communication between some persons in this place [Vincennes] and the Prophet." Assemblyman John Caldwell challenged the governor, asking him to "lay before the house such documents as were in his possession, proving the existence of a treasonable correspondence between persons of this place and the Indians, & to name such persons." Harrison responded first with confusion, then retraction, and finally by restating his previous conclusions. Harrison's paranoia reached such a pitch that he pushed the legislature to pass a law punishing treasonous activity. He hoped to have a legal means by which to silence those whom he suspected of undermining his authority. The law would have made real what Harrison could not accomplish through lies and innuendo. Harrison went so far as to withdraw his recommendation for John Caldwell to become a deputy surveyor. Although Caldwell had done nothing wrong in questioning the governor's assertions, Harrison continued to punish anyone whom he perceived to be an enemy. In letter after letter, he detailed the militant designs of the Prophet and the intrigues perpetrated by men such as William Wells.[30]

While Harrison made sure to appear imperturbable in public, the opposition to his governorship weighed heavily on his mind. The antislavery petitions, efforts to raise impeachment proceedings, and the whispers of his critics made him worry that he might be replaced. He hoped that President James Madison was "too just to censure an officer for unintentional error or to lend a favourable ear to the calumnies which are so industriously circulated." Yet in a letter to Secretary of War William Eustis he worried that the president may judge him "a man of feeble judgement and credulous disposition" for not actually knowing what the Prophet planned. Moreover, Harrison worried that President Madison would begin to lose faith in him if he could not offer proof of the Prophet's plans. He admitted as much to Eustis, saying that the Prophet probably did not intend war. But, fearful of not being reappointed, Harrison demanded that a "decisive and energetic measure [be] adopted to break up the combination formed by the Prophet" or the United States would soon "have every Indian tribe in this quarter united" against it.[31] Harrison's motives for demanding such actions were questionable given the divisive politics that strangled Vincennes. Was Harrison demanding action because he needed proof that his enemies were wrong, or did he believe his own rhetoric about the Prophet's militancy? In the face of pressure from his fellow Americans, Harrison routinely acted in a way that demonstrated his authority as governor. He rarely chose caution when his political enemies challenged him to be more pragmatic.

Tecumseh's 1811 visit to Vincennes provided the governor with a much-needed opportunity to reassert his power but also to silence those who questioned the motives of the Prophetstown Indians. In advance of the visit, Miami Indians and French traders stirred up yet more rumors: Tecumseh's visit was merely a prelude to an attack. Harrison responded with a series of public theatrics meant to make an impression on Indians and Anglo-American settlers alike. Parading the militia around town, warning the territorial assembly of citizens who were plotting with the Indians, and confronting his enemies in public created a visual pageant of Indian militancy for settlers to consume. Stout primed readers of the *Western Sun* by informing them that the "insolent banditti" (the Shawnee brothers) were indeed violent and determined to attack Vincennes. For his part, Harrison used the visit to draw a strict racial line between whites and the Indians, and also to make a political statement. He portrayed the Indians as bloodthirsty savages who were looking to murder the residents of Vincennes. When Tecumseh approached Vincennes, Harrison met him with [number] of townsmen in tow. In an effort to remind themselves that they could stand toe-to-toe with their Indian neighbors, Harrison and the militiamen wore hunting shirts, and, according to Badollet, Harrison "drew an animated picture of the meditated bloodshed with such success, that it was with difficulty, that [his supporters] could be refrained from running to Tecumseh's camp" and slaughtering the inhabitants. The hunters lined the street with their weapons, creating an imposing sight for Tecumseh as he walked toward Grouseland to negotiate with Harrison. In a letter to Eustis, Harrison recognized the "metamorphosis" that took place in Tecumseh's attitude as he walked Harrison's gauntlet. It "was entirely produced by the gleaming & clanging of arms, & by frowns of a considerable body of hunting Shirt men." Harrison's "hunting shirt men" were likely a purposeful design by the governor to echo the republican spirit of 1776 when the rebel Virginia Shirtmen fought to stop Lord Dunmore's force from ravaging the colony. The governor then reminded the militia that there were people in Vincennes who were "friends" to Tecumseh, but these comments were nothing new to the anti-Harrisonians. According to Badollet, the governor had "conceived an unextinguishable hatred against [Ewing and Badollet], because [they had] assisted in defeating his favorite scheme of introducing slavery."[32]

Despite his ability to marginalize his enemies in Vincennes, Harrison feared that the anti-Harrisonians might have too much influence in Washington DC and succeed in replacing him as governor. Both Jennings's presence there but also the letters Badollet penned to Albert Gallatin on a routine basis threatened the Harrisonian machine. Although Harrison knew his enemies were writing Gallatin and other officials, he did not know exactly what was being said. Harrison wrote to Eustis and asked him to disregard any statements that his actions toward the Prophet had been "premature and unfounded." The governor also sought out the support of the religious men of Vincennes in order to legitimize policies that had come under attack. He had succeeded at intimidating Tecumseh but had failed to silence the anti-Harrisonians, which fueled his fear that Madison might "censure" him. Harrison learned of Jonathan Jennings's continued efforts in Washington DC to sway Congress against the embattled governor. Jennings gleefully distributed "depositions and certificates with charges against Harrison" to several members of Congress. Jennings was confident enough in Harrison's political demise that he described to a friend his plan to "lay the ground work of an impeachment."[33] Harrison rightly feared that his life as a politician was soon to end.

Prophetstown presented a perfect opportunity for Harrison to extend his career as a military man. As rumors spread that Jennings was trying to remove Harrison, two local clergymen formed a committee that would openly support an attack on Prophetstown. Joining the committee was Francis Vigo, a proslavery man who became something of a town hero when he served as an informant for George Rogers Clark during the Revolutionary War. The clergymen went so far as to write President Madison, claiming that the governor's measures against the Prophet had saved Vincennes from destruction. Most of these men had a stake in seeing Harrison and his policies succeed. Yet any opportunity to evaluate the Prophet in a rational manner vanished as Harrison's supporters strove to defend his name and authority over Indian affairs. The public meeting of Harrisonians in Vincennes was less diplomatic. The infamous Indian-hater Daniel Sullivan gathered a large number of citizens of Knox County to demand action. In his mind, the safety of Americans on the frontier would "never be effectually secured but by breaking up of the combination formed by the Shawanese prophet." More importantly, Sullivan echoed much of what the French and Miami Indians had been saying since the founding of Prophetstown. If Prophetstown was not destroyed, "it is highly probable that the threatened destruction of *this place* and the *massacre of the inhabitants,* would have been the consequence."[34]

With residents of Vincennes calling for an attack on Prophetstown, Harrison found ways to use personal disputes to do the same. When Tecumseh and the Miamis claimed that white people were telling the Indians that Harrison was soon to be replaced as governor, Harrison claimed "the scheme originated with a Scotch tory," William McIntosh, who lived in Vincennes and with whom Harrison had a very hostile relationship. Initially the two men had been friends, but land speculation pitted them against each other, culminating in a legal decision that awarded Harrison monetary damages for McIntosh's calumnies. The governor concluded that the white men of whom Tecumseh spoke were in fact McIntosh and William Wells. Recognizing an opportunity to amplify the threat against Vincennes, Harrison challenged Eustis to imagine the "villainous intrigues" that were "carried on with the Indians in this country by foreign agents and other disaffected persons." These accusations, however, demonstrate that Harrison often acted on limited intelligence if not personal animosity. Two months later, Harrison called for Wells to be reappointed. In reference to Wells and his treasonous activities, Harrison stated that

> the supposed agency of Mr [William] Wells in produceing [*sic*] the late disturbances amongst the Indians is not Supported by any positive proof but that of Indians most of whom were his enemies [*sic*] before his removal from office—circumstances indeed are strongly against him but Knowing that he can be a very useful officer I would recommend to give him another trial by an appointment in the Indian Department if a Suitable Situation Could be found for him.

Yet months after that, Harrison warned Eustis that Wells could not be trusted, that he should be placed in the "Interior of our settlements where he would never see and scarcely hear of an Indian" so that he would be so "limited as to prevent his doing mischief."[35] Whether he intended it or not, he was showing Eustis just how personal the debate over Prophetstown had become and the extent to which Harrison would use his political power to sway federal leaders as influential as the secretary of war.

Even Harrison's lawsuit against William McIntosh drifted toward Prophetstown. A host of characters attended the general court to give testimony so that Harrison could prove that he did not defraud the Indians at Fort Wayne as McIntosh had claimed. Harrison and his supporters also denied responsibility for causing the "danger apprehended by the Americans from the Shawnee Prophet and his tribe of Indians." The court found in the governor's favor and awarded him four thousand dollars in damages. Although the case itself is insignificant, it once again brought Prophetstown into the spotlight and allowed the governor and his supporters the opportunity to describe the Prophet's militant ambitions in public theater.[36]

Harrison's paranoia and anger toward dissenters led him to demand obedience from the Indian communities of the Wabash-Maumee Valley. Harrison believed that the Prophet had instigated several murders in the Illinois country to divert attention from his town. Also, according to Harrison, Tecumseh boasted that a "considerable number of the Wyandots" and "some of the Six Nations" planned on joining the Shawnee brothers that fall. Fearful that an attack was near, Harrison wrote several communities of Miamis to determine their loyalties:

> I now speak plainly to you—What is that great Collection of people at
> the mouth of the Tipecanoe [sic] intended for? I am not blind my Children. I can easily See what their object is, these people have boasted
> that they will find me asleep, but they will be deceived. My children, do
> not suppose that I will be foolish enough to suffer them to go on with
> their preparations until they are ready to Strike my people. . . . I now
> inform you that I consider all those who join the Prophet & his party
> as hostile. . . . [T]hose who keep me by the hand must keep on one side
> of it and those that adhere to the Prophet on the other.

In Harrison's view, the Miamis either supported American interests or stood against them. Harrison had a very difficult time understanding how Indians could oppose both Vincennes and Prophetstown. Harrison's concluding comment ignored the difficult situation in which many of the Miamis found themselves. The governor continued to place Indians in the Vincennes/Prophetstown dichotomy that the Miamis and French had helped to create. Harrison's threat put the Miamis in a problematic position: if they followed his dictates, they would undermine their own interests. Harrison forced the Miamis to take sides even when he questioned the Prophet's militancy. Privately he averred that he wanted to know the Prophet's real intentions.[37] Publicly, he offered no such qualifications. Identifying Tenskwatawa's intentions proved quite difficult because the governor was already primed to believe that any Indians who resisted his help were allied with the Prophet. Harrison's policies, loyalties, and rhetoric prevented him from reaching any real understanding of the dynamics in the Wabash-Maumee Valley.

Many Indian leaders responded angrily to Harrison's demands that they take sides. They believed that Harrison exaggerated the situation for the Americans' benefit and ignored the real motives of the Miami, Potawatomi, and Lenape leaders. Some Indians did their best to maintain their distance from both Americans and Prophetstown by meeting their fellow Miamis in council during the fall of 1811. Lapoussier, a Wea leader, reminded Harrison that it was a mistake to think the Weas were connected to the Prophet. Frustrated with Harrison's suspicions, he said: "We have not let you go; we yet hold you by the hand: nor do we hold the hand of the Prophet with a view to injure you. I therefore tell you, that you are not correct when you supposed we joined hands with the Prophet to injure you." Lapoussier's metaphor reflected the ways in which most of the French and Miamis thought about the situation during this period. The Miamis sought to defend the physical and cultural spaces that separated them from the Americans and nativists. The Weas asserted that "no information from any quarter has reached our ears" that asked them "to injure any of your people [the Americans], except from your self [sic]." They recognized the extent to which Harrison's fears fueled the rumors of war, but they also realized that the Prophet played a part in fomenting hostilities. Lapoussier closed with a declaration: "We have our eyes on our lands on the Wabash [River], with a strong determination to defend our rights, let them be invaded from what quarter they may. When our best interests are invaded, we will defend them to a man."[38] They always had. From the era of French and British colonialism to the arrival of George Rogers Clark, the Miamis had defended themselves and their borders.

But given the intellectual context and diplomatic intrigue that polarized relations between Indians and whites, few people understood Lapoussier's comments within their cultural and historical context. Instead, he could only be understood in terms of the threat posed by Prophetstown. Harrison saw a bordered reality that was very different from the cultural borderland envisioned by the Miamis; he saw a physical space where an American homeland temporarily abutted a nativist one. One Miami leader claimed that an alliance with the Americans or the nativists threatened the Weas' "best interests," but Harrison continued to fear that the Weas were secretly in league with Tenskwatawa.[39] The Weas, like their fellow Miamis, continued to protect their homeland and village interests and did not want to associate with the Americans or the Prophet.

As the council ended, several Indian leaders stated their desire to remain independent even though they strongly objected to Tenskwatawa's actions. Miami leaders, including Pacanne, Negro-Legs, Osaga, and others, signed Lapoussier's speech as a gesture of support but also as an expression of the bordered world in which they lived. Nonetheless, their efforts were in vain. The Cincinnati newspaper *Liberty Hall* reported that the Miami leaders had threatened Little Turtle's life if he were to receive any annuities that fall, but the paper's editors contextualized the actions of the Miamis as a by-product of the Prophet's militancy. Harrison concluded that the Miamis rejected the annuities because they feared an attack from the Prophet, but this conclusion ignored reliable intelligence that the Prophet's force remained divided. As if Harrison's inability to understand Miami factionalism was not enough to cause trouble, Toussaint Dubois stated that "almost every Indian" north of Fort Wayne had gone to [Fort] Malden," which convinced many Americans that war was near. Secretary of War Eustis, preoccupied with the threat of conflict with Britain, opened the door for Harrison to make his own decision about the Prophet. Eustis told Harrison that peace was Madison's goal, but that frontier murders, robberies, and violence should not go unpunished. Yet the Prophet "should not be attacked and vanquished" unless "such a measure should be rendered absolutely necessary."[40]

By the late summer of 1811, Harrison and many of his supporters believed that action was necessary. The Prophet had not "abandoned his projects," Benjamin Parke worried, and "his partisans are now found from the Wabash to the Mississippi and up to the Lakes . . . and nothing but the appearance of a force much larger than that contemplated by the . . . Secretary of War will dissolve the [Indian] confederacy." Traditionally, historians couch the resulting violence at the Battle of Tippecanoe as a fight between two nations *necessitated* by Prophetstown's militancy, the British-Indian alliance, and frontier American communities desperate to protect their lands. Yet historians have fallen into the same trap as Harrison and his agents by failing to interpret Indian behavior outside of the Prophetstown/American dichotomy. Americans continued to misinterpret Indian actions because they compared Native peoples in the West with the Indians farther east, with whom they had much more experience. Most settlers were acquainted with Pontiac, the Iroquois Confederacy, and Shawnee militancy during the Revolutionary War, but few understood that Miami hegemony was the product of trade, not violence. The Shawnees had fought the colonists during Lord Dunmore's War, the rebels during the Revolutionary War, and the forces under Arthur St. Clair and Hosiah Harmar during the early federal era. The few Shawnees who supported neutrality had moved west, which left the more militant Shawnees under Blue Jacket, and later Tenskwatawa and his brother, to oppose the Euroamerican settlers. Harrison indulged Euroamerican memories by referring to Tecumseh's affinity for the great Pontiac, which directly associated the Shawnee leader with a militant past. The governor wanted the Americans to view the actions of the Shawnee brothers as the continuation of long-established patterns of violence. Yet scholars have failed to recognize the cultural violence within the American community of Vincennes and the extent to which their own cultural debates had clouded their perceptions of the Prophet. In fact, when Parke spoke of the Prophet's "artifice and intrigues . . . within our boundary," he was speaking of a Harrisonian boundary and not necessarily one that all Americans recognized or even imagined.[41] The Harrisonians' comments negated Tecumseh and Tenskwatawa's cultural context, not to mention that of their own white neighbors, for a more familiar one. For the Americans, Prophetstown symbolized their past violent experiences with Indians rather than a progressive Indian community or even the actual world in which the Miamis continued to operate.

After three years of difficult negotiations with the Prophet, the Miamis, and a host of other Indian communities, Harrison believed that he had no option left but to attack Prophetstown. A large contingent of Miami-speaking Indians refused to support the Americans openly, several traitorous Americans were possibly planning a coup, and Tenskwatawa refused to negotiate any further or to recognize the right Harrison had to buy Indian lands. Most of all, Harrison had already constructed his own idea of a militant Prophetstown, and he believed that Indians, especially the Prophet, were predisposed to war. There was little Tenskwatawa could do except to defend his town.

Having spent several years negotiating treaties with the nearby Indian communities, Harrison recognized the extent to which his policies had upset and in some cases polarized relationships between Indians and settlers. Tecumseh's trip to the American Southeast in the summer and fall of 1811 to gain support for his pan-Indian confederacy worried Harrison. More Indian converts to Prophetstown could overwhelm Harrison's capacity to defend American settlements. Believing that Prophetstown was the logical result of this growing polarization and represented an immediate threat to the region, the governor moved to destroy the nativist settlement. However, he encountered problems mobilizing an effective fighting force, which, by October 1811, was not nearly as large as he had hoped. Numbering fewer than eight hundred men, or just over half of what he expected, Harrison attributed this problem to his personal enemies who had "united with the British agents" and characterized the expedition as "entirely useless" and the Prophet as "one of the best and most pacific of mortals." Harrison's excuse may have been another example of him using Indian affairs to hide the events that transpired at Fort Harrison. In October 1811, he marched his force eighty miles north of Vincennes to construct the fort. The Americans constructed the fort as a staging area near present-day Terre Haute, Indiana. It was a halfway point for Harrison's men to prepare, if need be, for an assault on Prophetstown. Henry Swearingen detailed the near collapse of Fort Harrison due to internal divisions. While laying the foundation for the fort, the regulars and militia argued "to such a pitch that both parties were ready to fall on each other but by the interference of the officers" whose efforts stymied "their mutinous conduct."[42] A full-scale fight had nearly erupted within the ranks of Harrison's army, which likely convinced many militiamen to go back to their farms. Rather than admit his failure to unite the militia, Harrison blamed the factionalism in Vincennes.

Residents worried that Harrison's march toward Prophetstown during the fall of 1811 was in part a reaction to his failed policies. The only option he had left was to destroy the Indian town at Tippecanoe with minimal casualties and hope that the corresponding accolades would reinvigorate his leadership. John Badollet used his son Albert to spy on the activities of the militia, who then wrote his father a few times during their march toward Prophetstown expressing his anxieties. After reminding his son that he was on that mission involuntarily, he asked his son to keep a journal. More importantly, the elder Badollet asked that Albert "note down *every* occurrence as they take place, such an exercise [would] have the advantage of making time hang less heavily upon [him]." John Badollet's requests to his son may have indeed been part of his larger effort to undermine the governor, given his actions during the previous months. The anti-Harrisonians doubted claims that the Prophet and his brother planned a massive attack, which is why they questioned the intelligence behind an article in the *National Intelligencer* reporting Tecumseh's plan to sack Vincennes. Badollet could not have said it better when he lamented: "All I fear is that such a madman [Harrison] will goad the Indians into some act of despair to make good all what he has got published of their pretended views. Oh God! Oh God!"[43]

Vincennes was not only a community riven by factionalism; it was also a town where rumor and exaggeration shaped everyday life and identity. There was a historical continuity to the place as well. Debates about the meaning of republicanism, the Founders, and the legacy of the Revolution demonstrated the extent to which the people of Vincennes elevated their roles as settlers as a, if not the, determining factor for the fate of the republic.

So convinced were they of their importance, they willingly put their territory—in their eyes the heart of the republic—on the line in order to create the world they saw as truly reflecting republican values. And in that process they abandoned a cornerstone of republicanism—the public good—in order to dismiss and destroy their neighbors. A national issue like slavery soon became overshadowed by and intertwined within local debates about power and Indians. Harrison, Stout, Jennings, Badollet, and many others willingly participated in the politics of fear not to undermine an international threat like Britain or to drive off an Indian confederacy, but to ruin each other.[44]

And so as Harrison marshaled his force to march on Prophetstown, he did so not as the representative of a nation or even a town but of a faction. He trudged north to fight two battles: one against Prophetstown and one against his American enemies. Although his rhetoric suggested that the British and Indian alliance would lay waste to the western frontier, the American inhabitants were not helpless victims. Many Americans had helped create a frontier primed for violence because it was through violence that they could create and subsequently vocalize the world they imagined.

Perceptions of Prophetstown and explanations for the violence at Tippecanoe also played out on a national and international stage. As Americans debated war with Great Britain, frontier violence such as that at Tippecanoe reinforced pervasive fears among Americans that the British were indeed plotting for war by arming the Indians of the Ohio Valley.[45] The French and Miamis had already realized the benefit of using Prophetstown to their advantage; the Americans and British followed suit as they positioned themselves for war. While both created a more militant image of Prophetstown, they did so for different purposes. The Miamis were protecting their homeland and the Americans were trying to secure one. As the Wabash-Maumee Valley edged toward war, the fight for a borderland would not be determined simply by the outcome of the ensuing violence but also in the ways in which both sides used and even remembered the conflict.

5 /   The Battles of Tippecanoe

The violence at Tippecanoe was not the logical consequence of American nation-building, nor did the fight end with the Miamis and French bowing to the demands of their more powerful neighbors. Rather, the Battle of Tippecanoe was the denouement of a complicated tale—one in which Natives and non-Natives alike constructed an image of Prophetstown through which each party hoped to empower themselves at the expense of others. Though the people of the Ohio River Valley shared an idea of Prophetstown, they did not do so out of a sense of common experience. Instead, they used the symbolic and real portent of the town and the battlefield to defend their homelands. As the War of 1812 came to an end, the Americans, Miamis, and the French used violence—violence of their own creation—to secure their place in the Wabash-Maumee Valley.

Contemporary discussions of an American bordered land in the Ohio River Valley often point to the fact that within fewer than twenty years, a dynamic Native borderland had been swept away. Shawnees, Miamis, Potawatomies, Kickapoos, and other peoples had traversed a region without boundaries, largely respecting the hegemony of established peoples. But Anglo-American settlement meant lines on a map, fences on the ground, and other mechanisms that drove indigenous people apart. Their homelands fractured, it was all Indians could do to hold on to the last scraps of land remaining to them. Our historical memory of the American borderland is informed by a false narrative—one in which our memory has been skewed by the Battle of Tippecanoe and the War of 1812, where Harrison, according to one scholar, emerged an "undisputed hero." Historians have echoed this triumphalist narrative: the historian Richard White wrote that Indians were destined for "years of exile and the legacy of defeat and domination." Sean Wilentz remarked that Native peoples' "power to resist expansion east of the ninety-fifth meridian was forever destroyed." But few events have been as misinterpreted as the Battle of Tippecanoe.[1] Scholars have almost always characterized the battle, fought in the winter of 1811, as a fight between Native peoples and whites. But the conflict was not merely another example of racial violence on the frontier. Instead, the battle was brought on by American factions and Miami communities who helped create an image of a militant Prophetstown when they lied about the Prophet's motives and exaggerated the strength of his town. The battle did not produce any important diplomatic or military changes for the Indians and the Americans, nor did it facilitate greater ideological unification in either community. The divisions within each community prevented the full-scale mobilization that was necessary for either community to strike a decisive blow against the other.

The violence at Tippecanoe continued a pattern of constructive violence evident in the Miami world of the eighteenth century. By creating and using violence to their advantage, the Miamis and French positioned themselves to defend their lands and economic interests in the Wabash-Maumee Valley. They survived and in their traditional spaces. But the outcome at Tippecanoe also demonstrated that the Miami world had changed in irreversible ways. The Miamis no longer assumed a position of unquestioned prominence in the region after the fight, and for that reason, they were not the only benefactors in the battle's wake. In effect, by manipulating the Americans into a confrontation with the Prophet, the Miamis successfully incorporated the Americans into a borderland of violence they had been shaping for decades. This conceptual and physical borderland was not simply the product of Americans dispossessing Natives; it was also created by the Miamis and French (those who were being dispossessed) making real the many lies they told.

Yet the fight for victory on the battlefield, as well as the fight to control the narrative of Tippecanoe, consumed the town of Vincennes and the Indian inhabitants of the valley during the War of 1812. This mania continued well into the 1820s and 1830s.[2] While historians have tended to focus on the actual battle, Tippecanoe was in fact fought four times. There was the contest from 1808 to 1811 to determine the intentions of the Prophet's community at Tippecanoe; the second was the actual battle, fought on November 7, 1811; the third round occurred in the months after the battle as local factions used the fight to their advantage, and the fourth comprised the years and decades after the War of 1812. Throughout the remainder of the nineteenth century, Indian leaders, the French, and American politicians sought to rework their memories of the battle to explain (if not justify) the changing nature of political and cultural sovereignty in the region.

The Violence at Tippecanoe

By the end of October 1811, large patches of ice hugged the edges of the Wabash River. Most people busily prepared for the arrival of winter by storing grain for their cattle and horses, organizing their foodstuffs in underground cellars, and splitting the wood that would heat their homes through the bitterly cold months ahead. The Americans at Fort Harrison, though, were preparing for war. Having heard that Tenskwatawa had fortified his town in anticipation of an attack, Harrison marched his forces north to present-day Terre Haute, Indiana, and constructed the fort as a staging area for an expedition to Prophetstown. Many Americans believed that such a fort was necessary to prevent the Prophet from attacking Vincennes. Access to the Wabash River meant that the Prophet's followers could move quickly and that the dense thickets, swamps, and small lakes around the river would prevent an attack by cavalry and slow any infantry advance. Clinging to the belief that many Potawatomies had abandoned the Prophet, Harrison continued to plan an assault, all the while ignoring the militia's dwindling confidence in him. Men deserted his camp by the hundreds, leaving him with only 742 soldiers. Relations between his men had soured so much during the building of Fort Harrison that the regulars and militia nearly came to blows. Harrison blamed the squabbling on sickness, too proud admit that his actions had contributed to the near-mutiny.[3]

Despite the defections from Prophetstown, Harrison remained focused on confronting Tenskwatawa. The Prophet himself employed a similar tactic, hoping to force a small skirmish. Prophetstown lacked the unity Tenskwatawa desired; a clear victory against the Americans might convince hundreds of Indians to support his nativist ideals. If reticent Indians—especially members of the Miami factions—joined Prophetstown, Little Turtle and William Wells would see their influence decline. The Prophet knew that he risked disaster if he started a fight near his settlement, for that would give the Americans ample reason to destroy the town.

Marching along the north bank of the Wabash, Harrison and his men saw no Indians; this convinced Harrison that it was safe for his forces to camp eleven miles northwest of Prophetstown. The next day, several soldiers realized that Indian warriors watched them from the forests. On November 6, troops stopped in a sodden clearing just south of Burnet's Creek, assuming that the open land would prevent an Indian ambush. Harrison wanted to delay the attack until the next day, but several of his officers begged him to reconsider, urging him to attack Prophetstown as quickly as possible lest their men lose confidence.[4]

Meanwhile, the Prophet hoped to meet Harrison's forces and express his desire for peace in order to prevent an attack on Prophetstown and possibly pick a fight where Harrison would be ill-prepared. Tenskwatawa instructed several of his supporters to meet Harrison's force and question Harrison as to why they had moved so close to Prophetstown. Harrison claimed that he only wanted to speak with the Prophet; he vowed that he would not assault Prophetstown unless the Indians rejected his demands.[5] Harrison wanted to pick a fight so that he could prove that he was right about the Indian threat and to demonstrate that he was indeed capable of protecting the territory. A victory would also prove to federal authorities that his detractors were wrong and that they should dismiss calls to replace him. Dispersing the Prophet's force would reinvigorate his leadership at a time when his support was declining. The Prophet recognized that a fight might unite his divided community but that it could also force his followers to flee. Both men knew that a victory in battle would reinforce their leadership, but they also recognized that defeat could do exactly the opposite. Prepared to negotiate first and attack second, Harrison decided to camp along Burnet's Creek while the Prophet took refuge at Prophetstown.

Yet bloodshed erupted between the two groups despite their efforts to prevent it. The historical record places the blame on the Prophet for ordering a surprise attack on Harrison's encampment during the night. But this interpretation is based on Harrison's word alone. In fact, the fighting surprised both sides. Before dawn on November 7, 1811, a melee developed near the militia's bivouac at Burnet's Creek. The fighting began when American pickets shot and wounded two Ho-Chunk Indians trying to slip by the edges of the camp. Despite their injuries, the warriors struggled to their feet and tomahawked the soldiers. Tenskwatawa pleaded with his people not to rush to judgment, but to no avail. Roughly two hundred Indians rushed to Burnet's Creek to aid their compatriots, while other Indians departed Prophetstown because they did not want to suffer the consequences of war. Most Miamis fled the area near Prophetstown; they did not want the Americans to associate them with violence, for that would allow Harrison to strip their rights to the area. Other Indian communities withdrew when the Americans advanced and set fire to harvest and homes.[6]

Despite the fact that Harrison's troops outnumbered the Indian warriors by two to one, the battle raged for a few hours. Militiaman Josiah Bacon watched as musket flashes lit up the darkness, revealing Indians with "their faces painted black." The battle continued until sunrise; in the end, between 30 and 50 Indians and almost 188 Americans were left dead or wounded. Tenskwatawa abandoned his town in order to avoid capture by the American forces. Once again, he proved that he could not control his followers. Harrison ordered the razing of the entire town—all of the wigwams, the meetinghouse, and five thousand pounds of stored food. But this vengeful action did not mean the end of Tenskwatawa's influence in the Wabash-Maumee Valley. In fact, Tenskwatawa remained a significant force in the region, rebuilding his town during the winter of 1811 and 1812.[7]

Why did Harrison believe that the Prophet was such a threat? That answer is bound up in a complicated mess of interethnic and intercultural factionalism. Examining the competing ethnic interests in the region allows us to more completely understand the motives of those involved. By expanding our chronology and framing Harrison and the Shawnee Prophet within the history of the Wabash-Maumee Valley, we see the two men, and their communities, as products of regional and historic forces that were well outside their control. Despite decades of marginalization following the Revolutionary War, the French and Miamis identified opportunities and discovered avenues through which they could protect themselves, even if that meant amplifying the threat posed by an Indian community that was also at odds with the Americans. The French and Miamis were unwilling to subvert their ethnic and cultural identity to a larger racial polity. Even these groups could have allied themselves with Prophetstown in an attempt to stall or redirect American settlement, doing so would have still undermined their cultural foundations.

It is increasingly clear that Tenskwatawa never ordered the attack at Tippecanoe, despite many claims to the contrary.[8] The Prophet said as much four years later when he spoke to the governor of Michigan, Lewis Cass; he claimed that the Ho-Chunks had attacked Harrison's forces first. He asked Cass: "Who began the war? Did not General Harrison come to my village? . . . If we had come to you, then you might have blam'd us, but you came to my village for this you are angry at me." Tenskwatawa's inability to control the residents of his community was the logical outcome of the factionalized nature of Prophetstown.[9] The Prophet's attitude was both defensive and pragmatic. He had not spent three years constructing a community only to throw it all away by attacking Harrison's army camped outside Prophetstown.

As Harrison's forces marched back to Vincennes with nearly 130 wounded, they feared an attack from the many Indians who roamed the area. It was one thing for the soldiers to burn Prophetstown to the ground, but the soldiers were well aware that having desecrated an Indian burial ground was unforgiveable in the minds of the Indians. Nonetheless, the Americans returned to Vincennes safely, minus 37 soldiers who had died on the field of battle. The death count included Thomas Randolph, who had been Jennings's main challenger for territorial representative to Congress. It was ironic that the violence at Tippecanoe had resulted in Randolph's death. Many anti-Harrisonians believed that the governor's rhetoric about Prophetstown was the result of his frustration at not getting Randolph elected. In a way, Harrison had killed his ally Randolph. Many of the soldiers believed that more would die when the Indians counterattacked, but the counterattack never came. Many of the neutral Miamis had fled the area around Prophetstown, while the other Indian communities withdrew after witnessing the destruction. The Prophet had not organized the first attack, nor would he want to put his community at further risk with another. As Harrison's forces marched into Vincennes, they were not greeted by victorious fanfare or congratulatory cheers.

The Battle of Vincennes

The violence at Tippecanoe did nothing to change the dynamics among Indian and white populations; nor did it alter the power dynamics in the valley. Moreover, it did not secure the territory for the American nation. In fact, the violence at Tippecanoe only further exacerbated divisions among the Americans while undermining the little security they enjoyed. Initially, residents of Vincennes mourned the loss of their loved ones, but when rumors of an Indian war continued to spread, the factions quickly turned to blame each other for Harrison's failed expedition instead of unifying in face of the Indian threat. The violence at Tippecanoe thus became symbolic of much deeper ills in the territory.

Residents saw Harrison's march as the culmination of the governor's misguided Indian policies and therefore representative of his poor leadership. With each death, residents were reminded of the price they paid for Harrison's aggression and ineffectiveness. There was a funeral every day, sometimes two, as injured soldiers died from their wounds. One resident of Vincennes described the coffin processions "followed by a soldier . . . marching to the tune of 'Roslein Castle' beat upon muffled drums."[10] Rumors spread throughout the territory that militia had tried to retreat during battle because of Harrison's ineffective leadership. When reports surfaced that the Indians were resettling Prophetstown, residents of Vincennes, eyeing the many fresh graves, could not help but wonder just who had benefited from the battle.

Within weeks the factions in Vincennes began using the battle as a way to attack each other. They had a well-established tradition of using territorial politics in this way, and Tippecanoe proved no different. Harrison reported that his "personal enemies" had spread word that "the expedition was entirely useless & the Prophet as one of the best & most pacific of Mortals." Newspapers to the east called the fight a "most distressing disaster" and a "horrible butchery." John Badollet felt that Harrison had driven the Prophet to violence "in spite of their repeated cries for peace." Badollet was also quick to challenge stories that depicted the Prophet as a killer. About a month after Tippecanoe, a story spread through the territory that the Prophet's supporters had murdered a local Frenchman. But Badollet discovered that the man had died when his gun discharged by accident.[11] Rumors circulated through town that one of the sentinels who had heard the first shots had actually shot himself by accident or been shot by one of his fellow soldiers. If the stories were true, the townspeople reasoned, then the battle had started due to someone's incompetence and not because the soldiers had tried to protect themselves.

Rumors were also rampant that Harrison was responsible for the death of several soldiers during battle because he had panicked. The anti-Harrisonians decided to publish a letter in the local paper praising Colonel John P. Boyd's efforts during the battle, namely the conduct of the regular army that he commanded. The anti-Harrisonians intentionally neglected any praise of Harrison. The Harrisonians took offense to such blatant libel. In response, Benjamin Parke gathered several militiamen at a local inn on December 7, 1811, and adopted resolutions that rejected the public appraisals of Boyd. They "resolved unanimously" that the address put forth by the anti-Harrisonians was done so to "injure the character of Governor Harrison." Parke's group believed that the praise for Boyd was really another attempt by the governor's enemies to discredit him. Many were the "avowed enemies of the Commander in Chief," who had opposed "every measure of the government, in respect to the Shawnee Prophet and his party."[12] To Parke, this was just a continuation of the debates that preceded Tippecanoe. To stoke the fire, Stout published these resolutions in his January 4, 1812, edition of the *Western Sun*. The short-lived newspaper debate quickly engulfed the town in yet another dispute. For the Harrisonians, the attack on their governor was personal. The Boyd faction challenged Harrison's leadership at Tippecanoe, a major symbol of Harrisonian politics. American settlers provoked the Indians in an effort to end Harrison's governorship; now the Regular Army assaulted the governor. Although Harrison was used to people challenging his authority, the explosion of violence at Prophetstown made his effectiveness as a leader (and challenges to it) a national issue. Reports of his misconduct might make real the rumors that he would be replaced.

As a result, he could no longer simply bully his enemies into silence by tying them to Prophetstown. Harrison realized that national leaders were now quite concerned with the Prophet and the events at Tippecanoe. The Prophet's supposed attack, many reasoned, may have been the first battle in a full-scale war. Therefore, Harrison was quick to discredit those who threatened to destroy the narrative of Tippecanoe he worked so hard to create. His Indian agent at Fort Wayne, John Johnston, was the first victim. Shortly after the battle, Johnston concluded that the Indian force at Prophetstown had been far fewer in number than Harrison's command. Such a low estimate of Indians would have looked very bad considering the much larger number of Americans who had died. Harrison, always on the defense, claimed that "it was impossible to believe that there were less than seven hundred Indians in the late action," an estimate that would have made the American and Indian forces relatively equal. He questioned Johnston's "false" report and concluded that Johnston's estimate reflected unreliable information provided by the Indians. To discredit him further, Harrison claimed that Johnston had failed at his duty by replenishing "the powder horns and pouches of many of those Indians whom he knew" to have participated at Tippecanoe.[13] Such an accusation could lead not simply to Johnston's replacement, but possibly his imprisonment if indeed the agent's actions had led to the death of American soldiers.

Johnston was not the only person questioning the governor's efforts at Tippecanoe. Residents of Vincennes wrote to several national newspapers to show Harrison's perceived incompetence as a leader. Now that the eastern states had a watchful if not paranoid eye fixed on the violence in Indiana Territory, Harrison's enemies could finally detail the governor's corrupt behavior to a waiting audience. One newspaper, Pennsylvania's *Reporter*, claimed that Harrison was to blame for the death of Major Joseph Hamilton Daviess, the leader of Harrison's cavalry during the fight. Upon hearing that the *New York Commercial Advertiser* published a derogatory letter about him, Harrison told his ally Elihu Stout that he would pay for the author's name.[14] Rumors had once again surfaced that President Madison disapproved of Harrison and was soon to replace him.[15]

Harrison's supporters were quick to participate in the national debate over Harrison's actions at Tippecanoe. They said that the governor "was calm and deliberate—that his orders were precise and distinct" during the battle and that "victory was obtained by [the governor's] vigilance and activity." Harrison saw himself as only following orders from the government that were designed to "protect its citizens, but if possible, to spare the effusion of human blood." Other newspapers seemed to taunt Harrison, calling the frontier violence a "most 'un-prophet-able contest.'"[16] The debates raging in Vincennes, although framed around the meaning of Tippecanoe, fell across the same factional lines that had crystallized during the debate over slavery. Only now, given the significance the violence might have for the United States, the debate over Tippecanoe was truly becoming national.

The factions of Vincennes would not be outdone. After learning that Colonel Boyd—commander of the regulars—planned to travel east on a furlough (an undeserved trip in Stout's eyes), Stout publicly mocked Boyd's leadership and commitment. He closed with a highly inflammatory and sarcastic paragraph:

> We cannot withhold from the Colonel [Boyd] our sense of his *merit* and the great *loss* our country will sustain by being deprived of *his* services. Should there be a second expedition against the Indians, the Man, who by his *personal* skill and bravery decided the action of the 7th November, and took with his own hands the *war club* of their great warrior, the *magic cup* of the Prophet, and the scalp of a Chief, together with a number of other acts of bravery not necessary here to mention, but which will forever immortalize the Hero.[17]

Stout's language demonstrates the extent to which frontiersmen had begun to think of the Prophet as an abstraction, as a symbol for the cultural and political disputes in Vincennes. Tenskwatawa's "war club" and "magic cup" were not real; they symbolized Americans' interpretations of the significance of the fight. For a loyal Harrisonian such as Stout, the victory at Tippecanoe represented the final culmination of years of political and cultural disputes with his neighbors. From Stout's point of view, it was the Harrisonians who had earned the right to hoist the magic cup and war club, but not as prizes they stole from the infamous Shawnee Prophet. Instead, the cup and club were symbolic trophies the Harrisonians had earned in the hotly contested fight to control the territory by defeating their white neighbors.

Stout refused to reveal who had written the slanderous piece, and when an irate Boyd stormed into his crowded office, Stout angrily told him, "You may consider me as the author!" Boyd swung at Stout with his cane, but the nimble printer grabbed Boyd and his stick and then struck back in self-defense. Boyd's orderly, Bacon, tried to restrain Stout, but another militiaman yanked Bacon away from the printer and hurled him to the office floor. Boyd retreated, leaving Stout to gloat in victory, and gloat he did in that week's newspaper. "ANOTHER BATTLE *on the Wabash, or Colonel* JOHN P. BOYD's DEFEAT!!" the paper proclaimed. Wrote Stout: "[Is] not everyone ready to cry out shame! That such an *experienced* officer who has so highly boasted of his superior skill and abilities, should be thus ingloriously defeated, by a man who had never seen a 'tented field?' –Can such a man be trusted with the defense of our common country? Has he talents adequate to a corporals command? The Printer pronounces he has not!"

Stout elevated a minor skirmish inside his office into a "Battle on the Wabash," a fight Stout saw as equal in importance to Tippecanoe. While it may seem that Stout was only exaggerating, he was in fact communicating the larger significance of the dispute to his readers. The fight with Boyd—a representative of the anti-Harrisonians—was about an inherent difference in the values, beliefs, and identity of the Vincennes factions. It was also about the future identity and existence of the nation. The anti-Harrisonians could not be trusted with, according to Stout, "the defense of our common country" because they lacked the experience, skills, and proper vision to govern a territory.[18]

These impassioned remarks demonstrate that Tenskwatawa remained influential in Vincennes despite his defeat. His presence was inescapable. Physically the Prophet was always an outsider, but as a tool for the factions in Vincennes, he became central to their political and even cultural identities. For years, the people of Vincennes feared that the Indians at

Prophetstown would strike. Few could have imagined that the only substantive attacks in Vincennes would be initiated by Americans attacking one another. Such violence was the logical result of the deeply personal and cultural debates that had created great schisms in Vincennes. As the factions separated the Prophet from his physical reality, and did the same to the violence at Tippecanoe, they found ways to argue about much bigger issues by manipulating information about the Prophet. By tying their larger ideological debates to the practical realities of Indian affairs, the factions made certain that a quick—and possible deadly—resolution would be reached.

In addition to the fight in the streets of Vincennes, the factions persisted in their war of words. Badollet continued to speak of Prophetstown as a peaceful and industrious community. What happened at Tippecanoe enraged Badollet. Harrison's march was not simply an abuse of power but a reflection of the failures of the territorial system. "When I see intrigues & depravity triumphing . . . my respect for the republican system is on the wane," he told Gallatin.[19]

Harrison, though, remained convinced that his enemies were using every means at their disposal to deprive him of his governorship. He had received word from Josiah Snelling that his enemies were meeting in secret to destroy him. A couple of Miami leaders, William McIntosh, and others "had a council at midnight in the house of Joseph Basidon," where the Miami leaders, "at the instigation of McIntosh," signed a declaration declaring that their land cessions "had been taken from them without their consent." In doing so, they disavowed Harrison's power as governor. The informal gathering of Indians, Frenchmen, and Americans demonstrates that outliers had their own ways of becoming the final arbiter of land cessions. The declaration had since been forwarded to the territorial representative, Jonathan Jennings, in Washington City.[20]

The Harrisonians saw McIntosh's conspiratorial behavior as more than a threat to their power. It was a threat to their nation. By circumventing Harrison's rightful authority as governor, McIntosh disregarded federal and territorial laws. Despite McIntosh's efforts, many Harrisonians believed that the events at Tippecanoe would assure that the "sons of '76" (the Harrisonians) would remain in power. Badollet described a truly wretched sight in Vincennes in the months after Tippecanoe. Fear of retaliation left the town, as Badollet described, "crowded with fugitive families" taking up residence in more defensible buildings. To Badollet, the expanding boundaries of freedom and open diplomacy had regressed after Harrison's attack on Prophetstown. Not only were

Indians on the warpath, but the fundamental values of republicanism had been ignored and were quickly becoming overgrown with violence. Stout reminded readers that there was "no evidence" that the Indians desired peace and that "there is some secret communication between some person here and the Indians, by which the latter are informed of everything." Badollet believed that paranoia and fear that whites were aiding the Indians could lead to "darker deeds," possibly murder. Instead of cooperating in the face of an imminent war, the factions chose to use Indian affairs to promote their agendas. In that process, the territorial settlements were being abandoned, many homes simply left to be burned down, and the physical and conceptual boundaries of a republican frontier were quickly vanishing from the earth.[21] The violence ushered in by Tippecanoe was not simply a threat to the physical safety of frontier settlers but also an opportunity for the Harrisonians to enforce their policies arbitrarily and to attack their neighbors if necessary. In the minds of some, such arbitrary rule would destroy the territorial experiment and, with it, the nation.

People in Vincennes related to Prophetstown through their factionalism and fears and tended to ignore the interests of the Indians. For them, Prophetstown was a static place that represented Harrison's successes and failures. Although the anti-Harrisonians feared an Indian attack, many felt that if such a disaster occurred, it would be the fault of the governor's corrupt diplomacy. In that sense, their hatred toward Harrison determined how they saw Prophetstown, rather than the actions of the Indians within it. The more the factions vied for influence, the more their deep-seated biases toward each other shaped their perceptions of Indians and outsiders. In the long run, this served to undermine responsible governance as the factions could no longer fully grasp the reality of Indian affairs. Badollet even believed that "the object of the Governor was to bring on an Indian war."[22] Like the rest of the residents of Vincennes, he abandoned his wooden house after the battle for more secure buildings like the church, Harrison's mansion, or Nathaniel Ewing's brick residence.

The events after the battle demonstrate that the Wabash-Maumee Valley was no longer safe. American boundaries were not secure. Main Poc's Potawatomies attacked several American farms during the spring of 1812; most Americans interpreted the raids as a product of the Prophet's teachings. Hundreds of settlers left the area, including Harrison's family, whom he sent to Cincinnati. There were no pickets or scouts to warn of an Indian approach, and most of the settlers refused to venture outside.

Badollet hid at Ewing's residence, which was situated "one mile off in very [thick] woods" but posed a problem for making it to his office in town because he believed that a mile walk would place him in "danger of an ambush." Some residents built fences around their homes in an effort to remain safe, but the danger they faced appeared, at least to men like Badollet, to be a product of Harrison's abuses of leadership. Harrison had done little to protect the town. He was unsure how to handle the situation, even though he had been so direct in leading his forces against Prophetstown. He described the abandoned farms with unplanted fields and the homes full of "wretched people crowded together in places almost destitute of every necessary accommodation." Writing to the Secretary of War William Eustis, Harrison lamented that he was at a "loss as to the orders proper to be given in the present state of the country." He wrote to Eustis that he did not "conceive" himself "authorized to order out any militia at the expense of the United States," which meant that Vincennes would remain undefended.[23] The sheer helplessness of the people of Vincennes and their governor demonstrates the inherent weakness in the American territorial venture. Lacking even a rudimentary defense structure and an ability to assert American power, the territory was little more than a space no one—Native or American—could control.

The anti-Harrisonians still believed, as Badollet described in a letter to Gallatin, that the Indian war "was the only means that [Governor] possessed of escaping censure & punishment" for his erratic governance and his costly attack on Prophetstown. Harrison's reluctance to defend the town reflected his own confused reaction to the uncertainty and chaos that erupted after Tippecanoe. There was deeper significance in his inability to order out the militia—something he had done on a regular basis over the previous years. The aftermath of Tippecanoe had demonstrated that the United States was not in a position to defend its borders. Although the militia and regulars had burned Prophetstown, Harrison and the Americans had failed to enforce a permanent boundary by displacing the Indians from their settlements. Just the opposite had occurred. The Americans fled their homes to gather in "fortress" Vincennes for protection.[24]

Elihu Stout played an important role in maintaining a militant characterization of Prophetstown during this period. Rather than evaluate the various interests dividing Indian country, he conveyed biased reports from Harrison and the French traders. For instance, in May 1812, a large number of Indians gathered in council near the Mississinewa River to discuss the recent violence in the Wabash-Maumee Valley. Stout made little effort to detail the factionalism and open disagreements dividing the council; he said nothing about the accusations leveled by the Miamis against the Potawatomies, which would only serve to complicate the story of regional violence that Stout had worked so hard to silence.

Some Miamis argued that a pro-American Potawatomi leader, Winemak, had instigated recent attacks that resulted in several murders, an important piece of information considering that Harrison had favored Winemak and even invited him into Vincennes. The large meeting of Indians at the Mississinewa produced some positive results for the Americans, including a greater understanding of which Indians were actually attacking Euroamerican settlements, but Stout failed to report these details. Stout's article simply reinforced stereotypes that Indians were steadfast in their militant opposition to the Americans. Nor did the *Western Sun* mention anything about the various Indian communities who advocated peace. Such information might have strengthened the anti-Harrisonians' claims that the Prophet did not plan to attack Vincennes because it would invite retaliation against Prophetstown by those Indians advocating peace. Stout simply concluded that there was no "evidence of the return of the Indians to a friendly disposition."[25]

Stout had no qualms about spreading rumors that Americans were once again aiding the militant Indians. When the Miami leader Lapoussier confessed to knowing that the governor had detained a Lenape Indian and three children at Vincennes, Stout became suspicious. No Indians had visited Vincennes after these prisoners arrived, and so, according to Stout, only a white person could have shared the information with the Wea leader.[26] Such allegations were familiar, but now the likelihood of rumor-primed violence had increased tenfold.

Central to the inherent weaknesses of the territorial structure was Harrison's relationship with his Indian agents. These agents were key sources of information and tools for diplomacy when violence erupted. When Benjamin Stickney, Johnston's replacement as Indian agent, reported his findings about the machinations of local Indian communities to the secretary of war without first consulting Harrison, the governor penned a letter accusing the agent of subterfuge. Harrison argued that Stickney had already "produced mischief" by abusing his powers. Stickney told Eustis that a Wea leader had recently informed Captain Zachary Taylor that the governor would "shortly be deprived of office" without any knowledge of who had given the Indian leader that information. Even though Harrison stated that he had "no idea that Mr. Stickney [had] authorized such a report," the governor was "convinced it had its origin in [Stickney's] assertion of Independence" as Indian agent.[27] Just as Harrison had done many times before, he used Indian affairs to marginalize his enemies. Harrison believed that Stickney had operated outside the boundaries of his authority, and the governor questioned Stickney's loyalty to the American government. Having to share power frustrated Harrison to no end, and as the territorial system evolved, he seemed increasingly willing to marginalize his enemies through any means available. Harrison's frustrations are somewhat understandable given the gravity of the situation he faced after Tippecanoe. His anger, though, also speaks to a lack of control. It was not that Stickney lacked loyalty to an American government. It was that the territorial system mandated a level of diplomacy and communication that Harrison could not regulate. In such a world, Stickney, like Harrison, was forced to act on his own because the territory was simply too disorganized to allow him to operate systematically.

Given the lack of control in the territory, residents began to fear that their enemies would resort to murder. Badollet worried that these rumors would convince loyal Harrisonians or other people stricken with worry to "deprive us of our lives" while "under the appearance of an Indian."[28] John Badollet's concern that someone might dress up as an Indian and murder him seems foolish and exaggerated considering his great distaste for Harrison and his supporters. But Badollet's fearful letter about enemies playing Indian represents something more than a paranoid remark. Many of the residents had played Indian, including Harrison. They had used Indian affairs and manipulated Indian identities as a means to fight political battles in town and to define themselves and their territory. While the factions did not adopt Indian physical disguises per se, they did create a militant image of Indianness within the region. Stories of Indians plotting with French traders, rumors of treasonous Americans and Indians working together to destroy the governor, and Stout's biased characterizations of frontier diplomacy created an atmosphere conducive to threats, violence, and even death. In a world where boundaries were so permeable and chaos reigned, Badollet's fears seem valid given the desperate and often violent ways in which settlers used Tippecanoe to their advantage.

The French and Tippecanoe

French traders seized upon the opportunities wrought by the threat of an Indian war. For them, the permeable boundaries of nation and race were less a threat and more an opportunity. The French empire thrived because French men were willing to marry Indian women and to trade with Indian communities. French imperial diplomacy depended on interracial negotiation. In the minds of the French, national and racial identities prevented the very interethnic dialogues that were necessary to survive in North America. Such a mentality did not vanish after Tippecanoe; Anglo-Americans increasingly enforced rigid national and racial identities that excluded French and Indian people respectively. As a result, the French had to use the system created by the Americans to achieve their needs, which is why several Frenchmen likely joined Harrison's militia force that marched toward Prophetstown. They did so as spies and were in charge of evaluating Indian behavior as the American force moved north. They were in a perfect position to protect their Indian allies but also to guide Harrison's force toward their enemies. Serving with Harrison's militia would help these men to maintain and expand their role as diplomats and traders.[29] Furthermore, as the United States marshaled its resources for the war against Great Britain, trade goods and supplies meant to support the militia flooded places like Vincennes, Fort Wayne, and Fort Harrison. French traders seized these commodities and sold them to Indians as annuity goods.

The Americans had not quite succeeded in forcing the French to assimilate, and the necessities of war forced them to rely on the French to defend their territory more fiercely than they had in the past. This had to be especially galling for Harrison, who felt that the French made worthless soldiers. The French had successfully navigated the shrinking ground of diplomacy in order to protect their long-standing relationship with the Miamis and trade within the Wabash-Maumee trading network. By 1811, their carefully negotiated success was at risk. Trade to Prophetstown was almost nonexistent, and French traders' work became increasingly dangerous. The Prophet limited trade by physically and verbally abusing the French traders, some of whom left the town in fear for their lives.[30] Ridding the region of Prophetstown would force many of the Indian communities into a greater dependency on the Americans, which would provide ample opportunity for the French traders to direct and profit from land cessions and trading missions.

As localized violence in Indiana Territory spread and became part of the War of 1812, French traders found their roles as translators, go-betweens, and soldiers strengthened by the necessities of war. French traders negotiated with Indians, provided much-needed intelligence, and guided American forces. Two all-French companies joined the Indiana militia, and other Frenchmen served as the mounted riflemen.[31]

The French traders used the advent of war after Tippecanoe to position themselves in the center of regional trade and diplomacy. Toussaint Dubois was quite successful in this endeavor. As the captain of spies in Harrison's army, he proved himself worthy of navigating the difficult geographical and cultural terrain of the region. Men such as Benjamin Parke believed that Dubois was "more competent" than he in handling frontier diplomacy during the War of 1812. Reliance on the French—people the Americans were still resistant to accept as Americans—demonstrates the continued relevance of the colonial system in the early years of the American republic.

The experiences of Toussaint Dubois during the war demonstrate the ability by some French to exert greater influence. During the War of 1812, Dubois facilitated American efforts to negotiate with the local Indians and traveled routinely between his trade shop in Vincennes and Fort Harrison. When word reached the Americans during the winter of 1814 that a group of Indians were approaching Fort Harrison, Parke instructed Dubois to handle the affair. It was Dubois who could patch up relationships between the militia and the Indians. That same year, Dubois even had the opportunity to take over the Indian agency, but declined. His role as trader was lucrative enough since he was supplied with rations and authorized, according to Benjamin Posey, to "issue provisions for the Indians . . . for the best advantage to promote the public welfare." If they did not empower Dubois, Parke believed, the Indians would "go to the British." The Americans were powerless to influence the Indians without men such as Dubois. Dubois earned three dollars per day in payment for his services, plus whatever trade he completed outside of his diplomatic role. For his mission to Fort Harrison—which was one of many—he profited thirty dollars for ten days of work. Dubois not only enjoyed the commercial opportunities available to him through the trade, but he was also able to regulate affairs between the Americans and Indians. In one case, a Potawatomi Indian wounded several cattle as he left Fort Harrison, and although the Americans seized him, Dubois convinced them to let the man go.[32] Military policy was not hard-and-fast on the frontier, and imprisoning an Indian for harming cattle could easily have created bigger problems for the isolated frontier outpost. In that difficult position, Parke chose Dubois to protect the public welfare. Once hopeful of banishing all the French from the region, the Americans now depended on the French to secure the territory.

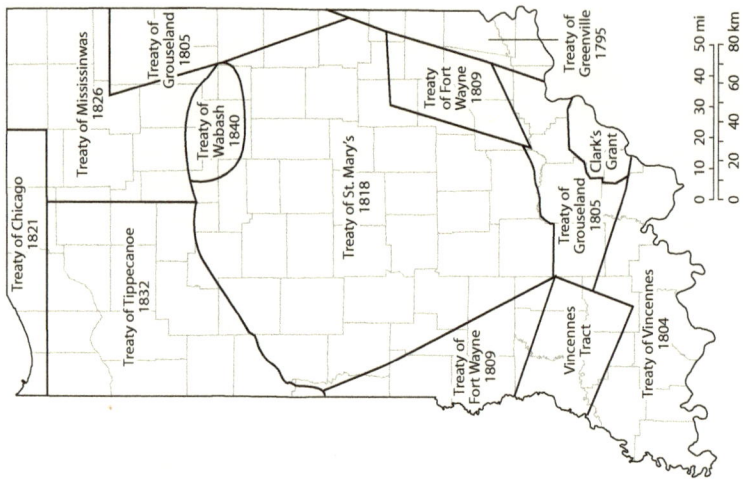

A. June 7, 1803 at Fort Wayne, with Delaware, Shawnee, Potawatomi, Miami, Eel River, Wea, Kickapoo, Piankashaw, and Kaskaskia.

B. August 13, 1803, at Vincennes, with Kaskaskia.

C. August 8 and 27 1804, at Vincennes, with Delaware and Piankashaw.

D. November 3, 1804, at St. Louis, with Sauk and Fox.

E. August 21, 1805, at Grouseland with Delaware, Potawatomi, Miami, Eel River, and Wea.

F. December 30, 1805, at Vicennes, with Piankashaw.

G. September 30, 1809, at Fort Wayne, with Delaware, Potawatomi, Miami, Eel River, and October 26, 1809, at Vincennes, with Wea.

H. December 9, 1809, at Vincennes, with Kickapoo.

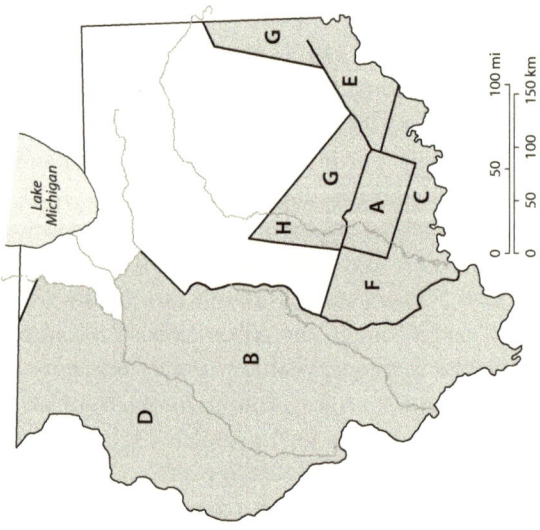

MAP 3. Land-cession treaties before and after the Battle of Tippecanoe. Land-cession treaties left the heart of the Miami homeland relatively intact until 1818. Note that land-cession treaties do not reflect settlement of non-Indians.

As Dubois facilitated trade and diplomacy out of Fort Harrison and Vincennes, he regularly came into contact with his fellow Frenchmen. Joseph Barron and Hyacinthe Lasselle were regular visitors throughout the region. Barron served as a guide for American armies, filled in for Dubois as an interpreter at Vincennes, and traveled throughout the valley conversing with Indians in order to determine their motives. Hyacinthe Lasselle was key to gathering intelligence on the Miamis and served as an officer in the American army, drawing one dollar per day as payment. Although Michel Brouillet and Jean Baptiste LaPlante continued to facilitate American diplomacy, they played a much less conspicuous role than before Tippecanoe.[33]

The increased reliance on these traders reflected a growing acceptance of the French as members of the white community. Much of this was likely necessitated by the inability of white Americans to protect the territory on their own. When territorial governor Thomas Posey wrote to the secretary of war in 1814 about the troublesome Indians, he spoke very highly of Dubois. He was a man "very much respected and to be relied on, who had been an old Indian trader, is well acquainted with a great many [Indians]; speaks the Indian language, and has been a resident at Vincennes for at least thirty years."[34] Posey made no mention of Dubois's ethnicity, nor did Benjamin Parke. John Badollet, one of the most vocally anti-French residents in the region, was also silent on the French after Tippecanoe. Yet such silence was not a product of a sudden disappearance of the French people from the region. Instead, it demonstrates that their ethnicity was no longer *the* determining factor for how most whites looked at French residents. Instead of destroying the French-Miami system of trade and diplomacy, the violence ushered in by Tippecanoe forced the Americans to continue to rely upon the help of outsiders.

The opportunities provided by the Battle of Tippecanoe, therefore, provided the French with an opportunity to retain cultural stability. Underneath American snobbery, one can detect the persistence of French habits. People traveling through Vincennes continued to speak disparagingly about backwardness of the European community. One traveler, John Bradbury, wrote that "nothing can induce [the French] to abandon their old practices." Another visitor commented that the "cabin bounded [French] views in architecture," upon which he could "bestow no commendations." Decades after the war, the French retained a cultural presence in the region. In the early 1830s, local officials imposed criminal charges on numerous Frenchmen for playing Lew, a "favorite card game among the French." Affluent French people refused to abandon their cherished institutions; Lasselle took out a subscription in *Le Courier des Etats Unis*, a French newspaper established by French immigrants. One French descendent commented that the French were the "controlling factor in all elections in Knox County until 1855," demonstrating their continuity as an ethnic group well into the nineteenth century.[35] Much of this was possible because the French traders successfully defended their economic and cultural interests. Lasselle's profits from the Indian trade and his service in the army funded the Lasselle Ballroom in Vincennes; considered the nicest hall in town, the building served as a gathering place for many Anglos and French settlers in the years after the war.

Despite what outsiders thought, residents of the region increasingly looked at the French as an integral part of a nationalizing process in which those of European heritage shaped the culture and boundaries of the frontier. As diplomats, soldiers, and traders, the French contributed immeasurably to the security of the territory and safety of white residents. More important, it was the French who had made possible two centuries of trade with native nations. Nevertheless, unity would remain elusive until both Anglo-Americans and the French shared a similar historical narrative. The stories they told of the "Battle" of Tippecanoe were central to this process of creating shared collective memory. Though the Americans bickered over the meaning of the battle, they made sure to include the heroic Dubois in the tale. In June 1812, Elihu Stout included a poem in his paper entitled, "AN EULOGY, On the Heroes of the 7th of November 1811." "Let Dubois never be forgot," begins the seventh stanza; even more curious is the fact that Dubois is mentioned before Harrison and Boyd.[36] The poem ends by thanking God for protecting American lands by spoiling the serpents' nest, which they hoped would give "our country rest." Not only was Dubois a central part of the "victory" at Tippecanoe; he was part of the process through which the United States gained a secure western boundary. Years later, Mary Brouilette remembered the French and the Battle of Tippecanoe similarly. A glance at the names of the Frenchmen who marched to Tippecanoe would "convince even the most skeptical that the Creoles ranked high in patriotism and must be credited with materially helping make the territory that is now Indiana safe." As the stories of Tippecanoe were told and retold, residents of the territory created an invisible but permanent boundary of beliefs that incorporated once disparate groups of people into a single memory. The Americans welcomed the French into the boundaries of their national narrative as they took what Patrick Hutton claims is "possession of the past by crowding out the traditions of its competitors" and "by reshaping them to conform to [their] own conceptions"; thus, not only had the Americans pressured the French to abandon their ramshackle homes and their *taverns*—they had convinced them to remember the past in a specific way.[37] And in an ironic turn, many of these stories and celebrations of an "American" victory took place in the Lasselle Ballroom, a French institution established by a family whose roots extended well into the colonial era and who routinely played imperial and national interests against each other to their own benefit. Although the Americans failed to recognize it, they were not simply celebrating the past in a French establishment. They were celebrating a past that was both French, Miami, and American.

The Miami Homeland

While the violence at Tippecanoe presented a threat to the nascent American and Indian communities in the region, it presented the Miamis with a unique opportunity to deflect violence to their benefit. If they could continue to shape the narrative of violence—something they had done repeatedly—by pinning the blame on their enemies, they could retain a foothold by positioning themselves as key diplomats and allies. Different Indian communities were quick to profess peaceful intentions after the battle; scholars suggest that this submissive behavior grew from Indians' fear of Harrison's army. Yet the Battle of Tippecanoe (and the battle for Vincennes) demonstrated just how weak the Americans were at defending their boundaries.

Given the weakness of the American army and the destruction of Prophetstown, the Miamis were in a key position to exercise their role as diplomats. By shaping the narrative of the post-Tippecanoe state of affairs, the Miamis could once again situate themselves between the Americans and nativists. One Wea leader, Little Eyes, quickly propagated a story of Prophetstown's weakness. He described a tense situation in the days after the battle when some of Tenskwatawa's followers vowed that they would kill him; many others simply abandoned him. These baseless assertions were designed to temper hostilities by praising the Americans' victory, thus helping to situate the Miamis as key intermediaries.[38]

Historians have struggled to decode Little Eyes' motives because they continue to frame his actions within the American-nativist dichotomy. Alfred Cave places Little Eyes with the Prophetstown Indians shortly after the battle; John Sugden, on the other hand, suggests that Little Eyes was an intermediary of the Americans, sent to negotiate with the Prophet three days before the battle.[39] Little Eyes' motives remain clouded in the records, but it is likely that he followed a philosophy similar philosophy to that of Pacanne—he hoped to interpose the Miamis between hostile parties and thereby make them indispensable to all. Harrison concluded, as he had with Pacanne, that Little Eyes worked on the Prophet's behalf. Yet it is far more likely that Little Eyes' story about the Prophet was designed to keep the Americans out of Miami lands.[40] By describing a Prophetstown that was no longer a threat to the Americans, Little Eyes lessened the likelihood that the Americans would return. Moreover, by describing the valley Indians as divided, Little Eyes' story made diplomacy a much more viable option.

Other Miami Indians manipulated information about the battle to condemn Indians who had threatened Miami interests in the valley. The Owl, Pacanne's loyal lieutenant, made sure to enlarge the blame when it came to the violence at Tippecanoe. In order to protect Miami interests, the Owl told Harrison that Potawatomi warriors had traveled to Prophetstown in advance of the battle; moreover, the Owl talked large about his own struggle to prevent his young men from joining Tenskwatawa. The Miamis had suffered from the Potawatomies' subterfuge during treaty negotiations, making the latter likely targets for Miamis. In an echo of the Miamis' own behavior, Little Eyes pointed out the Potawatomies' habit of, as Badollet termed it, "robbing the Red & White & carrying falsehoods between them."[41] Yet such games had the potential to backfire, and backfire they did.

Anglo-American leaders' refusal to think outside of racial, color-based categories meant that men such as Harrison would invariably conclude that all Indians were enemies. Despite the Owl's record of opposing American policies to protect Miami interests, Harrison seized upon the information the Owl provided and concluded that the Potawatomies, along with the Miamis, backed the Prophet.[42] Harrison continued to see Prophetstown as a staging area, a community that resembled an army camp.

The Owl's knowledge of what transpired there proved to Harrison that the Miami leader was indeed a nativist. In reality, the Owl and Little Eyes intended something else entirely. When they spoke of violence at Prophetstown and the many Indians who flocked to the town, they hoped to broaden the blame for the violence at Tippecanoe so that Harrison would condemn more of the outsiders who had invaded the Miami homeland. Harrison stated that a Wea Indian guaranteed him that "many of [the

Wabash Indians] still retained their confidence in the Prophet."[43] By encouraging the Americans to confront the Prophet—and convincing the Americans that the enemies of the Miamis were responsible—the Miamis could protect their homeland when negotiations resumed.

For his part, the Miami intermediary William Wells remained devoted to the destruction of the Prophet. The violence at Tippecanoe was destructive for Tenskwatawa, but it provided a unique opportunity for Miami leaders such as William Wells and Little Turtle, who were more than eager to regain their influence in the Tippecanoe region. By claiming that he knew the outlines of British strategy for war in the southern states, Wells tried to exacerbate Harrison's fears of a catastrophic race war. Wells claimed that the "Creeks & all the Southern Indians as well as the Negroes" would soon have all of the "necessary implements of War" and that the Creeks would "raise the Negroes in that Quarter Against the Whites."[44] Wells's position as a Miami leader and a white American meant that he could understand the cultural values of both societies. He understood that Harrison saw African slaves as inferior and threatening and employed the rhetoric of race to shape Harrison's response. In Harrison's mind, Creek militancy, coupled with the Prophet's army, would prove disastrous for the Euroamerican settlements in the territory. With Little Turtle dead and the Miami community fractured, Wells's tremendous efforts to orient the Americans against Prophetstown had few results. Harrison's forces had burned the town, but this had not helped the Miamis. Wells's letters to Harrison were likely a desperate effort to force Harrison to attack the Prophet's followers, even though the town itself no longer mattered.

The Shawnee brothers were just as devoted to controlling the post-Tippecanoe narrative. Tecumseh and Tenskwatawa joined a council of nearly six hundred Indians at the Mississinewa River in May 1812. They hoped to use the public conference—attended by various Indian communities and British and American agents—to condemn recent frontier murders that many people tied to the Prophet. During the council, several Potawatomi Indians pinned the frontier violence on Tenskwatawa, knowing full well that Harrison was likely to believe them. Many of the Indians rejected these accusations. Tecumseh responded by blaming the Potawatomies and reminding those present that he could not be held responsible for Indians who did not choose to accept the locus of his authority. Many Indians present likely recognized Main Poc's responsibility for the frontier murders. Main Poc's followers had raided American settlements throughout April and May, in direct disobedience of the

Prophet. Main Poc had ignored the Prophet's dictates before, when he continued a trade in alcohol and Euroamerican trade goods; he knew that Tenskwatawa's settlement would be a convenient scapegoat for the cause of frontier violence. The Miamis used the opportunity to assert their independence and to demonstrate that intrusive Indians such as the Shawnees and Potawatomies were causing trouble. They had not "hurt our white brethren since the Treaty of Greenville" and wished that "all of the other nations present could say the same."[45] The Miamis were desperately trying to position themselves between American suspicions and Indian militancy given the fallout from Tippecanoe and in turn remind them that it was the Miamis who were the original inhabitants of the region. Such recognition had proved fruitful in the Fort Wayne Treaty negotiations, and many Miamis hoped it would continue in the post-Tippecanoe world as well.

Despite their best and often successful efforts to sway public opinion in the Wabash-Maumee Valley, the Miamis could do very little to control the deteriorating relationship between the United States and Great Britain. President James Madison declared war on Britain during the spring of 1812, when the two powers failed to reach a compromise over free trade and sailors' rights. Madison signed the declaration of war against Great Britain on June 18, 1812, a decision that drastically altered the dynamics in the Wabash-Maumee Valley.[46] Britain could distribute goods to its Indian allies throughout the Ohio Valley, and many of the Indian communities gladly accepted them. War presented Indian groups with an opportunity to renew their relationships with the British but also to acquire weapons they could use to defend themselves in a region flooded by American settlers. This was a welcome opportunity for Indian communities like Pacanne's more conservative Miamis, and Tecumseh's supporters, who hoped to gain traction and stability in a region that was becoming increasingly unstable.

News of war did not reach the Wabash-Maumee Valley until July 1812. Each Indian and Euroamerican group in the Wabash-Maumee Valley arrived at the War of 1812 for reasons far outside the international crisis that was so central to President Madison. Most of Harrison's militia joined his ranks because of threats to their homes and to the capital of the territory—threats created by Harrison and his French and Miami sources. The beginning of war helped Harrison immensely as it seemed to confirm much of the governor's rhetoric about the British and Indians. After resigning as governor, he seized upon the opportunity to serve as a general in the Kentucky militia and eventually assumed charge of the western theater of war as a major general in the U.S. Army. Harrison was involved in the war in order to further his career and to avoid censure, but also because he believed so much of the damning information regarding the Prophet. These beliefs also led him to think that the Indians were conspiring with the British on a far greater scale than they were. The Miamis were there because they were involved in a civil dispute with their own polity, few of whom wanted to cement Prophetstown as a fixture in the Wabash-Maumee Valley. Tenskwatawa and other residents of Prophetstown were there because of the divisions within their community but also because they hoped to find some stability in a rapidly changing environment. The War of 1812 was only the most recent layer of violence in a valley that had seen constant conflict for decades. While war may have been declared on Britain in June 1812, the inhabitants of the Miami homeland had declared war upon their enemies four years earlier.

The Prophet recognized the benefits of the war as well. He sent runners throughout the Illinois country and northern Great Lakes region to rally the Indians. He knew that the opportunities provided by war were more persuasive than his nativist rhetoric. The chance to attack American settlements and to receive trade goods from the British was more important than the Prophet's efforts to revitalize Indian peoples. Tenskwatawa was coming to realize that the ability to beat the Americans mattered more than his principles. His actions, though, were a reaction to Tippecanoe, a product of uncontrollable violence that he had helped initiate.

However, as the war evolved in the western Ohio Valley, it became more destructive and violent than the Miamis anticipated. Harrison was certainly focused on ridding the region of the Prophet and his followers, but he was far more concerned with limiting the access Indians had to guns, ammunition, and other resources that would strengthen their destructive wrath. Geographically the war spread from Fort Dearborn (present-day Chicago) to Detroit and south to New Orleans, mobilizing large numbers of Americans and Indians throughout the valley and nation. Fort Dearborn and Fort Detroit fell to the Indians and British in August 1812, which meant that two of the central forts of the Ohio Valley were no longer controlled by the Americans. Such a development meant that the lands in between—the Miami homeland—would be of central importance if the Americans had any chance to stop the British incursion into the region.

Instead of carving a powerful diplomatic position between the warring sides, the Miamis quickly became victims of violence they had helped create. Harrison originally planned to attack Prophetstown and the Potawatomies that September, but he quickly turned his eye toward the Miami settlements in northeastern Indiana after the United States lost Dearborn and Detroit. Harrison's commission as a major general effectively removed him as governor of the territory and gave him free reign to do as he pleased. Also, William Wells's death during the Battle of Fort Dearborn left the Miamis largely voiceless in terms of challenging Harrison's decisions. Harrison remained focused on the areas around Fort Wayne even after a group of Indians from Prophetstown had attacked Fort Harrison and nearly taken it. Several Weas and Miamis had warned Zachary Taylor's command at Fort Harrison of the impending attack, but Harrison disregarded the intelligence. Rather, he instructed troops to destroy Little Turtle's town even though he "had no evidence of the inhabitants of that Town having joined in the hostilities against" the Americans. Harrison feared that militant Indians might take the food and materials from Little Turtle's town and use it to feed and arm Indian militants. William Clark, the governor of Illinois Territory, warned that many of the Indian towns would sue for peace and that "protection should be extended towards them." Harrison, frustrated by the Indian raids on American settlements, abandoned any efforts to negotiate with the Miamis. He likely recognized that war with Britain and its Indian allies provided too great an opportunity to rid the valley of Indians once and for all. Harrison had also concluded that it was impossible to discriminate between the peaceful and militant Indians.[47]

Harrison's concern over the loss of Chicago and Detroit paled in comparison to his fear that the Prophet's and Tecumseh's confederacy had found new life. While the Prophet struggled to gain large numbers of adherents, Tecumseh won the support of 3,500 warriors living in Indiana, Illinois, and Wisconsin. Tecumseh could promise them an alliance with the British, which included easier access to trade goods, while the Prophet's teachings advocated separation from the polluting influences of Europeans. Tecumseh's success in constructing such an alliance was largely the product of the Indian communities hoping to use an impending war to protect their interests and not necessarily because they supported the Prophet's nativist ideology. Receiving goods from the British went against the Prophet's teachings, but it also allowed the pan-Indian confederacy to mobilize more effectively than it had under the Prophet. As important, it provided individual Native communities with the tools—guns, ammunition, and supplies—to protect themselves in an increasingly violent world.

The British alliance with Tecumseh's pan-Indian confederacy proved successful in the early days of the war, but the situation changed after Detroit fell. Tecumseh's confederacy was unable to take Fort Meigs in August 1812 at the same time that Oliver Hazard Perry commanded the American navy to victory on the Great Lakes when he defeated a British squadron in September 1813. Harrison mirrored Perry's successes by defeating a British Indian force at the Battle of the Thames in October 1813, the battle in which Tecumseh died. During the same period, American militias periodically ravaged the Wabash-Maumee Valley, in particular any Indian settlements near Prophetstown. Harrison's successes against Tecumseh proved beneficial for the Miami villages that were largely in ruins by 1813. Tecumseh was dead and his brother the Prophet had resettled in British-held territory, which left the Wabash-Maumee Valley outside of the central theater of war.

As the Miami homeland stabilized in 1814 and 1815, memories of Tippecanoe remained central to the formation of postwar boundaries. Both Harrison and the Miamis sought to expand their sphere of influence by delicately navigating the postwar memory of frontier violence. The Miamis came out of the war weakened by the destruction of their croplands, but they were also stronger diplomatically; many of the nativist Indians who had once inhabited Prophetstown were either dead or in Canada. Better able to situate themselves in relation to the legacy of Prophetstown, the Miamis focused on their needs as a people; from this stance, they could articulate their peaceful postwar intentions. Furthermore, they now approached an American government that was far more willing to accommodate Native interests. Concerned that the frontier war would soon reignite, the Americans made every effort to appease the Miamis and recognize their rightful claim to the region. The last thing the Americans wanted was for the militant Indians to resettle near Prophetstown. Harrison continued to attack the Prophet through rhetoric, drawing attention to the threat he posed despite British promises that he would not return to the United States. No longer the governor of Indiana Territory, Harrison was less concerned with defending the actual physical boundaries of the region and far more interested in using his military experiences to propel himself into national politics. By politicizing the role that he had played on the battlefield, Harrison fashioned himself as a national leader by reminding the public that he had successfully defended the northwestern frontier during the war. Other frontier residents saw changes in the postwar era as a new beginning, a moment when Americans would finally unify and assert themselves in the trans-Mississippi West. They identified diminishing violence as proof that the Americans united with a national identity.

The Americans confronted emboldened Miamis once the war ended. The Treaty of Ghent, signed in December 1814, did not indicate an end to hostilities. Neither did Andrew Jackson's victory in New Orleans. Captain Andrie of the U.S. Rangers reported in February 1815 that "the Indians have received fifty cags [sic] of powder, lead and flints" and that the Indians planned to "make an attack on Ft. Harrison and would return to the British immediately after the attack." Rumors had it that the Wea leader Lapoussier had also joined the British and brought Little Eyes with him. This was nothing new to the Miamis, many of whom continued to operate within a colonial mind-set. The Kickapoos and Potawatomies allied with the British that May, but the Miamis refused to join them. They made sure to position themselves between militant Indians and fearful Americans. Benjamin Parke mournfully observed that whites roamed the countryside, hunting and murdering Indians. He lamented this "sad state of society" that he hoped "never again to witness."[48]

The actions of the Miamis in late 1814 and 1815 do not reinforce the larger metanarratives of the War of 1812. They were not a defeated people. Given the ratification of the Treaty of Ghent by the U.S. Senate in February 1815, the continued use of violence by British and Indian peoples in the Wabash-Maumee Valley indicates circumstances outside of the Anglo-American diplomatic crisis. In fact, the treaty itself stipulated that the two sides would restore their borders to prewar status, but it did little to address the problems in the western Ohio River Valley. Indian warfare was part of a much longer conflict over boundaries and influence in a region that had not reached any real resolution. In fact, British diplomats asked that the northwest territories from western Ohio to Wisconsin (a large swath of Miami territory) be made into an Indian state. Although such a plan had no chance of being implemented, it did speak to the value many Indians placed on the region and the extent to which Indians remained present. Although James Madison rejected the notion of an Indian state, the northern areas of Ohio, Indiana, and Illinois remained contested and lacked a distinct boundary. Despite years of violence and destruction, the Wabash-Maumee Valley remained a contested space where the Miamis and Americans continued to fight for greater stability.

While the Americans and British hoped to remake the region to suit their plans for North America, the Miamis found the situation suitable to their needs for independence. A full year after the signing of the Treaty of

Ghent, Pacanne still found himself in a position to trade with the British, who were more than willing to send their traders into the region despite "American protests." Some Indian communities hoped to join the Miamis as part of an Indian-British alliance in the valley, but the Miamis at Mississinewa refused to make war on the Americans. For Pacanne and the Miamis now based at Mississinewa and Eel River, allegiance to the Kickapoos and Potawatomies was as dangerous as an alliance with the Americans. More importantly, such an agreement was not necessary because the Miamis had successfully defended their status as the original inhabitants of the valley. Pacanne sought to draw the Miamis together at a permanent village on the Eel River. Under his leadership, the Miamis would "establish their village in the old form." Pacanne's words are striking because they demonstrate his confidence that the Miami world had not undergone a fundamental alteration—both their physical and cultural boundaries remained secure. In fact, Indian agent Benjamin Stickney remarked that the Miamis had not acculturated. They had "no uniform place of residence," and the "respective bands assemble in the spring at their several ordinary places." Their population had increased, they remained devoted to their traditional spiritual way of life, and they had succeeded in large part at avoiding missionaries. Like Stickney, Pacanne was confident that he had successfully defended Miami boundaries by protecting his community. In fact, many Indians continued to dispute the boundaries established by the 1809 Fort Wayne Treaty.[49]

Despite the ravages of war and the death of many of their brethren, valley Indians saw the boundary as ill-formed. In fact, Pacanne's boundaries remained traditional in the sense that they reflected the prewar Miami world. When he signed the Treaty of Greenville of 1814, he certainly took to heart article four, which read, "In the event of the faithful performance of the conditions of this treaty, the United States will confirm and establish all the boundaries between their lands and those of the . . . Miamies, as they existed previously to the commencement of the war." The violence of the War of 1812, much like the violence of the Revolutionary War, or even the colonial period, was still reinforcing Miami interests. The Americans recognized the lack of a permanent boundary between the United States and British North America as well. Benjamin Parke worried that the Miamis—namely Pacanne—would be invited to Malden in the winter of 1816 to discuss "British merchants being invited into their country." This was especially important given that the white inhabitants of the territory declared their right to statehood just two months later.[50]

Surprisingly, both the Miamis and territorial settlers of Indiana asserted their right to sovereignty at the exact same time, but on a complete different scale. Scholars often dismiss Miami actions as desperate attempts to protect their remaining territory in the face of superior American numbers. In fact, they were only trying to protect Miami society as they understood it and operating in a world where boundaries were far more permeable than scholars have suggested. Unlike the Miamis, the Americans were increasingly moving away from their parochial worlds. Vincennes would now be a town within a state. It was no longer a symbolic or political capital in which factions contested local politics. Vincennes had become, according to one traveler, a "frontier town of a new race," a town that embodied the unified ideals of a white nation increasingly hopeful to remove Indians from their homelands.[51]

Yet some of the Miamis were just as hopeful as the Americans that their towns would identify a Miami world free of interference. Their desire to remain independent does not indicate failure. Pacanne's effort to resettle the Miamis at Eel River had succeeded. Having avoided an alliance with Little Turtle and William Wells, the Americans, and the nativists, Pacanne emerged from the war a much stronger leader because he had resisted accommodation and alliances with outsiders. The destruction of Prophetstown and removal of nativist troublemakers had placed the Miamis in a position to be secure. Americans such as Benjamin Parke could not look north and see only a static boundary between the United States and British North America. He saw a world in which whites and Indians continued to attack each other and where the British remained an influential force. In between the British and the Americans stood the Miamis, who remained in their homeland and who continued to assert their right to maintain a Miami world. Despite the death of Pacanne in 1816, his nephew Jean Baptiste Richardville, born at Kekionga, assumed a leadership role. As though a phoenix, the Miamis emerged from the fires of violence still living, trading, and even dying in the same region as their ancestors.

The aftermath from the Battle of Tippecanoe did more than provide the Miamis with an opportunity to remain on their homelands. It also forced the Americans to recognize the Miamis as the legitimate inhabitants of the Wabash-Maumee Valley. In dealing with the many claims put forth by Native groups during the War of 1812, Harrison was quick to tell the secretary of war that the "Miamies, Maumees, or Tewicktovies, are the undoubted proprietors of all that beautiful country which is watered by the Wabash and its branches" and that "all the neighboring tribes . . .

are either intruders upon them, or have been permitted to settle in their country."[52] This was a distinct shift from Harrison's pre-Prophetstown mentality. Richardville used this legitimacy—a legitimacy earned by his uncle Pacanne in decades of successful diplomacy and in part through the events at Tippecanoe—to his advantage. Despite efforts by the Americans to negotiate removal treaties with the Miamis in 1826, Richardville defended Miami autonomy by seizing upon the many lessons he had learned as a member of an "in-between" people.

When the Americans and British signed the Treaty of Paris in 1783, they ignored the Indian inhabitants who controlled most of the lands being ceded. Historians have rightly challenged the ethnocentric nature of those decisions to demonstrate the continued viability of many Indian peoples in the Ohio Valley. Yet it seems we have allowed the Treaty of Ghent to perform a similar whitewashing. From 1816 to 1846, the Miamis' populations actually increased despite some who removed and others who died of impoverishment and alcoholism. After the Treaty of St. Mary in 1818, they still controlled their winter hunting grounds in what was known as the Miami National Reserve, some 875,000 acres. Even by 1823, only a few white families lived in northern Indiana, and those who did were largely of French descent. What was once Kekionga (now Fort Wayne) housed fewer than four hundred people in 1829, most of whom were métis or American traders present because of their desire to trade with the Miamis. Such a circumstance was not entirely unfamiliar from when Kekionga stood at the same site. Even by the 1830s, Miami people were certainly acculturating, but marriages and burials continued to follow Miami customs.[53] It is not surprising that one scholar of the Miamis concluded that by the 1840s, the "Miami people were doing as they always had, seeking opportunity and adapting to change, but remaining Indian."[54]

Northern Indiana was at once Miami and American. Even Miami agriculture spoke to the longevity of Miami farming practices. By this period in their history, the Miamis enjoyed a relatively large land base and a federal annuity to promote the "Civilization of Indians" through the implementation of western agricultural practices. Although the Indian agent John Tipton accepted the money for use among the Miamis, the Miamis instead used the money to hire outsiders—much as they had with the Lenapes and Shawnees at Kekionga—to prepare and farm their lands.[55] However, in hiring outsiders to farm their lands, Miami women were quickly losing control over a commodity (corn and other agricultural foodstuffs) that had been key to their ability to influence trade and diplomacy. Coupled with the increased settlement on their former homelands, non-Natives no longer needed to trade with the Miamis for food. Increasingly, Miami women were also marrying outside their community, a key reason why the number of Miami speakers experienced a noticeable decline in the 1830s and 1840s.

Yet not all Miami women experienced such drastic changes, nor should such change suggest a decline in Miami culture. Many Miami women continued farming out of necessity because their husbands had died or because their husbands were off trading for extended periods of time. Dependent upon their farm economies, Miami women typically stayed near their reserves, where they continued to speak their language, as did their children, unlike their husbands, who needed to speak English in order to converse with whites for trade. In one instance when many Miamis were removing west, Congress allowed an elderly Miami woman to keep her reserve in Indiana because of her advanced age and familial responsibilities.[56] Although Miami women had lost much of their diplomatic influence by the 1820s and 1830s, they nonetheless remained an important part of Miami cultural persistence in the region.

Why did the Miamis remain? What about the Miamis made them unique when so many other groups and people (the Prophet included) had been forced to remove west? As they had done many times before, the Miamis used their geographical advantage to their benefit while playing different communities against each other. When Indian agent John Tipton attempted to remove the Miamis in the 1830s, he had to confront a Miami community that skillfully played the land speculators and traders, who profited greatly from the Miamis being present in Indiana, against the State of Indiana, which hoped the Indians would disappear forever. Trading families such as the Ewings regulated the annuity payments due and regularly extended credit to the Miamis. The northern Indian economy, whether through the Ewing family or the trading houses at Fort Wayne, depended upon the Miamis.[57] The Miamis were indeed in a weakened position and certainly beginning to acculturate in ways not before witnessed, but they still wielded a degree of economic power that they used to maintain their historic identity and relationships.

When state officials tried to force the Miamis to move west, the Miamis seized upon their relationships with traders and land speculators—who benefited by keeping the Miamis in the state—to disarm state officials. As long as the Miamis controlled their lands, the traders would continue to profit by distributing annuity payments. The Miami leader Le Gros reminded the supporters of Indian removal that the Miamis would stay on the lands which the "Great Spirit gave us, from generation to generation, and not leave it." A veteran of the violence at Tippecanoe and the chief negotiator of the plan for Miami removal, John Tipton grew frustrated at the stubborn Miamis. Tipton understood that they had a "well organized . . . government" and "shrewd men" like Richardville in charge.[58] Forcing them to leave the region would not be easy. But by the 1830s the Americans had taken so much land from Indians that many simply left the region and moved west. With Richardville's help, the Miamis held on to large sections of their lands until November 1840.

"Settling" on the Narrative

The shift from a Native-white borderland to an American borderland occurred in the period after 1820; by this point, the Americans were seizing increasingly large sections of Miami territory. In total, the Miamis had ceded more than 10 million acres since the war. Yet the process of creating an American bordered land was contingent on a number of factors. The Americans also needed to reinvent the historical narrative framing the taking of Miami lands by continuing a tradition of remaking the story of Tippecanoe. They needed to take events and identities that had developed in private spaces—local quarrels, anonymous letters full of rumors and lies, personal vendettas—and make them public through institutionalized memory.[59]

The reinvention and re-remembering of Tippecanoe continued when Americans returned to the site in the 1820s. Heavy rains churned up the soil of the battlefield, bringing human bones to the surface. Apparently, the Indians returned to the battlefield shortly after Tippecanoe and desecrated the graves, but no one discovered this until ten years later, by which time white Americans felt safe to return to the area. According to John Tipton, in 1821, a company of soldiers from Fort Harrison discovered that the "bones of men and horses [lay] bleaching together" on the ground exposed to the elements.[60] As a result, the Americans buried the bones as if to affirm both the physical control over the lands and the cultural control over the historical narrative. In the end, the Americans were able to celebrate their dead by erecting a monument on lands once key to the Prophet's nativist movement. They had to satisfy their need for a monument by using only a large stone to mark the communal grave.

Yet the process of remaking Tippecanoe was far from complete. Nearly a decade later, as if to finally lay claim to both the narrative and the land itself, members of the Tippecanoe expedition reinterred the bones. In a letter to the *Indianapolis Journal*, John Tipton described the event where "a great number of people from different states attended" the memorial, including a few survivors. They even invited Harrison, but he could not attend. His absence, however, allowed for the continued abstraction of the events in November 1811. In the absence of the leading participants from the fight, memorialists were better positioned to create their own narrative. What had been a draw now became in John Tipton's eyes a "victory" that "shortened the war" by "crippl[ing]" Tecumseh's "operations." And while the narrative of power relations became more one-sided, identities became more rigid and defined. Gone were the factions and disagreements. Instead, it was the "united skill and courage of the army of the United States," Tipton wrote, "and the volunteers and militia of Kentucky and the Indiana Territory *jointly* . . . . [I]t was an *American* army, led by Gov. Harrison . . . and followed by many of the first citizens of our country."[61] It was an American victory, not a parade of dysfunction, and it was unified effort rather than a contest of factions.

In burying the bones for the third time, the Americans performed both a physical and symbolic ritual that embodied the formation of an American bordered land. The memorialists exerted their control not only over the decayed bodies but also over the soil and earth, the physical boundary. One of soldiers who had participated at Tippecanoe in November 1811 reminded those gathered that Harrison's firm leadership had not only defeated the Prophet, but secured the western boundaries as well. Like those before him, he continued the history of lies surrounding Tippecanoe. Tipton stated that through Harrison's victories over the Indians during the War of 1812, a "British army was conquered, the famous Tecumseh slain, and all our foes humbled." For the soldier, American reigned supreme, and thanks to Harrison, "others have reaped a rich harvest of his well-earned laurels."[62]

The Miamis were a decade away from losing the last of their lands, and the northern boundaries of the United States were firmly established in Michigan, Indiana, and several western states. The disputed memories of Tippecanoe were vanishing in the face of a national narrative that was glorifying American expansion and the removal of Indian peoples. Remembering Tippecanoe became a way for Americans to make real the "bordered" reality of 1830s America by re-creating the past. They were involved not only in the "invention of tradition" but also in creating new physical boundaries and with it a sense of self. For them, the War of 1812 was no longer a draw and near disaster for the United States, but a victory where both their British and Indian "foes" had been defeated and an Americanism had been born.[63] As Americans increasingly redefined the war, they used Tippecanoe as a type of theater where they could act out the new national narrative that was central to an evolving American identity.

In fact, it should be no surprise that Elihu Stout, a cornerstone to the violence that flared at Prophetstown, would in later years turn against the narrative of Tippecanoe that he helped create. Stout refused to publish any celebratory stories about the Battle of Tippecanoe during the 1830s because Harrison had created the greatest of treasons and joined the Whig Party. As he spoke highly of the Democratic candidates for office, Stout made sure to undermine Harrison's narrative. The battle "displayed neither generalship on the part of Governor Harrison, nor that caution which is never forgotten by an able commander."[64] For Stout, Tippecanoe was now currency for understanding party politics and the weakness of the Whig Party's presidential candidate.

Tippecanoe did not simply represent a violent episode on November 7, 1811, between the Prophet and Harrison, but instead a symbolic exercise through which non-Native settlers made their, according to one scholar, "inner subjective impressions" of nation, race, and culture into "forms that have a stabler . . . objective existence."[65] In defining a border, they defined themselves. Even after the Battle of Tippecanoe, even after the French traders fled and Harrison attacked the town, neither Vincennes nor Prophetstown joined together under a banner of racial unity. The Prophet strove to unite his community but watched as the Potawatomies and Miamis continued to challenge him. Their desire to place local interests above racial and nativist ideals prolonged factionalism within the region.

If anything, Prophetstown, like Vincennes, was unable to change the historical dynamics and factional nature of the Wabash-Maumee Valley. Local and cultural interests ruled the region for over a century, and the two "new" towns simply could not overcome the issues fueling factionalism. The Prophet and Harrison believed that they represented the racial interests of Indians and Euroamericans, respectively. In fact, their interests, like their relationships, overshadowed the complicated issues connecting Indian histories with Euroamerican ones. Although the Prophet and Harrison likely looked at the War of 1812 as the logical result of their peoples' inability to compromise, their beliefs did not reflect the feelings of their communities at large, nor would the roots of regional violence ever mirror those framing the conflict between the United States and Great Britain.

By framing the fight for Prophetstown as essentially a fight between the American nation-state and an allied British-Indian force, scholars too easily connect these violences within the larger international conflict between Great Britain and the United States during the War of 1812. By assuming the overarching influence and power of the American nation-state and the British Empire, the bloodshed at Tippecanoe becomes the first act to the War of 1812.[66] Yet the violence that spread throughout the Wabash-Maumee Valley during the early 1800s was rooted in both the colonial past and the American present. American and British imperial endeavors quickly fell prey to the factional and ethnic conflicts of the Miami world, enabling communities and even individuals to empower themselves through lies, manipulation, and deceit.

Conclusion

The work of Benjamin Drake is the apotheosis of the scholarly tendency to see the Battle of Tippecanoe as William Henry Harrison's decisive victory over the Prophet's radical and militant Indians. Nearly forty years after the battle, Drake concluded that "peace on the frontiers was one of the happy results of this severe and brilliant action. The tribes which had already joined in the confederacy were dismayed; and those which had remained neutral now decided against it." Drake made Harrison into a heroic figure who miraculously survived the battle because of his "coolness and bravery." In this seminal work, Drake lavished attention on the details of Harrison's injuries: a musket "ball [passed] through his stock, slightly bruising his neck; another struck his saddle, and glancing hit his thigh; and a third wounded the horse on which he was riding." A "fanatical" Indian Prophet was no match for the heroic William Henry Harrison. Harrison's victory, though, has often revolved around the concomitant decline of the Prophet. According to Drake's variety of historical myth, "the defeated Indians were greatly exasperated with the Prophet: they reproached him in bitter terms for the calamity he had brought upon them, and accused him of the murder of their friends who had fallen in the action."[67] Drake's story, like that of the Tippecanoe memorialists, reflects the racialized world in which Americans lived by the 1840s and 1850s, not the lived experiences of Americans in Indiana or the Miamis in the Wabash-Maumee Valley.

Tippecanoe was never just a battle. Yet it is the battle that has silenced a very different tale that took place among the Miamis and American settlements along the Wabash-Maumee Valley. The Miamis sometimes suffered through and at other times benefited from French and British colonialism, Indian nativism, and American expansionism, and while this may be said of many Indian communities, few did so while remaining in their homelands. Indeed, treaty negotiations, land sales, and removal policies whittled away at the traditional Miami land base, but such changes, though at times destructive, did not stop the Miamis from living in a place that they knew quite well. Should we ignore their persistence simply because the Miamis of the 1840s did not quite resemble those of a century earlier? Should we allow the Miamis to vanish from the histories we tell of antebellum Indiana because we hold them to a rigid, static, and unchanging definition of what it meant to be Miami? Most of all, should we call this region an American bordered land simply because the Miamis were weaker than in years previous?

In effect, what existed in the 1820s and 1830s was quite similar to what existed in the 1770s, a Wabash-Maumee borderland in which the Miamis continued to play an important role in the economic and social organization of the region's settlements. This borderland was at once Miami and American. While not all parties—whites and Miamis—were happy with the other's presence, they nonetheless cooperated and lived within a world that combined aspects of both. Whether economically, socially, or even historically, the Miamis and Americans shared a space and past that was at times quite similar. In effect, they had both benefited from a borderland of violence they had created.

By the 1830s, the Miami borderland was gone. There is no doubt in that. But the American borderland in Indiana was still dependent upon Miami trade, land cessions, and fear. And the stories Indianans and Americans told about their violent past was in large part dependent upon the violence the Miamis helped to generate. Yet despite sharing the narrative of a militant Prophetstown, the Miamis and Americans differed starkly over what the battle produced. One soldier remembered that Tippecanoe shortened the War of 1812 and undermined Tecumseh's confederacy, and that Harrison's actions at Tippecanoe and beyond resulted in a "Province conquered."[68] Such language is startling given its avoidance of historical fact, but also because it demonstrates a secure northern boundary of the 1830s that did not exist in the 1810s. It also ignores the fact that the Americans were not the only beneficiaries of the battle. In fact, without the help of the Miamis, the Americans might have lost control of their territory altogether, and without the Miamis, the state would not have functioned as it did.

Simply put, the Miamis were not your average group of Indians, if indeed such a claim can be made about any Native people. Their unique relationship to the Wabash and Maumee Rivers, and their ability to benefit through incorporation, allowed the Miamis to exert a type of power and influence we do not typically associate with Indian peoples in the historically violent Ohio River Valley. Our failures to fully evaluate the ill-formed nature of Indiana's northern border is largely the result of scholars maintaining the racial perspective embodied in American memories of Tippecanoe as well as a historical lens that looks west more than north. In the rigidly racialized past, the Miamis could only be accommodationists or nativists. We have told stories of the Miamis as a people without tying them to the territorial system, tales of the French and métis without understanding their centrality to American diplomacy or their relationship to the Miamis, and evaluated the western expansion of the United States without examining the ways in which groups such as the Miamis facilitated it, but we have not combined the three in one study. The Miamis are easy to ignore when we only ask questions about single ethnic or national groups or when our only goal is to understand the formation of the nation-state. But when we look at the roots and power of violence in reshaping the Ohio River Valley during the early republic, the story becomes much more complicated, and the narrative changes as a result.

By looking at the parties that invaded the Miami borderland and the ways in which Prophetstown served as a lens through which the French, Americans, and Indians exerted influence, we are better able to understand the delicate and limited nature of western expansion. By focusing so heavily on the Prophet and Harrison, scholars have too easily taken their racialized rhetoric at face value. Their rhetoric was in fact more a reaction to disunity within their communities than a reflection of a shared set of cohesive beliefs and actions. While these two men were certainly important to the remaking of the Miami homeland, their actions and especially their words have too easily silenced those who were indeed as influential but often not as vocal.

The paths Harrison and the Prophet followed post-Tippecanoe were more reflective of the hyperracialized narratives scholars often tell of Prophetstown. These two men spent a great deal of their time trying to maintain, if not expand, the influence they enjoyed during the conflict. Their efforts were frustrated. The Prophet no longer had the support of his brother, Tecumseh, who had died at the Battle of the Thames in 1813. Many of the Prophet's supporters had moved back to the Wabash-Maumee

Valley, but Tenskwatawa was unable to follow suit because the federal government had banned him from returning to the United States. Federal Indian agents feared that letting him to return to the Wabash-Maumee Valley would mean the renewal of hostilities against American settlements. War seemed a distinct possibility, for some of the Prophet's former supporters, including Shawnee, Kickapoo, and Sac Indians had resettled near the Tippecanoe River in 1816. The Treaty of Ghent authorized Native peoples to return to the territories they occupied before the war, based on the stipulation that the United States grant "tribes or nations . . . all the possessions, rights, and privileges" that they possessed before the war.[69] As head of the commission charged with negotiating the return of these Indian groups, Harrison must have rankled at the fact that so many of them returned to Tippecanoe. Neither would he have been pleased at the Miamis' triumphant embrace of their sacred lands. While the Prophet endured exile in Canada, Harrison suffered as well. The people of Ohio elected him as a representative to Congress in 1816, but he was relegated to Ohio's state senate by 1819 and subsequently lost an election to Congress in 1822. Despite these reversals, both men found ways to use the American political structure to reassert their influence.

In turn, to utilize their historical relationship to Tippecanoe for personal benefit, both Tenskwatawa and Harrison started an important process through which Americans moved away from fears of British aggression and the return of Indian militancy. During the summer of 1824, Lewis Cass, then governor of Michigan Territory, sent a letter to the Prophet requesting his presence at Detroit. Cass believed that the Prophet was "restless and discontented" and that the Shawnee leader had little left in life but "disappointment." Cass hoped that the isolated, aging, and politically weakened Prophet might aid the federal government's plans to force Indians from the Ohio Valley. The chance to take part in plans for Indian removal provided an excellent opportunity for Tenskwatawa to undercut the influence of an old Shawnee adversary, Black Hoof. To a certain extent, Cass hoped for the same thing; Black Hoof's Shawnees resisted efforts to push them from their homes. The Prophet had accepted the fact that he would not return to Prophetstown, but he also recognized that helping the Americans would let him reassert his authority within the Shawnee community. By moving west, he would be able to escape from the Americans and be closer to the Kickapoos, Potawatomies, and other Indian communities that had lived with him at Prophetstown. The meeting between Cass and the Prophet proved beneficial. Cass recognized the Prophet's cooperative nature but also echoed the stereotypes of the Prophet that had originated in Vincennes. He declared that the aging Shawnee leader was "'radically cured . . . of his Anglo-mania.'"[70] In fact, the Prophet had grown increasingly angry with the British for not compensating him fully for his services during the war; he no longer had trusted allies outside of his immediate relations.

Isolated for nearly a decade from his community in Indiana, Tenskwatawa had little choice but to pacify Cass in order to survive. The Prophet deftly used Cass to work his way back into the United States by agreeing to lead a contingent of Shawnees west to the Kansas River in the late 1820s. In 1828, he set up a village separate from more influential Shawnee leaders such as Cornstalk and Big Snake. But just as at Prophetstown, many of the Indians at Tenskwatawa's Kansas village soon departed because he could not provide them with the supplies necessary to survive. Most traveled east to the Shawnee settlements in Missouri that were friendlier to the Indian agents. Two years later, a large contingent of Ohio Shawnees arrived in Kansas from Ohio, but few cared to associate themselves with the Prophet. Resentful at losing influence among his people, he moved east to present-day Kansas City, Kansas, where he constructed another village.[71]

Like Tenskwatawa, Harrison used his connections to Prophetstown as a means to improve his circumstances. Rather than return to Vincennes after the War of 1812, Harrison hoped to exploit his reputation as a military leader and Indian fighter to climb the political ladder. After failing to win a congressional seat in 1822, Harrison won election to the United States Senate in 1824. Harrison served as chairman of the Senate Committee on Military Affairs, a post previously held by Andrew Jackson. He became minister to Columbia four years later, and retired from public life in 1829. Frustrated at his lack of wealth, Harrison welcomed James Hall's biography *A Memoir of the Public Services of William Henry Harrison,* from which he derived some profit. In 1836, he ran for president and lost, but he won the office in 1840, largely due to the popularization of American politics wrought by the rise of the secondary party system and an American populace that was increasingly anti-Indian. The Whig Party recognized how Andrew Jackson used his identity as an Indian fighter to propel him into office, and party leaders hoped to do the same with Harrison. Harrison had made a career by demonizing Indians to his advantage, a talent perfectly suited for an American populace demanding removal. By 1840, more than twelve biographies portrayed Harrison as a national hero who had won the day at Tippecanoe and defeated the great Shawnee leader Tecumseh.[72] The Whig Party continued using this portrayal of Harrison and his famed efforts during the War of 1812 to get him elected to the White House. As had been the case when he was territorial governor of Indiana, Harrison used the power of words to protect his interests and marginalize his political opponents.

As Tenskwatawa constructed yet another Prophetstown several hundred miles west of the original settlement, Harrison built a symbolic Prophetstown for political purposes. Remarkably, his campaign chose Tippecanoe rather than the Battle of the Thames, where Harrison defeated the British and Tecumseh died. Harrison capitalized on his connection to Prophetstown by organizing a presidential campaign built upon the myth of his victory at Tippecanoe. National rallies of more than fifty thousand Whigs expressed their support for Harrison by singing the eight stanzas of "Tippecanoe and Tyler too."

> What's the cause of this commotion, motion, motion,
> Our country through?
> It is the ball a-rolling on
>> For Tippecanoe and Tyler too.
>> For Tippecanoe and Tyler too.
>> And with them we'll beat little Van, Van, Van,
>> Van is a used up man.
>> And with them we'll beat little Van.

The song, like the campaign slogan, identified William Henry Harrison as "Tippecanoe" to remind Americans of Harrison's "heroic" actions against the Shawnee Prophet's forces. But the politicization of the town, river, and battle ignored the historical context of "Tippecanoe." The nickname Tippecanoe recalled a famous Indian battle but made no mention of the public quarrel in Vincennes that framed it or the Miami and French, who were equally to blame. Tippecanoe was, in fact, the Euroamerican name for a small stream that ran perpendicular to the Wabash River. The Prophet established Prophetstown at the confluence of these two rivers. The Potawatomi Indians called it *Ke-tap-e-kon*, and the Miamis named it *Ke-tap-kwa-na*. Euroamericans identified the village at the mouth of the Tippecanoe as *Ke-tap-e-kon-nong*, which they corrupted initially as *Keth-tip-pe-can-nunk* and eventually as Tippecanoe.[73] The various spellings reflect the different peoples who lived near these rivers. The word Tippecanoe became synonymous with Harrison and heroism, not Tenskwatawa or the Miamis. For Harrison and his supporters, Tippecanoe was about power, not place. While Harrison's nickname evoked faint memories of his battles against Indians, by 1840 the moniker largely symbolized national and racial values centered on the continued westward expansion of Anglo-Americans. His supporters recognized that they could use the battle to refashion Harrison into a heroic Indian fighter much like Andrew Jackson. They colonized the word much as they had colonized the Indians' lands.

Several biographies continued to refashion Harrison's image. One of the many biographies characterized Harrison as "the idol of the northwestern army" because "no general had a higher reputation for bravery, skill, and perseverance." In fact, "they knew that if they were sick, they would not be left to suffer. If there was only a crust of bread, their general would share it with them." They hailed "the gallant Harrison!, Who often fought and ever won, The glorious wreath of victory." Whig supporters mythologized Harrison through the Battle of Tippecanoe and the events surrounding it, which reflected more of the sociopolitical atmosphere of the late 1830s and 1840s than the reality of life in the Wabash-Maumee Valley during the early 1800s. By 1840, the United States government had forced thousands of American Indians west of the Mississippi in order to create separate worlds for the two races.[74]

This more rigid racial divide played out most clearly in the lives of Harrison and Tenskwatawa. Tenskwatawa remained at the last iteration of Prophetstown near the Argentine district of present-day Kansas City, Kansas, until his death in 1836. He isolated himself from the majority of the Shawnees, who had begun working with the missionaries and government agents. Few Indians sought his council largely because he did not support any sort of collaboration with the Americans. He spent his last few years in relative obscurity.[75] Harrison failed to win the presidency the same month that Tenskwatawa died, but he continued his efforts and won the presidential election in 1840. A few months later, Harrison stood on the east portico of the Capitol Building, where Chief Justice Roger Taney administered the presidential oath of office. Shortly thereafter, Harrison, then sixty-eight years old, delivered an inaugural address that lasted almost two hours. Only once did he mention "aboriginal" peoples. His imagined nation, like his community at Vincennes, simply had no room for them. Harrison contracted a cold during his first month in office, and his condition deteriorated quickly into full-blown pneumonia. He passed away thirty days into his term as president. Like the Prophet, he died never having constructed his ideal community.

In terms of survival, the Miamis enjoyed greater success. While the Miamis too had suffered their fair share of disruption and displacement, many Miami communities remained living on community reservations in the Wabash-Maumee Valley. In an 1840 treaty, the federal government in collaboration with the Miamis privatized portions of the 875,000-acre Miami National Reserve. The federal government hoped that as private landholders, the Miamis would assimilate into mainstream American society. In fact, the opposite occurred. One Miami leader, Papakeechi (Flatbelly), constructed a brick home on a reservation where he continued to live with members of his village. Other Miamis resettled on Lafontaine's reserve near Huntington and Richardville's reserve near Fort Wayne. Still others joined Pa-Lonz-Wa (Francis Godfroy) and his family, who lived in several two-story homes along the Mississinewa River. This community was built, as one historian describes, "in a traditional pattern within a square enclosure."[76] Various log cabins and other dwellings dotted the Miami lands, most of which the federal government paid to construct in exchange for Miami participation in treaty negotiations. In fact, the Miamis often remained in the area despite removal and the loss of their lands. So stable was Miami society in Indiana that Godfroy constructed several cabins when Miami refugees returned to the Wabash-Maumee Valley from Kansas.

Miami women were also crucial in efforts by the Miamis to stay in the Wabash-Maumee Valley. Although intermarriage with white traders no longer presented Miami women with opportunities to secure influence through trade, they still used their relationships with the white world to their benefit. The story of Moconnoqua (Frances Slocum) is instructive in this regard. Despite appearing to be as "Indian" as her fellow Miamis, and unable to speak English, Moconnoqua was also Frances Slocum, a white woman who had been kidnapped by the Miamis at a young age. She deftly withheld this information until removal threatened to destroy the village of her deceased husband, Deaf Man, in the mid-1830s. By telling her story, Moconnoqua secured recognition as white from her family in Pennsylvania, who confirmed Moconnoqua's story after visiting her in Indiana. With the help of a lawyer, Moconnoqua convinced the federal government that a white person and her immediate family should not be removed. Both the House of Representatives and Senate agreed. Once again the Miamis had used the system to their advantage because, as Susan Sleeper-Smith has demonstrated, Moconnoqua's "immediate family" was in fact her entire village.[77] Congress allocated her and her "family" a reserve of 620 acres, which remained immune from removal. Like many Miami women before her, Moconnoqua served as a key intermediary with outsiders.

These reserves were more than remnant villages where impoverished Miamis sat waiting to vanish. These were stable communities where many Miamis continued to prosper. Key to their survival was farming and a reinvigorated fur trade. Trappers turned away from the few remaining beaver to hunt and sell black raccoon pelts, a resource that played an important part of the regional economy well into the nineteenth century. One scholar even concludes that the Indiana Miamis "lived better" than their white and "emigrant neighbors," suggesting that the Miamis had benefited by resisting removal.[78] Such success was not an aberration or a twist of fate. The Miamis were skilled diplomats and artisans of violence, skills they used to survive European imperialism, nativist militancy, and American expansion. And despite or possibly because of an American society that could only see Indians as static and unchanging, the Indiana Miamis remained on their ancestral homelands. Even the federal government refused to recognize the Indiana Miamis after 1897 in response to their stubborn refusal to leave.

Thoroughly enmeshed in American identity by 1840, the political and racial narrative of Tippecanoe was actually the product of several cross-cultural narratives that exposed the fragility of the Prophet's nativist endeavor, the Miami homeland, and the frontier republic. The fight for the Miami homeland and for Tippecanoe revealed a world where conceptual and physical boundaries were equally permeable and organic. The cross-cultural conflicts were not simply one strand of American nationalism but what one scholar calls its "marrow."[79] For the Miamis, French, nativists, and Americans, the Miami homeland was at once a borderland, frontier, territory, and home. It eventually became part of a nation and a country. Through lies, deceit, violence, and bigotry, Indians and Euroamericans created narratives about the Wabash-Maumee Valley and its inhabitants in order to defend their homelands. Many of these actions seem commonplace, the stuff of a violent frontier, because they were the "ordinary" means through which different and often conflicting cultures constructed and remade local narratives that helped determine the identity of the valley.[80] In the end, Euroamericans laid claim to an American borderland and secured their sovereignty not simply by occupying space but by lying together with the Miamis about their past.

Notes

Preface

1. The longue durée references the French Annales school of history and the preference its scholars had for analyzing broad historical structures over distinct events and personalities. Our understanding of the violence at the Battle of Tippecanoe has long been framed by the personalities of William Henry Harrison, Tecumseh, and the Shawnee Prophet, not to mention the discrete time period of the War of 1812. For the purposes of *The Borderland of Fear*, I wanted to examine violence and social interaction over a broader expanse of time in order to understand the ways in which long-term historical relationships and networks shaped key events such as the Battle of Tippecanoe in November 1811. For more on the longue durée, see Peter Burke, *The French Historical Revolution: The Annales School 1929–1989* (Stanford: Stanford University Press, 1990).

2. Pekka Hämäläinen and Samuel Truett, "On Borderlands," *Journal of American History* 98, no. 2 (2011): 349.

3. David L. Preston, *The Texture of Contact: European and Indian Settler Communities on the Frontiers of Iroquoia, 1667–1783* (Lincoln: University of Nebraska Press, 2009), 12.

4. A second group of publications offer more expansive considerations of the region but continue to frame the actions of individuals and communities within a strict binary of American expansionism versus Indian resistance and nationalism. Cayton's *Frontier Republic*, Gregory Dowd's *A Spirited Resistance*, and Patrick Griffin's *American Leviathan* are considered the definitive texts in the history of pan-Indianism and American territorial expansion during the (I accept all changes on this page) early republic, yet all tie Indian and Euroamerican behavior to the growth of American nationalism. These seminal works tell us a great deal about the growth and unification of the American nation-state and Indian nationalism during the 1790s and early 1800s, but typically assume the inevitable expansion of American nationalism.

Introduction

1. John Badollet to Albert Gallatin, June 7, 1812, in John Louis Badollet and Albert Gallatin, *The Correspondence of John Badollet and Albert Gallatin, 1804–1836*, ed. Gayle Thornbrough (Indianapolis: Indiana Historical Society, 1963), 242.

2. Prophet to William Henry Harrison, August 1, 1808, in *Messages and Letters of William Henry Harrison*, ed. Logan Esarey (Indianapolis: Indiana Historical Commission, 1922), 1:299–300.

3. Alfred A. Cave, *Prophets of the Great Spirit: Native American Revitalization Movements in Eastern North America* (Lincoln: University of Nebraska Press, 2006), 66.

4. Joshua Piker, "Lying Together: The Imperial Implications of Cross-Cultural Untruths," *American Historical Review* 116 (2011): 985. Gregory Dowd looks at a similar process of using lies to stabilize frontier society in his article "The French King Wakes up in Detroit: 'Pontiac's War' in Rumor and History," *Ethnohistory* 37, no. 3 (Summer 1990): 254–78. He argues that "the idea of the French return [to the Ohio Valley after the Seven Years' War] reflected an Indian attempt to manipulate France, to bring back, through war and ceremony, the French counterweight to Anglo-American expansion" (255).

5. Paul Gilje, *The Making of the American Republic, 1763–1815* (Upper Saddle River NJ: Pearson Prentice Hall, 2006), 273.

6. By Miami homeland, I mean the geographical areas moving from present-day northwest Ohio along the Maumee River into present-day Indiana along the Wabash River down to its connection with the Ohio River. The northern reaches of this homeland would be bound at the St. Joseph River in present-day Michigan. For a deeper and more thorough conceptualization of the Miami homeland, see Michael P. Gonella, "*Myaamia* Ethnobotany" (PhD diss., Miami University of Ohio, 2007). Susan Sleeper-Smith challenges scholars to "identify the myths that conditioned past cultural perceptions and reshaped the ideas, ideologies, and discourses of historical narrative" (Sleeper-Smith, *Indian Women and French Men: Rethinking Cultural Encounter in the Western Great Lakes* [Amherst: University of Massachusetts Press, 2001], 148).

7. Several scholars have proven influential for my argument about the Miami homeland and the eventual conflict over Prophetstown. Joshua Piker's *Okfuskee: A Creek Indian Town* (Cambridge: Harvard University Press, 2006) and David Preston's *The Texture of Contact: European and Indian Settlers on the Frontiers of Iroquoia, 1667–1783* (Lincoln: University of Nebraska Press, 2012) engage Native histories on a community level. This has not been done in regard to Prophetstown or the Miami communities on a case-by-case basis. Adam Jortner's *The Gods of Prophetstown: The Battle of Tippecanoe and the Holy War for the American Frontier* (New York: Oxford University Press, 2011) offers an intriguing interpretation of the town itself, but as part of a larger discussion of the "religious" debate between Harrison and the Prophet. Among the most influential studies on these questions include Tracy Neal Leavelle, *The Catholic Calumet: Colonial Conversions in French and Indian North America* (Philadelphia: University of Pennsylvania Press, 2011); Michael Whitgen, *Infinity of Nations: How the Native New World Shaped Early America* (Philadelphia: University of Pennsylvania Press, 2011); and Richard White, *The Middle Ground: Indians, Empires, and Republics in the Great Lakes Region, 1650–1815* (New York: Cambridge University

Press, 1992). John Hall's *Uncommon Defense: Native Allies in the Black Hawk War* (Cambridge: Harvard University Press, 2009) explores the reasons why various Native communities aided the American cause during the Black Hawk war, concluding that they did so within a Native context and hoped to inflict damage upon a historic enemy, the Sauk Indians. For pan-Indianism and Indian militancy, see Gregory Evans Dowd, *War under Heaven: Pontiac, The Indian Nations, and the British Empire* (Baltimore: Johns Hopkins University Press, 2004); David Dixon, *Never Come to Peace Again: Pontiac's Uprising and the Fate of the British Empire in North America* (Norman: University of Oklahoma Press, 2005); Kathleen DuVal, *The Native Ground: Indians and Colonists in the Heart of the Continent* (Philadelphia: University of Pennsylvania Press, 2007); David Silverman, *Red Brethren: The Brothertown and Stockbridge Indians and the Problem of Race in Early America* (Ithaca: Cornell University Press, 2008); and Patrick Griffin, *American Leviathan: Empire, Nation, and the American Frontier* (New York: Macmillan, 2008.

8. Peter Silver, Patrick Griffin, Richard White, Ned Blackhawk, Matthew Jennings, and Stephen Warren have broadened our understanding of the formative nature of violence in early America. See Peter Silver, *Our Savage Neighbors: How Indian War Transformed Early America:* (New York: Norton, 2008); Griffin, *American Leviathan*; Ned Blackhawk, *Violence over the Land: Indians and Empires in the Early American West* (Cambridge: Harvard University Press, 2008; Matthew Jennings, *New Worlds of Violence: Cultures and Conquests in the Early American Southeast* (Knoxville: University of Tennessee Press, 2011); and Stephen Warren, *The Worlds the Shawnees Made: Migration and Violence in Early America* (Chapel Hill: University of North Carolina Press, 2014). In *The Middle Ground*, White details the Americans' refusal to negotiate with Indians, which ushered in a new era of violence in the western Ohio Valley. Both Griffin and Silver build on the violence of the Ohio Valley as a means to discuss the growth of national and racial unity among Euroamerican frontier communities. Ned Blackhawk looks farther west to the Indian peoples of the Great Basin and argues not only that violence not only shaped their world but that several of the Great Basin Indian communities redirected and refashioned violence in order to protect themselves. One group, the Ute, grew in power because of their ability to shape regional violence. Matthew Jennings shifts our focus east in an edited collection that details the complicated nature of competing cultures of violence. He challenges scholars to look at the roots of violence from multiple perspectives and to see it outside of culturally specific boundaries like war and peace. By doing so, we are better situated to include those peoples who have been historically marginalized from the dominant narrative centered on "morality plays about Manifest Destiny and Western Expansion." Stephen Warren's recent work on the Shawnees explores the unique ways in which the Shawnees adapted to various migrations through time to survive the violent outbursts of the Ohio Valley from the fifteenth to the eighteenth century.

9. Pekka Hämäläinen and Samuel Truett, "On Borderlands," *Journal of American History* 98 (2011): 352.

10. Stephen Aron and Jeremy Adelman, "From Borderlands to Borders: Empires, Nation-States, and the Peoples in between in North American History," *American Historical Review* 104 (June 1999): 816; Jane Burbank and Frederick Cooper, *Empires in World History: Power and the Politics of Difference* (Princeton: Princeton University Press, 2010), 8.

11. Hämäläinen and Truett, "On Borderlands," 340, 348. The French, British, and American empires struggled to "maintain distinction and hierarchy as they incorporate[d] new people" and as Indian peoples were able to coerce Europeans into their own systems of power.

12. Thomas A. Chambers, *Memories of War: Visiting Battleground and Bonefields in the Early American Republic* (Ithaca: Cornell University Press, 2012), 16; Ana Maria Alonso, "The Effects of Truth: Re-Presentations of the Past and the Imagining of Community," *Journal of Historical Sociology* 1 (March 1988): 41; Ana Maria Alonso, "The Politics of Space, Time and Substance: State Formation, Nationalism, and Ethnicity," *Annual Review of Anthropology* 23 (1994): 382.

13. An important contribution of this work is the examination of the ways in which local relationships and conflicts fueled the development/construction of ethnic identities and the ways in which institutional memory eventual pulled cultural values and identities forged in private spaces into public ones. For a discussion of ethnicity and nationalism in relation to public and private spaces, see Alonso, "The Politics of Space, Time and Substance," 392, 391.

14. Some recent scholars have challenged the nationalistic dichotomies that have framed examinations of Native-white relationships on the Miami frontier. Robert Owens in *Mr. Jefferson's Hammer: William Henry Harrison and the Origins of Indian Policy* (Norman: University of Oklahoma Press, 2011) examined the extent to which territorial governor William Henry Harrison, rather than President Thomas Jefferson, shaped and defined Indian policy for the western territories. While Owens frames frontier relationships within a traditional nationalistic dichotomy, he nonetheless challenges scholars to examine how local actors reshaped national ideologies. Jay Gitlin's *Bourgeoisie Frontier: French Towns, French Traders, and American Expansion* (New Haven: Yale University Press, 2010) took this one step further. He argues that the French as an ethnic group should be considered as an important influence on frontier society and regional identities. Rather than see the French as subsumed into the American nation-state, Gitlin demonstrates that they found ways to defend their interests despite the influx of American settlers.

15. We must look deeply into the collaborative efforts that Richard White so skillfully evaluated in *The Middle Ground* in order to uncover the ways in which accommodation could be used to defend one group at the expense of another.

16. Hämäläinen and Truett, "On Borderlands," 352; Piker, "Lying Together," 969.

1 / Facing East from Miami Country

1. C. C. Trowbridge, *Meearmeear Traditions*, ed. W. Vernon Kinietz, Occasional Contributions from the Museum of Anthropology of the University of Michigan 7 (Ann Arbor: University of Michigan Press, 1938), 76.

2. Ibid., 75.

3. For more on the constructive nature of violence in early America, see Pekka Hämäläinen, *The Comanche Empire* (New Haven: Yale University Press, 2009); Ned Blackhawk, *Violence over the Land: Indians and Empire in the Early American West* (Cambridge: Harvard University Press, 2008); Peter Silver, *Our Savage Neighbors: How Indian War Transformed Early America* (New York: Norton, 2009); Patrick Griffin, *American Leviathan: Empire, Nation, and the Revolutionary Frontier* (New York: Hill and Wang, 2008); Eric Hinderaker, *Constructing Colonialism in the Ohio Valley,*

1673–1800 (Cambridge: Cambridge University Press, 1999); Gregory Dowd, *A Spirited Resistance: The North American Indian Struggle for Unity, 1745–1815* (Baltimore: Johns Hopkins University Press, 1992); and Richard White, *The Middle Ground: Indians, Empires, and Republics in the Great Lakes Region, 1650–1815* (Cambridge: Cambridge University Press, 1990).

4. Griffin labels the contest between the Americans and British as a "world of failed sovereignty," where self-sovereignty was the only option (Griffin, *American Leviathan*, 150).

5. M. M. Quaife, ed., *A Narrative of Life on the Old Frontier: Henry Hay's Journal from Detroit to the Mississippi River* (Madison: Historical Society of Wisconsin, 1915), 221–32, 225, 231.

6. Ebenezer Denny, *Military Journal of Major Ebenezer Denny* (Philadelphia: Lippincott, 1859), 145; Thomas Hutchins, *A Topographical Description of Virginia, Pennsylvania, Maryland, and North Carolina, Comprehending the Rivers Ohio, Kenhawa, Sioto, Cherokee, Wabash, Illinois, Mississippi* (London: Burlington House, 1778); Wallace A. Brice, *History of Fort Wayne* (Fort Wayne IN: D. W. Jones and Son, 1868), 38.

7. Tracy Neal Leavelle, *The Catholic Calumet: Colonial Conversions in French and Indian America* (Philadelphia: University of Pennsylvania Press, 2011), 8; Theodore Calvin Pease and Raymond Werner, eds., *The French Foundations, 1680–1693*, vol. 1, Collections of the Illinois State Historical Library (Springfield: Illinois Historical Society, 1934), 23, 392–93; Emily J. Blasingham, "The Depopulation of the Illinois Indians," *Ethnohistory* 3, no. 4 (Autumn 1956): 363–73. Estimates from Father Jacques Marquette, Louis Jolliet, and James Mooney placed the number of Illinois Indians between nine thousand and ten thousand during this period. Beauharnois to the French Minister, May 3, 1733, "1733: Letters from the Upper Country Intercepted; Ravages of Smallpox," in *The French Régime in Wisconsin*, ed. Reuben Gold Thwaites, pt. 2, *1727–1748*, Collections of the State Historical Society of Wisconsin (Madison: Wisconsin State Historical Society, 1906), 17:175; Blasingham, "The Depopulation of the Illinois Indians," 14; Harvey Lewis Carter, *The Life and Times of Little Turtle: First Sagamore of the Wabash* (Urbana: University of Illinois Press, 1987), 14; Alfred T. Goodman, ed., *Journal of Captain William Trent from Logstown to Pickawillany* (Cincinnati: Robert Clarke, 1871), 12–34.

8. Trowbridge, *Meeearmeear Traditions*, 4; Michigan Historical Collections, *Historical Collections of the Michigan Pioneer and Historical Society* (Lansing: Michigan Historical Society, 1904) 33:38, 436; Thwaites, ed., *The French Regime in Wisconsin, 1634–1727*, 16:375; Pierre Francois Xavier, S.J., *The History and General Description of New France*, vol. 5 (New York: John Gilmary Shea, 1871), 141; Michael P. Gonella, "*Myaamia* Ethnobotany" (PhD diss., Miami University, 2007), 83.

9. This book references a number of Miami communities that include the Miami proper at Kekionga, other Miami communities at Eel River and Mississinewa, as well as the Weas near Ouiatenon and the Piankashaws near Vincennes. Although this study looks at the distinct differences between these various communities, it also emphasizes that all of these groups were members of a singular Miami ethno-polity marked by a shared Illinois-Miami dialect of Algonquian, similar descent patterns and political structures, and cultural markers.

10. Thwaites, ed., *The French Régime in Wisconsin, 1634–1727*, 16:375. Bert Anson notes that the "Miamis also had a prime source of revenue in the corn they supplied

to traders, soldiers, and other tribes" (Anson, *The Miami Indians* [Norman: University of Oklahoma, 1970], 56–57). Stewart Rafert states that the "Miami strengthened their independence by trading their specialized soft white corn and by levying tolls at the Wabash-Maumee portage" (Rafert, *The Miami Indians of Indiana: A Persistent People, 1654–1994* [Indianapolis: Indiana Historical Society Press, 1996], 33). "As the Miami were beginning to understand economic needs and resources on their own," Rafert notes, "they occupied key portages and learned to trade their soft white corn, in effect diversifying their . . . economy away from the undependable fur market where prices could collapse unexpectedly" (ibid., 23). Thwaites, ed., *The French Régime in Wisconsin, 1634–1727*, 16:285n2, 375; "Memoir on the Savages of Canada as Far as the Mississippi River, Describing Their Customs and Trade, 1718," in *The French Régime in Wisconsin, 1634–1727*, ed. Thwaites, 16:375. For more on this white corn, see Gonella, "*Myaamia* Ethnobotany," 90. Eric Hinderaker states: "Nearly every feature of the empires of trade constructed in the Ohio Valley during the late 17th and 18th centuries worked against the preservation of insularity; like trading contacts everywhere, they tended to create powerful channels of intercultural influence and to blur the lines of power and interest" (Hinderaker, *Elusive Empires: Constructing Colonialism in the Ohio Valley, 1673–1800* [Cambridge University Press, 1997], 2).

11. Henry Rowe Schoolcraft, *Information Respecting the History, Conditions, and Prospects of the Indian Tribes of the United States* (Philadelphia: Lippincott, 1853–57), 5:194–95; Jacob P. Dunn Notebook, 4:75, Jacob P. Dunn Papers, Indiana Division, Indiana State Library, Indianapolis; Gonella, "*Myaamia* Ethnobotany," 89.

12. H. Joutel, *A Journal of the last voyage perform'd by Monsr. De la Sale, to the Gulph of Mexico, to find out the mouth of the Mississippi River* (printed for A. Bell, B. Lintott, and J. Baker, 1714), 110–14; Elizabeth J. Glenn, "Miami and Delaware Trade Routes and Relationships in Northern Indiana, in *Native American Cultures in Indiana: Proceedings of the First Minnestrista Council for Great Lakes Native American Studies*, ed. Ronald Hicks (Muncie IN: Minnetrista Cultural Center and Ball State University, 1992), 63; Rafert, *The Miami Indians*, 34–35.

13. Ramezay and Begon to French Minister, November 7, 1715, in *The French Régime in Wisconsin, 1634–1727*, ed. Thwaites,16:327; Susan Sleeper-Smith, *Indian Women and French Men: Rethinking Cultural Encounters in the Western Great Lakes* (Amherst: University of Massachusetts Press, 2001), 75–76. Anthony Wayne recognized the amount of corn present at Kekionga. He had never "before beheld such immense fields of corn in any part of American from Canada to Florida" (Wayne, Fort Defiance, to Secretary of War, August 14, 1794, in *American State Papers*, Class II, *Indian Affairs*, 1:490–91). Joutel, *A Journal of the last voyage*, 176; Quaife, *A Narrative of Life on the Old Frontier*, 225. In another case, French traders hoped to gain permission from an Indian community so that the Frenchmen could live among Indians. Part of the negotiation process involved a meal: "When the discourse ended, that Chief caus'd meat to be set before us, as dried flesh, bread made of Indian corn of several sorts, and watermelons, after which he made us smoke and then we returned to our house" (Joutel, *A Journal of the last voyage*, 178; Sleeper-Smith, *Indian Women and French Men*, 76–78). In one instance, "three Frenchmen returned . . . from Michilimackinac, who informed us it was not without reason that we had been told that we risked much in attempting to go to Michilimackinac. For eight days the occupants of that post had been as if the tomahawk were suspended over their heads. Two of the principal women in the

village, who had always until then appeared very friendly to the French, went weeping from hut to hut, demanding the death of the French who had killed their brother" (Thwaites, ed., *The French Régime in Wisconsin, 1634–1727*, 6:234).

14. Letter from Governor Vaudreuil, October 14, 1716, in *The Frénch Regime in Wisconsin, 1634–1727*, ed. Thwaites, 16:345; Governor Vaudreuil to Council, October 28, 1719, ibid., 16:382; Governor Vaudreuil to Council, October 22, 1720, ibid., 16:395.

15. *Henry Hamilton and George Rogers Clark in the American Revolution with the Unpublished Journal of Lieutenant Governor Henry Hamilton,* ed. John D. Barnhart (Crawfordsville IN: R. E. Banta, 1951), 134–35.

16. The French recognized early on that they needed to be in close proximity to the Miamis in order to engage the Miami trade. Ramezay and Begon to French Minister, November 7, 1715; Governor Vaudreuil to Council, October 28, 1719, in *The French Régime in Wisconsin, 1634–1727*, ed. Thwaites, 16:332; from Bienville and Salmon to the Minister, dated May 20, 1733, in Jacob Piatt Dunn, *The Mission to the Ouabache* (Indianapolis: Bowen-Merrill, 1902), 301. This is a comparison made to U.S. efforts to destroy Miami agriculture in the late eighteenth century by burning Miami crops, destroying their villages, and razing Kekionga. Rafert, *The Miami Indians,* 24; Report of de Bienville, July 27, 1734, in Dunn, *The Mission to the Ouabache,* 330; Speeches by Indian Tribes to Beauharnois, July 8, 1742, in "Speeches of the Ouyatanons, Petikokias, Kikapoux, and Maskoutins," in *The French Régime in Wisconsin, 1634–1727,* ed. Thwaites, 17:380–87; "Reasons for Establishing a Colony in Illinois," July 10, 1766, in *The New Régime, 1765–1767,* ed. Clarence Alvord and Clarence Carter, Collections of the Illinois State Historical Society (Springfield: Illinois State Historical Library, 1916), 11:250.

17. Jervase Cutler, *A Topographical Description of the State of Ohio, Indiana Territory, and Louisiana* (Boston: Charles Williams, 1812); Beauharnois and Hocquart to the French Minister, October 14, 1733, in "1733: Indians of the Upper Country; Foxes; Shawnee; Illinois," in *The French Régime in Wisconsin,* ed. Thwaites, 17:184–87. Croghan describes Kekionga as consisting of "forty or fifty cabins, besides nine or ten French houses," with "soil rich and well watered" ("August 1st" in *Early Western Travels, 1748–1846,* ed. Reuben Gold Thwaites [Cleveland OH: A. H. Clark, 1904], 1:149–50).

18. Raymond to La Jonquiere, October 11, 1749, in *Illinois on the Eve of the Seven Years' War,* ed. Theodore Calvin Pease and Ernestine Jenison (Springfield IL: State Historical Society, 1940), 119–21; White, *The Middle Ground,* 216. The report to Raymond states that Memeskia's band "had won all the Miami of Le Pied Froid's band who had promised them to abandon their village to settle them at Great Miami River," demonstrating that the destruction of Le Pied Froid's settlement at Kekionga was more about incorporation than killing one's fellow Miamis. Charles de Raymond to La Jonquiere, September 4, 1749, in Archives Nationales, Ministere des Colonies, C11A 93:62, and in *Illinois on the Eve,* ed. Pease and Jenision, 105–8; Raymond on the Miami, October 1749, ibid., 122–24; Reports to Raymond, March–April, 1750, ibid., 169, 166–88; Raymond to Rouillé, October 1, 1751, ibid., 393–401; Reports to Raymond, March–April, 1750, ibid., 169; Reports to Raymond, May 1750, ibid., 194.

19. "In the year 1749, of the reign of Louis the 15th, King of France, we Céloron, commander of a detachment sent by Monsieur the Marquis de la Galissoniere, Governor General of New France, to reestablish tranquility in some Indian villages of these cantons, have buried this Plate of Lead at the confluence of the Ohio and the

Chadakoin, this 29th day of July, near the river Ohio, otherwise Belle Riviere, as a monument of the renewal of the possession we have taken of the said river Ohio and of all those which empty into it, and of all the lands on both sides as far as the sources of the said rivers, as enjoyed or ought to have been enjoyed by the kings of France preceding and as they have there maintained themselves by arms and by treaties, especially those of Ryswick, Utrecht and Aix-la-Chapelle" (in William J. Campbell, *Speculators in Empire: Iroquoia and the 1768 Treaty of Fort Stanwix* [Norman: University of Oklahoma Press, 2015], 40). Celeron to Vaudreuil, April 23, 1751, in *Illinois on the Eve*, ed. Pease and Jenison, 194.

20. Here our vocabulary for discussing diplomatic relationships between the Miamis and Europeans is ineffective. The term "faction" itself speaks to partisan interests, which in the case of the Miamis typically refer to their relationships with Europeans. Does the term "faction" adequately address the ways in which the Miami saw themselves and their neighboring communities? Erminie Wheeler-Voegelin, Emily J. Blasingham, and Dorothy R. Libby, eds., *An Anthropological Report on the History of the Miamis, Weas, and Eel River Indians—Summary of Piankashaw Locations*, 2 vols. (New York: Garland, 1974), 1:31; English Translation of Margry, 6:710–72, in Pierre Margry, *Decouvertes et establissements des Francais dans l'Ouest et dans le sud de l'Amerique septentrionale (1614–1754). Memoires et documents originaux recueillis et publies par Pierre Margry*, 6 vols. (Paris, 1888). Three Miamis signed the Treaty of Lancaster with the British in July 1748. Wheeler-Voegelin, Blasingham, and Libby, eds., *An Anthropological Report*, 1:30. Although the Miamis used violence to their advantage, Europeans were often not so fortunate. By the mid-1700s, the Piankashaws found themselves the target of a trade war between the French and British. Traditionally, the Piankashaws had migrated back and forth between Vincennes, the Vermilion River village, and Fort Ouiatenon. However, in 1752 many Piankashaws settled along the White and Great Miami Rivers near British settlements such as Pickawillany to trade with the English. In a desperate attempt to regain influence among the Miamis, the French attacked the pro-British settlement in 1751. Word that some of the Miamis had signed a treaty of friendship with the British in 1748 and again in 1750 had made its way to the French. But the French failed to displace the British until a métis leader, Charles de Langlade, and a force of Ottawa and Ojibwe warriors destroyed Pickawillany in 1752. Playing the middle, very few Miamis joined the fight to defend the British trade center. Like Memeskia's attack on Piedfroid's settlement in 1747, the violence did not prove disastrous for the Miamis or polarize relationships between them and the French. Instead, the Miamis who settled near the British moved to their former settlements at Ouiatenon and Kekionga, where the French eagerly welcomed them back. Charles Raymond to La Jonquiere, October 11, 1749, in *Illinois on the Eve*, ed. Pease and Jenison, 122–24; Charles Raymond to La Jonquiere, October 11, 1749, ibid., 120.

21. Captain Trent to Governor Dinwiddie, July 6, 1752, in *Journal of Captain William Trent from Logstown to Pickawillany*, ed. Alfred T. Goodman (Cincinnati: Robert Clarke., 1871), 87–90; Wheeler-Voegelin, Blasingham, and Libby, eds., *An Anthropological Report*, 1:37; Marquis Michel-Ange, Duquesne de Menneville, to Rouillé, October 31, 1753, in *Illinois on the Eve*, ed. Pease and Jenison, 843.

22. Lois Mulkearn, ed., *George Mercer Papers: Relating to the Ohio Company of Virginia* (Pittsburgh: University of Pittsburgh Press, 1954), 19; Sieur de Vincennes to St. Ange, March 7, 1733, in Dunn, *Mission to the Ouabache*, 302–4.

23. Arrell Gibson, *The Kickapoos: Lords of the Middle Border* (Norman: University of Oklahoma Press, 1976), 21; Raymond to La Jonquiere, in Archives Nationales, Ministere des Colonies, C11A 93:62, and in *Illinois on the Eve*, ed. Pease and Jenison, 105-8.

24. White, *The Middle Ground*, 174-77.

25. Rafert, *The Miami Indians*, 33-34; Adelman and Aron, "From Borderlands to Borders," 816. Stewart Rafert lists the various commodities the Miamis incorporated into their communities (Rafert, *The Miami Indians*, 33-34).

26. Stephen Aron and Jeremy Adelman describe the ability of the Miamis to play the French and British against each other as only preserving "the patina of Indian autonomy" (Adelman and Aron, "From Borderlands to Borders," 821).

27. Hämäläinen and Truett suggest looking at Native boundaries of power outside of traditional Western concepts. Indeed, the Miami world was "characterized by informality, autonomy, fluidity, and isolation from states" (Hämäläinen and Truett, "On Borderlands," 345). Mulkearn, ed., *George Mercer Papers*, 19.

28. The Miami situation reflects Pekka Hämäläinen's assertion that scholars ought to revisit "North American history as a history of entanglements—of shifting accommodations—rather than one of expansion" (Hämäläinen and Truett, "On Borderlands," 347).

29. Capt. Donald Campbell to Col. Bouquet, December 11, 1760, in *The Papers of Col. Henry Bouquet*, ed. Sylvester K. Stevens and Donald H. Kent, ser. 21645 (Harrisburg: Pennsylvania Historical Commission, 1941), 223-25; Rafert, *The Miami Indians*, 41; Carter, *Life and Times of Little Turtle*, 68.

30. "The Journal of Captain Thomas Morris of His Majesty's XVII Regiment of Infantry," in *Early Western Travels, 1748–1846*, ed. Thwaites, 1:316, 316-18.

31. "The George Croghan Journal, May 15, 1765–October 8, 1765," in *The New Regime, 1765-1767*, ed. Alvord and Carter, 11:36; White, *The Middle Ground*, 325.

32. Duquesne to Rouille, October 27, 1753, in *Illinois on the Eve*, ed. Pease and Jenison, 838-39; Duquesne to Rouille, October 31, 1753, ibid., 843-44, 838-45. As Rafert argues, "Change for the Miami was selective and permissive rather than coercive" (Rafert, *The Miami Indians*, 34).

33. Rafert, *The Miami Indians*, 27-30. Though Kekionga increasingly served as the center for trade in the Wabash-Maumee region after 1763, the Miamis had not forgotten about their historical connection to Vincennes and its importance to trade. Located between Kekionga and St. Louis, and north of New Orleans, Vincennes proved to be an important stopping point for trade missions given its location along the Wabash River, which connected the waters flowing south from the Great Lakes to the western run of the Ohio River. Vincennes was a heterogeneous village of close to 250 French settlers, African and Indian slaves, several British traders, and Indians, mostly Piankashaws. Although the fur trade dominated the local economy, French agricultural production boomed as well, contrary to British and American claims that the French were lazy and unproductive. The French purposely produced an agricultural surplus—more than 10,000 bushels of corn and 36,000 pounds of tobacco in 1767 so that they could purchase rum, wine, and manufactured goods from New Orleans, which they in turn exchanged for furs from Indian communities. Furthermore, after Britain defeated France in the Seven Years' War, the Miamis continued to court trading relationships with whomever they pleased and eagerly sought out French and Spanish traders near St. Louis. According to Spanish records, several representatives

of Miami-speaking Indians traveled to St. Louis in 1769 to receive gifts, despite the efforts by George Croghan and the British to expand British influence throughout the Illinois country. Griffin, *American Leviathan*, 143.

34. "The Unpublished Journal of Henry Hamilton, 1778–1779," Vincennes, December 18, 1778, to February 22, 1779, in *Henry Hamilton and George Rogers Clark in the American Revolution*, ed. John D. Barnhart (Crawfordsville IN: R. E. Banta, 1951), 112, 152–53, 151–52; 164–65.

35. Joseph Bowman, journal, January 29, 1779–March 20, 1779, in *George Rogers Clark Papers, 1771–1781*, ed. James Alton James, vol. 8 of *Collections of the Illinois State Historical Library* (Springfield: Illinois State Historical Library, 1912), 163; Arent S. De Peyster to McKee, June 13, 1782, in Michigan Pioneer and Historical Society, *Pioneer Collections: Collections and Researches Made by the Pioneer Society of the State of Michigan* (Lansing: Wynkoop, Hallenbeck, Crawford, 1908), 10:378–79; Wheeler-Voegelin, Blasingham, and Libby, eds., *An Anthropological Report*, 1:50–52, 51; "Hamilton's Councils, June and July 1778," in *Collections of the Illinois State Historical Library*, H. W. Beckwith (Springfield: R. W. Rokker, 1903), 1:319–20; Gibson, *The Kickapoos*, 36; Arent S. De Peyster to McKee, June 13, 1782, in Michigan Pioneer and Historical Society, *Pioneer Collections*, 10:586.

36. According to Bradley J. Birzer, August de la Balme and his force "hoped ultimately to take their plunder from Kekionga (present-day Fort Wayne, Indiana) and Detroit [their eventual destination] to the early American capital of Philadelphia. There, they would present the claims of the French residing in Vincennes and Kaskaskia against the Virginia government." Birzer frames his discussion of de la Balme within American nationalism, stating that the ultimate goal of the French was to use the American government to protect themselves from the Virginians and British agent Charles Beaubien (Birzer, "French Imperial Remnants on the Middle Ground: The Strange Case of August de la Balme and Charles Beaubien," *Journal of the Illinois State Historical Society* 93 [Summer 2000]: 138–40).

37. Rafert, *The Miami Indians*, 44; M. P. Le Gras to Clark, December 1, 1780, in *George Rogers Clark Papers, 1771–1781*, ed. James, 469; Anson, *The Miami Indians*, 91; Birzer, "French Imperial Remnants," 147. "The Little Turtle is not considered a Miami. A Frenchman, who traded from the Mississippi to the Lakes, purchased in the west an Iowau [*sic*] girl and adopted her as his daughter. In one of his subsequent visits from Montreal he employed a Mohiccan [*sic*] Indian, partly civilized to accompany him in capacity of a servant. In the Kickapoo country the master & man became engaged in battle and the former was wounded in the thigh. The Mohiccan carried him, with incredible labour & fatigue to the Miami village and when he had reached there the grateful Frenchman poured out his lamentations because he had lost all his goods and had no means to reward him. The Mohiccan offered to accept of the Iioawau [*sic*] girl & the other consented. They were married, settled among the Miamies & had a great many children, of whom the eldest was Little Turtle" (Trowbridge, *Meearmeear Traditions*, 87).

38. "Flying under a French flag to ward off potentially hostile Indians, some one-hundred men accompanied de la Balme as they departed for Kekionga and Detroit. They arrived at Ouiatenon on October 20, 1780, and nearly forty men, for unknown reasons, deserted the expedition" (Birzer, "French Imperial Remnants," 144, 144–45). For more on this event, see Karen Marrero, "'She Is Capable of Doing a Good Deal

of Mischief': A Miami Woman's Threat to Empire in the Eighteenth-Century Ohio Valley," *Journal of Colonialism and Colonial History* 6, no. 3 (Winter 2005); Birzer, "French Imperial Remnants," 145. According to Birzer, "Whichever side controlled the Long Portage—the eight-mile strip of land connecting the Wabash and Maumee Rivers—controlled the entrance either to Detroit or to Vincennes. If the British and their allies controlled the portage, they could use it both to attack rebels to the south, and to protect Detroit from attacks from the south. The counter was true as well. If the rebels controlled the portage, they could use it as a base to attack Detroit. Control of the portage also meant controlling the interior of the continent, as it provided the shortest and most efficient link between the St. Lawrence and Mississippi river systems." Birzer goes on to say that "the portage, and the Miamis and their allies who controlled it, was the key to success in the West for both the British and the rebels," implying that it was the Miamis who controlled the portage. Four pages later, Birzer states that the Miamis asked the British for permission to attack Vincennes, once again framing the Miamis' behavior as a product of British imperialism, when in fact such rhetoric was likely more the product of a shared misunderstanding of power relationships underlying diplomatic negotiations as described in detail by Richard White (Birzer, "French Imperial Remnants," 149). A. S. de Peyster, Detroit, to Lt. Col. Mason Bolton, June 27, 1780, in Michigan Pioneer and Historical Society, *Historical Collections: Collections and Researches Made by the Michigan Pioneer and Historical Society* (Lansing MI: Robert Smith, 1891), 19:537; Le Gris and Le Gross Loup, Ft. Miamis, to Capt. Lernoult, June 28, 1779, ibid., 19:443; and A. S. de Peyster, Detroit, to Lt. Col. Mason Bolton, July 6, 1780, ibid., 19:540.

39. Journal of Henry Hay, from Detroit to the Miami River, December 9, 1789, to April 3, 1790, vol. 7 in M. M. Quaife, *Fort Wayne in 1790*, Indiana Historical Society Publications no. 7 (Greenfield, IN: William Mitchell, 1921), 317.

40. Josiah Harmar to Henry Knox, November 24, 1787, in *Outpost on the Wabash, 1787–1791*, ed. Gayle Thornbrough, Indiana Historical Society Publications (Indianapolis: Indiana Historical Society, 1957), 19:46–57; Harmar to General Knox, November 24, 1787, in Ebenezer Denny, *Military Journal of Major Ebenezer Denny* (Philadelphia: Lippincott, 1859), 218; Wilson, "Vincennes," 244; White, *The Middle Ground*, 429, 430.

41. Governor St. Clair to the Secretary of War including Mr. Gamelin's Journal, August 23, 1790, vol. 1 of *American State Papers: Indian Affairs and the Northwest Indians, March 3, 1789 to March 3, 1815* (Washington DC: GPO, 1832), 93.

42 Joseph Valliere to Miro, January 12, 1790, in *Spain in the Mississippi Valley*, ed. Lawrence Kinnaird (Washington DC: AHA, 1945), 3:292; Wheeler-Voegelin, Blasingham, and Libby, eds., *An Anthropological Report*, 1:72; Kathleen DuVal, *The Native Ground: Indians and Colonists in the Heart of the Continent* (Philadelphia: University of Pennsylvania Press, 2007), 161–62.

43. For Pacanne's speech on behalf of the English, in 1781, see Michigan Pioneer and Historical Society, *Historical Collections*, 19:595–96.

44. Wheeler-Voegelin, Blasingham, and Libby, eds., *An Anthropological Report*, 1:58; Joseph Valliere to Miro, January 12, 1790, in *Post War Decade, 1782–1791*, vol. 2 of Kinnaird, ed., *Spain in the Mississippi Valley*, 292–94; Arent S. De Peyster to McKee, June 13, 1782, in Michigan Pioneer and Historical Society, *Pioneer Collections*, 10:586–87; Arent S. De Peyster to Haldimand, May 3, 1783, ibid., 11:362–63; DuVal, *The Native*

Ground, 161–62; J. M. P. Le Gras to Clark, July 22, 1786, in *Spain in the Mississippi Valley*, ed. Kinnaird, 3:179, 335.

45. Secretary Sargeant to Governor St. Clair, August 17, 1790, in *The Territorial Papers of the United States*, ed. Clarence Edwin Carter, vol. 2, *The Territory North-west of the River Ohio, 1787–1803* (Washington DC: GPO, 1934), 300; Griffin, *American Leviathan*, 215, 194–202, 203.

46. St. Clair to President, May 1, 1790. in *The Territorial Papers of the United States*, ed. Carter, 2:245; Secretary Sargeant to Governor St. Clair, August 17, 1790, ibid., 301; Winthrop Sargent to John Francis Hamtramck, July 16, 1790, in *The Territorial Papers of the United States*, ed. Carter, vol. 3, *The Territory Northwest of the River Ohio, 1787–1803* (Washington DC: GPO, 1934), 320–21; Governor St. Clair to the Secretary of War, Fort Steuben, January 26, 1790, in *The St. Clair Papers*, ed. William Henry Smith, (Cincinnati: Robert Clarke, 1882), 132; Major Hamtramck to Governor St. Clair, March 19, 1790, ibid.,132.

47. Wilson, "Vincennes," 260.

48. "The Record of the Court at Upland in Pennsylvania, 1676 to 1681 and a Military Journal Kept by Major E. Denny, 1781 to 1795," in *Record of Upland, and Denny's Military Journal*, vol.7 of Pennsylvania Historical Society, *Memoirs of the Historical Society of Pennsylvania* (Philadelphia: Lippincott, 1860), 349; Rufus Putnam, *The Memoirs of Rufus Putnam*, ed. Rowena Buell (Boston: Houghton Mifflin, 1903), 119–21; Rufus Putnam to General Knox, Ft. Washington, July 5, 1792, ibid., 273–78.

49. John Marshall, qtd. in Steven Boyd, ed., *The Whiskey Rebellion: Past and Present Perspectives* (Westport CT: Greenwood, 1985), 97.

50. Walter Lowrie and Matthew St. Claire Clark, eds., *American State Papers: Indian Affairs*, 2 vols. (Washington DC: Gales and Seaton, 1832–34), 1:490; Land Ordinance of 1785 and Northwest Ordinance of 1787, qtd. in Andrew R. L. Cayton, *Frontier Indiana: A History of the Trans-Appalachian Frontier* (Bloomington: Indiana University Press, 1996), 109.

51. Timothy Willig, "Prophetstown on the Wabash: The Native Spiritual Defense of the Old Northwest," *Michigan Historical Review* 23, no. 2 (Fall 1997): 120.

52. Little Turtle in Council, July 22, 1795, *American State Papers: Indian Affairs*, 1:570–71; Lowrie and Clark, July 22, 1795, ibid., 1:570–71.

53. Ibid., 1:570–71, 571.

54. Ibid., 1:571.

55. Ibid., 1:574; Martha E Tyson, ed., *A Mission to the Indians from the Indian Committee of Baltimore Yearly Meeting, to Fort Wayne, In 1804. Written at the time, by Gerald T. Hopkins* (Philadelphia: T. Ellwood Zell, 1862), 66; Samuel G. Drake, *The Book of the Indians of North America* (Boston: Josiah Drake, 1833), 57.

56. Rafert, *The Miami Indians*, 53; Treaty of Greenville, 1795, in *Encyclopedia of Minorities in American Politics*, ed. Jeffrey D. Schultz, Kerry L. Haynie, Anne M. McCulloch, and Andrew L. Aoki, eds., vol. 2, *Hispanic Americans and Native Americans* (Phoenix AZ: Oryx, 2000), 724–26.

57. Lowrie and Clark, July 22, 1795, *American State Papers: Indian Affairs*, 1:577.

58. Rafert, *The Miami Indians*, 60; Gibson, *The Kickapoos*, 48–49.

59. Edmunds, *The Potawatomies*, 16–17; Stephen Warren, *The Shawnee and Their Neighbors, 1795–1870* (Urbana: University of Illinois Press, 2008), 25–26.

60. Henry Dearborn to William Henry Harrison, June 17, 1802, in William Henry Harrison, *The Papers of William Henry Harrison, 1800–1815* [henceforth cited as *WHH Papers*], ed. Douglas E. Clanin and Ruth Dorrel (Indianapolis: Indiana Historical Society, 1994), text-fiche, reel 1, 315–24; White, *The Middle Ground*, 430–31.

61. Carter, *The Life and Times of Little Turtle*, 170–71.

62. Clarence Edwin Carter, ed., *The Territory of Indiana, 1800–1810*, vol. 7 of *The Territorial Papers of the United States* (Washington DC: GPO, 1939), 92; Moses Dawson, *A Historical Narrative of the Civil and Military Services of Major-General William H. Harrison, and a Vindication of His Character and Conduct as a Statesman, a Citizen, and a Soldier* (Cincinnati OH: M. Dawson, 1824), 52; Harrison to the Secretary of War, March 3, 1803, in *Messages and Letters of William Henry Harrison*, ed. Logan Esarey, vol. 1, *Governors Messages and Letters* (Indianapolis: Indiana Historical Commission, 1922), 76.

63. Wheeler-Voegelin, Blasingham, and Libby, eds., *An Anthropological Report*, 1:74.

2 / The National Trinity

1. Benjamin Stickney to William Eustis, July 19, 1812, in *Letter Book of the Indian Agency at Fort Wayne, 1809–1815*, ed. Gayle Thornbrough (Indianapolis: Indiana Historical Society, 1961), 162–63 Adam Jortner discounts the national trinity as a "ruse" because the Prophet continued to plan for war. But given the Prophet's own inability to control his followers and the Americans' desire for peace, the Prophet could easily have been marshaling his forces to defend Prophetstown instead of preparing for war. His suggestion of a national trinity may have been defensive instead of offensive. In fact, the Kickapoo Indian whom Jortner cites may have had his own agenda and may have used the idea of the Prophet to gather support. A deeper examination of the Kickapoos during this period is needed (Jortner, *The Gods of Prophetstown: The Battle of Tippecanoe and the Holy War for the American Frontier* [New York: Oxford University Press, 2012], 209). Clarence Edwin Carter, ed., *The Territorial Papers of the United States*, vol. 14, *The Territory of Louisiana-Missouri, 1806–1814* (Washington DC: GPO, 1949), 578; Stickney to Capt. Nathan Heald, April 29, 1812, in *Letter Book*, ed. Thornbrough, 114.

2. Jeremy Adelman and Stephen Aron, "From Borderlands to Borders: Empires, Nation-States, and the Peoples in Between in North American History," *American Historical Review* 104, no. 3 (June 1999): 815. Gregory Dowd breaks Indians into two groups—nativists and accommodationists—that either resisted or aided American expansion in *A Spirited Resistance: The North American Indian Struggle for Unity, 1745–1815* (Baltimore: Johns Hopkins University Press, 1992). In his analysis of the frontier republic, Andrew Cayton posits settlers as embodying Revolutionary political ideologies (Cayton, *The Frontier Republic: Ideology and Politics in the Ohio Country, 1780–1825* [Kent OH: Kent State University Press, 1986], x–xi). Eric Hinderaker concludes that the supremacy of whites and American law on the frontier "ensured rapid access to western property, and made every white person in the west an effective agent of empire" (Hinderaker, *Elusive Empires: Constructing Colonialism in the Ohio Valley, 1763–1800* [Cambridge: Cambridge University Press, 1997], 266). This dynamic extended into the early republic and should be expanded to nonwhites as well since

the Miamis and French found ways to defend their ethnic interests while also shaping the formation of Indiana Territory.

3. Amanda Cobb, "Understanding Tribal Sovereignty: Definitions, Conceptualizations, and Interpretations" *American Studies* 46, no. 3/4 (Fall/Winter 2005): 115–32.

4. C. F. Volney, *A View of the Soil and Climate of the United States of America: With Supplementary Remarks upon Florida; on the French Colonies on the Mississippi and Ohio, and in Canada; and on the Aboriginal Tribes of America* (Philadelphia: J. Conrad, 1804), 382; Henry Dearborn to William Henry Harrison, January 17, 1805, in *WHH Papers*, reel 2, 78.

5. Harrison to Dearborn, March 3, 1805, in *WHH Papers*, reel 2, 104; Harrison to Dearborn, August 26, 1805, ibid., reel 2, 324.

6. Moses Dawson, *A Historical Narrative of the Civil and Military Services of Major-General William H. Harrison, and a Vindication of His Character and Conduct as a Statesman, a Citizen, and a Soldier* (Cincinnati OH: M. Dawson, 1824), 48.

7. Harrison to Dearborn, Vincennes, March 3, 1803, United States National Archives RG 107, Old Army H-346(2), pp. 6, 7; Harrison to Secretary of War, March 3, 1803, in *Messages and Letters of William Henry Harrison*, ed. Logan Esarey, vol. 1, *Governors Messages and Letters* (Indianapolis: Indiana Historical Commission, 1922), 83; Dawson, *Historical Narrative of William Henry Harrison*, 52.

8. Robert Mann, "The Silenced Miami: Archaeological and Ethnohistorical Evidence for Miami-British Relations, 1795–1812," *Ethnohistory* 46 (Summer 1999): 402, 404.

9. Mann states that "the pivotal year in the renewal of the 'chain of friendship'" was 1807, when a "British naval action against a supposedly neutral U.S. vessel, the USS *Chesapeake* . . . led the British to turn once more to their Native American allies" (ibid., 407). Mann also says that after 1809 "some conservative Miamis had indeed rekindled fictive kin relations with the British who were invoking them in their struggle to maintain the ability to reproduce their identity" (ibid., 410).

10. William Wells to Gen. James Wilkinson, Ft. Wayne, October 6, 1804, United States National Archives RG 107, War Department Secretary of War, Letters Received, W-469(2); Minutes of a Council held at Fort Wayne, June 21, 1805, Signed J. J. [John Johnston?] Enc. with letter from Harrison to Dearborn, Vincennes, July 10, 1805, United States National Archives RG 107, Old Army H-325(2); Erminie Wheeler-Voegelin, Emily J. Blasingham, and Dorothy R. Libby, eds., *An Anthropological Report on the History of the Miamis, Weas, and Eel River Indians—Summary of Piankashaw Locations*, 2 vols. (New York: Garland, 1974), 2:226; Harrison to Secretary of War, August 26, 1805, *American State Papers: Indian Affairs and the Northwest Indians, March 3, 1789 to March 3, 1815*, vol. 1 (Washington DC: GPO, 1832), 1:701; *Messages and Letters of Harrison*, ed. Esarey, 162.

11. Treaty of Grouseland, art. 4, 1805; Treaty of Grouseland, art. 4, 1805; Harrison to Dearborn, August 26, 1805, in *Messages and Letters of Harrison*, ed. Esarey, 1:164.

12. Gerard T. Hopkins, journal, April 9–12, 1804, Collection Am. 081 Pennsylvania Historical Society (Phi 291), Philadelphia PA, n.p.; Volney, *A View of the Soil*, 362.

13. Volney, *A View of the Soil*, 378; Harrison to Dearborn, August 26, 1805, *American State Papers: Indian Affairs*, 1:702.

14. Alfred A. Cave, *Prophets of the Great Spirit: Native American Revitalization Movements in Eastern North America* (Lincoln: University of Nebraska Press, 2006), 65, 91–92.

15. Ibid., 92. Alfred Cave is the only scholar who offers an interpretation of the Greenville settlement as being devoted to Shawnee renewal. He states that "the brothers hoped that Greenville would be recognized as the new center of Shawnee life, that Shawnees from all over the continent would gather there. In that expectation they were disappointed, but Greenville did attract visitors from numerous other Algonquian nations" (ibid.). Yet Stephen Warren states that Tenskwatawa "founded a multiethnic religious community at Greenville, Ohio based on the principle of separation from Americans" (Warren, *The Shawnees and Their Neighbors, 1795–1870* [Urbana: Illinois University Press, 2005], 27). Gregory Dowd argues that the Prophet used his settlement at Greenville "to make provision to receive and instruct all from the different tribes that were willing to be good" (Dowd, *A Spirited Resistance,* 136). Given the contradictory statements, it makes sense to look at the primary sources cited for such conclusions. Dowd cites a nineteenth-century source by Richard McNemar on Kentucky revivals, and Alfred Cave uses sources from both the nineteenth and twentieth centuries (MacLean's "Shaker Mission," Andrews's "Shaker Mission," Sugden's *Tecumseh,* and Willig's "Prophetstown on the Wabash").

16. William Wells to Harrison, June 1807, in *WHH Papers,* reel 2, 827. Iroquois and Algonquian Indians gathered at the Glaize in the early 1790s to discuss a permanent boundary line between Indian country and the United States, but they divided over the benefits of continued militancy (Helen Hornbeck Tanner, "The Glaize in 1792: A Composite Indian Community," *Ethnohistory* 25, no. 1 [Winter 1978]: 15–39).

17. R. David Edmunds, "Forgotten Allies: The Loyal Shawnees and the War of 1812," in *The Sixty Years' War for the Great Lakes, 1754–1814,* ed. David C. Skaggs and Larry L. Nelson (East Lansing: Michigan State University Press, 2001), 339; Edmunds, "The Loyal Shawnees," 339.

18. Warren, *The Shawnee and Their Neighbors,* 47, 19.

19. Harrison to Dearborn, July 11, 1807, in *Messages and Letters of Harrison,* ed. Esarey, 224; Wells to Harrison, June 1807, in *WHH Papers,* reel 2, 829, 900.

20. Wells to Harrison, August 1807, in *WHH Papers,* reel 2, 900–901.

21. John Johnston to Dearborn, Ft. Wayne, May 31, 1807, Potawatomi File, Great Lakes Indian Archives; Wells to Harrison, August 1807, in *WHH Papers,* reel 2, 920.

22. R. David Edmunds, *The Potawatomis: Keepers of the Fire* (Norman: University of Oklahoma Press, 1978), 166–67.

23. Wells to Dearborn, April 20, 1808, in *The Territorial Papers of the United States,* ed. Clarence Edwin Carter, vol. 7, *The Territory of Indiana, 1800–1810* (Washington DC: GPO), 1939), 556.

24. Edmunds, *Keepers of the Fire,* 156.

25. Stewart Rafert, *The Miami Indians of Indiana: A Persistent People, 1654–1994* (Indianapolis: Indiana Historical Society Press, 1996), 71.

26. Stephen Warren and Randolph Noe, "'The Greatest Travelers in America': Shawnee Survival in the Shatter Zone," in *Mapping the Mississippian Shatter Zone: The Colonial Indian Slave Trade and Regional Instability in the American South,* ed. Robbie Ethridge and Sheri Shuck-Hall (Lincoln: University of Nebraska Press, 2009), 168, 350, 334. Warren and Noe argue that for the Shawnee, "diplomatic considerations outweighed any long-standing attachments to homeland. The vicissitudes of trade and alliance determined migration patterns" (167). Hinderaker, *Elusive Empires,* 48; Susan Sleeper-Smith, *Indian Women and French Men: Rethinking*

Cultural Encounters in the Western Great Lakes (Amherst: University of Massachusetts Press, 2001), 87–89.

27. Kathleen DuVal, *The Native Ground: Indians and Colonists in the Heart of the Continent* (Philadelphia: University of Pennsylvania Press, 2007), 5.

28. Andrew R. L. Cayton, "Race, Democracy, and the Multiple Meanings of the Indiana Frontier," in *Indiana Territory: A Bicentennial Perspective*, ed. Darrel E. Bigham (Indianapolis: Indiana Historical Society, 2001), 57.

29. Richard White, *The Middle Ground: Indians, Empires, and Republics in the Great Lakes Region, 1650–1815* (Cambridge: Cambridge University Press, 1991), 425. The existence of and debate over slavery in the western Ohio Valley, although unique to the Anglicized political culture of Vincennes in this case, was much older in the region, as explored in Brett Rushforth, *Bond's of Alliance: Indigenous and African Slavery in New France* (Chapel Hill: University of North Carolina Press, 2012).

30. *Western Sun* (Vincennes IN), September 3, 1808; Volney, *A View of the Soil*, 22, 23.

31. Volney, *A View of the Soil*, 23; John Badollet to Albert Gallatin, June 27, 1807, in John Louis Badollet and Albert Gallatin, *The Correspondence of John Badollet and Albert Gallatin, 1804–1836*, ed. Gayle Thornbrough (Indianapolis: Indiana Historical Society, 1963), 79; Badollet to Gallatin, January 1, 1806, ibid., 57; Badollet to Gallatin, June 27, 1807, ibid., 79; Hinderaker, *Elusive Empires*, 263.

32. Jennings to Mitchell, September 19, 1807, in Jonathan Jennings, *Unedited Letters of Jonathan Jennings: With Notes by Dorothy Riker*, ed. Dorothy L. Riker (Indianapolis: Indiana Historical Society Publications, 1932), 163; Allen Greer, "Commons and Enclosure in the Colonization of North America," *American Historical Review* 117, no. 2 (April 2012): 366; Charles Larrabee to Adam Larrabee, Ft. Knox, Indiana Territory, February 7, 1812, in Charles Larrabee, "Lieutenant Charles Larrabee's Account of the Battle of Tippecanoe, 1811," ed. Florence G. Watts, *Indiana Magazine of History* 57, no. 3 (September 1961): 225–47. Charles Larrabee (1782–1862) was a member of the Fourth Army Regiment who wrote five letters to his cousin Adam Larrabee (d. 1869), a second lieutenant. Charles had been stationed in Pittsburgh when he was transferred to Indiana Territory and traveled to Prophetstown under Colonel Boyd. Volney, *A View of the Soil*, 20–25.

33. James Hall, *A Memoir of the Public Services of William Henry Harrison of Ohio* (Philadelphia: Key and Biddle, 1836), 99.

34. Although this chapter examines the disputes over slavery and Indian affairs starting in 1807, there was indeed factionalism over Indian affairs before 1807. A person signing with the name "A Citizen of the World" wrote a lengthy treatise about the Indiana's territorial government in 1803 that included an explicit attack on Harrison: "I [Citizen of the World] have observed in the *American Literary Advertiser*, an extract of a letter to the editor of the Kentucky Gazette, dated St. Vincennes Sept 17, 1802, which reads as follows, 'I have to communicate the pleasing result of our council with the Indians. Every object for which it was holden [*sic*], so far as it relates to us, is completely obtained. They listened with attentions and apparent pleasure, to the plans proposed for their advancement in civilization. They *all* promised their firmest support in carrying the measures of the president into effect.' . . . And further, it was with the utmost difficulty that the Indians consented to relinquish their right to the twenty four leagues square on the Wabash. Besides, *all* the chiefs were not present,

and although sent for and solicited to come, *they absolutely refused!*—I am astonished, indeed! That men have not more regard to truth in their public assertations" (*Indiana Gazette*, January 1, 1803).

35. Jay Gitlin, "Old Wine in New Bottles: French Merchants and the Emergence of the American Midwest, 1795–1835," in *Proceedings of the Thirteenth and Fourteenth Meetings of the French Colonial Historical Society*, ed. Philip P. Boucher (Lanham MD: University Press of America, 1990), 42–43.

36. Esarey, ed., *Messages and Letters of William Henry Harrison*, 165; Governor St. Clair to the Secretary of War, August 23, 1790, *American State Papers: Indian Affairs*, 1:92. Michael Strezewski, Robert G. McCullough, Dorothea McCullough, Craig R. Arnold, Joshua J. Wells, James R. Jones, and Leslie Bush, *Report of the 2006 Archaeological Investigations at Kethtippecanunk (12-t-59), Tippecanoe County, Indiana* (Fort Wayne: IPFW Archaeological Survey, Indiana University–Purdue University, 2007), 233; John Francis Hamtramck to Josiah Harmar, November 2, 1790, in *Outpost on the Wabash, 1787–1791*, ed. Gayle Thornbrough, Indiana Historical Society Publications 19 (Indianapolis: Indiana Historical Society, 1957), 259–64; Jay Gitlin, *The Bourgeois Frontier: French Towns, French Traders, and American Expansion* (New Haven CT: Yale University Press, 2010), 67.

37. Esarey, ed., *Messages and Harrison*, 303; Henry Dearborn to William Henry Harrison, January 23, 1802, in *WHH Papers*, reel 1, 247.

38. Dearborn to Harrison, January 23, 1802, in *WHH Papers*, reel 1, 271; Esarey, ed., *Messages and Letters of Harrison*, 303; Dearborn to Harrison, January 23, 1802, in *WHH Papers*, reel 1, 271.

39. "Resolutions," *Western Sun*, August 22, 1807. Initially a small one-room schoolhouse where the local Catholic priest taught Latin, mathematics, and history, it eventually became Vincennes University (which exists to this day) and was the only four-year institution in Indiana until the founding of Indiana University.

40. "Resolutions," *Western Sun*, August 22, 1807. Stout printed a list of the people who had defaulted on their taxes in the January 27, 1808, issue of the *Western Sun*. The article also stated that all defaulted accounts would have their land sold that March.

41. Gitlin, "Old Wine in New Bottles," 47; Esarey, ed., *Messages and Letters of Harrison*, 113.

42. To Thomas Jefferson from the French Inhabitants of Vincennes, "Resolutions adopted at a meeting of the French Inhabitants of Vincennes," October 10, 1807, in *WHH Papers,* reel 3, 9; Hinderaker, *Elusive Empires*, 270.

43. Gitlin, "Old Wine in New Bottles," 50, 44; John D. Barnhart, ed., *Henry Hamilton and George Rogers Clark in the American Revolution with the Unpublished Journal of Lieut. Gov. Henry Hamilton* (Crawfordsville IN, 1951), 146. Hamilton states that after capturing Michel Brouillet Sr., they discovered that he had written orders from both Lieutenant Governor Abbott (British official) and Francois Bosseron (aide to George Rogers Clark). *Biographical and Historical Record of Vermillion County, Indiana* (Chicago: Lewis, 1888), 192. In *The Journals and Indian Paintings of George Winter, 1837–1839* (Indianapolis IN: Indiana Historical Society, 1948), 44, George Winter states that Jean Baptiste Brouillet was the half brother of a fiddle player named Brouillet in Logansport. This was Michel Brouillet's son Michel Bradamore Brouillet, who published *A Collection of Cotillions, Scotch Reels, &c. Introduced at the Dancing School of M B. Brouillett* (Logansport IN: Lasselle, 1834). Otho Winger, *The Lost Sister among*

the Miamis (Elgin IL: Elgin Press, 1936), 142, lists Jean Baptiste Brouillet as born in 1796. His obituary in the *Lafayette (in) Courier*, July 6, 1867, says he was born at Fort Harrison (near present-day Terre Haute): "his father was a Frenchman, and was made a captive when a youth." Harrison to Eustis, December 3, 1809, in *Messages and Letters of Harrison*, ed. Esarey, 395; Gitlin, "Old Wine in New Bottles," 40.

44. These traders include Joseph Barron, William Wells (not French), Michel Brouillet, Charles Beaubien, and Peter Lafontaine (Charles Poinsatte, *Outpost in the Wilderness: Fort Wayne, 1706–1828* [Allen County: Fort Wayne Historical Society, 1976]; Anson, *The Miami Indians*, 145; Harrison to Eustis, December 3, 1809, in *Messages and Letters of Harrison*, ed. Esarey, 395; White, *The Middle Ground*, 65).

45. Hinderaker, *Elusive Empires*, 267.

46. Gayle Thornbrough, "Introduction," in Badollet and Gallatin, *Correspondence*, 9–14; Badollet to Gallatin, August 31, 1805, ibid., 49; Francis S. Philbrick, ed., *The Laws of Indiana Territory, 1801–1809* (Springfield: Illinois State Historical Library, 1930), xxxviii.

47. William A. Hunter, ed., "John Badollet's 'Journal of the Time I Spent in Stony Creek Glades,'" November 25, 1793, *Pennsylvania Magazine of History and Biography* 104, no. 2 (April 1980): 168.

48. John B. Dillon, *A History of Indiana* (Indianapolis: Bingham and Doughty, 1859), 439; Judge Davis to the Attorney General, January 26, 1806, in *Territorial Papers of the United States*, ed. Carter, 7:335; "Petition to Congress by Citizens of Harrison Country," 1809, ibid., 7:703.

49. Ira Berlin, *Many Thousands Gone: The First Two Centuries of Slavery in North America* (Cambridge: Harvard University Press, 1998); In December 1807, Ann, an indentured servant labeled a "Mulatto" and "Negroe" in the judicial record lodged a complaint against her owner, James Trimble, for "ill usage & cruel treatment" in the Court of Common Pleas. The court ruled that Trimble "enter into recognizance" at the clerk's office and ordered that he "shall not in [the] future abuse or unreasonably chastise his said servant during the time she remains in his . . . controle" (Court of Common Pleas for Knox County, December 5, 1807, box 12, folder 856, Indiana State Archives). I use the term "slave" to describe the indentured African Americans in Vincennes because their owners forced them to sign ninety-nine-year indentures. They were de facto slaves. In 1808, authorities discovered a "coloured man" named Caleb dead in the town jail, but after the coroner, Jacob Kuykendall, and twelve other men inspected the body, they concluded that Caleb had died from "natural sickness & malady, and not otherwise." The town authorities made sure that the slave's rights had been protected (Court of Common Pleas for Knox County, October 1808, Indiana State Archives, file 1013, box 15).

50. Although Matthew Salafia in *Slavery's Borderland: Freedom and Bondage along the Ohio River* (Philadelphia: University of Pennsylvania Press, 2013) does not discuss the slavery debate that took place in Vincennes during this period, the patterns of debate and cultural disputes do reinforce Salafia's larger argument about slavery's borderland, the region north and south of the Ohio River that encompassed portions of Ohio, Indiana, and Kentucky.

51. Emma Lou Thornbrough, *The Negro in Indiana: A Study of a Minority* (Indianapolis: Indiana Historical Bureau, 1957), 9; Jacob Piatt Dunn, ed., *Slavery Petitions and Papers* (Indianapolis: Bowen-Merrill, 1894), 523; Gayle Thornbrough and Dorothy

L. Riker, eds., *Journals of the General Assembly of Indiana Territory, 1805–1815* (Indianapolis: Indiana Historical Bureau, 1950), 232–38, 257, 289, 301.

52. Philbrick, ed., *Laws of the Indiana Territory*, xlii; *A Century of Lawmaking for a New Nation: U.S. Congressional Documents and Debates, 1774—1875*, Annals of Congress, House of Representatives, 10th Cong., 2nd sess., p. 501.

53. Jesse B. Thomas and Sam Gwathmey to George Clinton, October 13, 1807, in *WHH Papers*, reel 3, 18.

54. Joyce Applebee, "Republicanism and Ideology," *American Quarterly* 37, no. 4 (Autumn 1985): 472.

55. Michael Warner, *The Letters of the Republic: Publication and the Public Sphere in Eighteenth-Century America* (Cambridge: Harvard University Press, 1992), xi; Warner, *Letters of the Republic*, 63.

56. Teena Gabrielson, "James Madison's Psychology of Public Opinion," *Political Research Quarterly* 62, no. 3 (September 2009): 434.

57. "To G. W. Johnston, Esq.," *Western Sun*, February 7, 1808; "To a Citizen of Vincennes," *Western Sun*, February 7, 1808. Dr. Elias McNamee wrote under the name "A Citizen of Vincennes," but Slim Simon did not know this. "To G. W. Johnston, Esq.," *Western Sun*, February 7, 1808; "To a Citizen of Vincennes," *Western Sun*, February 7, 1808; "To G. W. Johnston, Esq.," *Western Sun*, February 7, 1808; "To a Citizen of Vincennes," *Western Sun*, February 7, 1808.

58. "Pop Gun to the Editor of *The Western Sun*," *Western Sun*, February 8, 1808; "A Citizen of Vincennes to the Citizens of Indiana," *Western Sun*, February 8, 1808; "For the Western Sun," *Western Sun*, February 4, 1809; "A Citizen of Vincennes to the Citizens of Indiana," *Western Sun*, February 8, 1808; "For the Western Sun," *Western Sun*, February 4, 1809. Two articles appeared in the April 20, 1809, edition of the *Western Sun* that discussed the need to find common ground and to focus on the nation rather than on personal differences. They advocate focusing on an American identity and adhering to true republican principles. But in the same edition, McNamee accuses Thomas Randolph of trying to trick the voters until after the election: "Mr. Randolph wishes to lull the citizens asleep . . . till after his election." The men invoked other issues, such as religion, that showed that another sort of cultural divide was at hand. General G. W. Johnston, for instance, saw inaccuracies in Simon's argument that Abraham, Isaac, and Jacob owned slaves. They "were shepherds and shepherdesses of hirelings, and were not transferred as the slave holder sells his fellow creature, without his consent and with as little compunction as he would a bullock for the slaughter." The focus on biblical interpretation turned the slavery debate into a heated conversation about the essential truths of religion and Christianity, as well as character and faith. More study is needed of the divisive religious rhetoric within the factionalized white community because treating whites as a monolithic religious entity essentializes their religious identity. Yet, in Indiana Territory, such boundaries were not yet fixed. In Vincennes, Christians were not unified and were unable to enforce a singular white religious vision upon the Indians when they had yet to figure it out for themselves. Religion was just one of the many important ideas contested and debated by the inhabitants of the region. In fact, the factions quite often debated religion in one sentence and other issues in the next. Jeremiah Jingle did not allow Johnston's comments to go unnoticed. Accusing Johnston of trimming on the issue of slavery, Jingle demanded that he state his opinion on the division of the territory, the

embargo, and American relations with France and Britain. As a candidate to represent Knox County in the territorial assembly, he had, according to Jingle, supported and rejected the issue of slavery in the territory, gaining votes on both sides and election as the representative of Knox County.

59. "A Farmer," *Western Sun*, March 4, 1809; "A Farmer," *Western Sun*, March 18, 1809.

60. Jonathan Jennings beat Thomas Randolph in the election tally: 428 votes for Jennings, 402 for Randolph, and 81 for John Johnson (*Western Sun*, July 8, 1809).

61. Harrison to Gallatin, August 29, 1809, in Badollet and Gallatin, *Correspondence*, 108; 108-10; *Western Sun*, July 8, 1809; Harrison to Gallatin, August 29, 1809, in Badollet and Gallatin, *Correspondence*, 111, 113.

62. Badollet to Gallatin, November 13, 1809, in Badollet and Gallatin, *Correspondence*, 116-17.

3 / Prophetstown for Their Own Purposes

1. Prophet to Harrison, August 1, 1808, in *Messages and Letters of William Henry Harrison*, ed. Logan Esarey (Indianapolis: Indiana Historical Commission, 1922), 299.

2. This point echoes larger patterns of information control as discussed by Michel Foucault in *Ethics: Subjectivity and Truth* (New York: New Press, 1994), 17.

3. Alfred A. Cave, *Prophets of the Great Spirit: Native American Revitalization Movements in Eastern North America* (Lincoln: University of Nebraska Press, 2006), 66-79. R. David Edmunds's *The Shawnee Prophet* (Lincoln: University of Nebraska Press, 1983) also details the growth of Prophetstown. Edmunds argues that the Prophet's nativist vision shaped the early development of Prophetstown as an idea but that Tecumseh was the one who applied the idea of Indian unification to his pan-Indian movement after the Treaty of Fort Wayne in 1809. Gregory Dowd argues that Tecumseh did not necessarily supplant his brother after 1809 and that the two continued to forge a pan-Indian confederacy at Prophetstown. I build on Dowd's emphasis that Tenskwatawa remained relevant by showing that Indians and non-Indians were still so deeply suspicious of the Prophet's influence and behavior that they worked tirelessly to shape and control his message (rather than Tecumseh's) within diplomatic circles. We should be more critical of the idea of Prophetstown. Not only did the Prophet and Tecumseh have a vision and idea of what Prophetstown would become, but so, too, did the Miami, French, and Americans. David L. Preston, *The Texture of Contact: European and Indian Settler Communities on the Frontiers of Iroquoia, 1667-1783* (Lincoln: University of Nebraska Press, 2009), 232-33; David Brion Davis, *The Slave Power Conspiracy and the Paranoid Style* (Baton Rouge: Louisiana State University Press, 1969), 6, 11; Gregory Evans Dowd, "The Panic of 1751: The Significance of Rumors on the South Carolina-Cherokee Frontier," *William and Mary Quarterly* 53, no. 3 (July 1996): 556.

4. Gregory Evans Dowd, *A Spirited Resistance: The North American Struggle for Unity, 1745-1815* (Baltimore: Johns Hopkins University Press, 1990), 131-32. Although briefly, Dowd does address William Wells's attempts to condemn the Prophet by tying him to the British.

5. Speech by Tecumseh to Harrison, Vincennes, August 20, 1810, in *Messages and Letters of Harrison*, ed. Esarey, 465-66; Stephen Warren, *The Shawnee and Their Neighbors, 1795-1870* (Urbana: University of Illinois Press, 2008), 28.

6. Nathaniel Ewing to Albert Gallatin, June 26, 1810, and John Badollet to Albert Gallatin, September 25, 1810, in John Louis Badollet and Albert Gallatin, *The Correspondence of John Badollet and Albert Gallatin, 1804–1836,* ed. Gayle Thornbrough (Indianapolis: Indiana Historical Society, 1963), 159, 166; Susan Sleeper-Smith, *Indian Women and French Men: Rethinking Cultural Encounters in the Western Great Lakes* (Amherst: University of Massachusetts Press, 2001), 30. Andrew R. L. Cayton also discusses the power Native women exercised in this period in his chapter on the Miami world: "For Indian women, marriage to a European often brought with it increased influence and privileges for both herself and her kin, among them better access to European goods and technology" (Cayton, *Frontier Indiana,* 8). C. C. Trowbridge, *Shawnese Traditions: C. C. Trowbridge's Account,* ed. Vernon Kinietz and Erminie Wheeler-Voegelin (New York: AMS Press, 1980), 12–13.

7. Harrison to Henry Dearborn, November 9, 1808, in *WHH Papers,* reel 3, 302. Harrison states: "The part of the Shawanoe Tribe which is attached to the Shawnee Prophet having removed last Summer to the Wabash and being almost in a starving condition applied to me for relief—this I did not think it proper to afford them to the extent required but as the Annuities for their tribe have been generally engrossed by the Blackhoofs band I offered to advance them provisions to the Amount of one hundred dollars to be deducted out of their next years Annuity."

8. Stephen Warren, *The Shawnee and Their Neighbors, 1795–1870* (Urbana: University of Illinois Press, 2008).

9. John Tanner, *A Narrative of the Captivity and Adventures of John Tanner, during Thirty Years Residence among the Indians in the Interior of North America* (New York: G. C. H. Carvill, 1830).

10. Timothy D. Willig, "Prophetstown on the Wabash: The Native Spiritual Defense of the Old Northwest," *Michigan Historical Review* 23 (Fall 1997): 125; C. C. Trowbridge, *Meearmeear Traditions,* ed. W. Vernon Kinietz (Ann Arbor: University of Michigan Press, 1938), 4; "Speeches of Miami, et al. Chiefs," September 4, 1811, in *WHH Papers,* reel 4, 756; William Biggs, *Narrative of the Captivity of William Biggs among the Kickapoo Indians in Illinois in 1788* (Metuchen NJ: C. F. Heartman, 1922); Alexander Davidson and Bernard Stuve, *A Complete History of Illinois from 1673 to 1873* (Springfield: Illinois Journal Co., 1877), 222. Dissecting these differences remains a challenge for historians as well. Since the historical record provides so little evidence about Indian motivations for following the Prophet, historians have given greater weight to the Prophet's teachings.

11. Harrison to Eustis, August 28, 1810, in *Messages and Letters of Harrison,* ed. Esarey, 470; John Sugden, *Tecumseh: A Life* (New York: Henry Holt, 1998), 188; C. C. Trowbridge, "Native American material," box 1 (Keekarpo Indians—2 versions), Bentley Historical Library, University of Michigan.

12. Harrison to Eustis, August 6, 1810, in *WHH Papers,* reel 4, 668; Harrison to Eustis, October 5, 1810, ibid., reel 4, 218; Harrison to William Eustis, October 5, 1810, in *Messages and Letters of Harrison,* ed. Esarey, 1:471.

13. Wells to Secretary of War, July 14, 1807, in *Territorial Papers of the United States,* ed. Clarence Edwin Carter, vol. 7, *The Territory of Indiana, 1800–1810* (Washington DC, 1939), 465; Wells to Henry Dearborn, July 14, 1807, Shawnee File, Great Lakes Ethnohistory Archive; Wells to William Henry Harrison, August 20, in *WHH Papers,* reel 2, 900; Harrison to Henry Dearborn, September 5, 1807, ibid., reel 2, 925; Wells to Harrison, August 20, 1807, ibid., reel 2, 900.

14. Robert Mann, "The Silenced Miami: Archaeological and Ethnohistorical Evidence for Miami-British Relations, 1795–1812," *Ethnohistory* 46 (Summer 1999): 401.

15. Harrison to Dearborn, May 19, 1808, in *WHH Papers*, reel 3, 156; Harrison to William Eustis, July 14, 1809, in *Messages and Letters of Harrison*, ed. Esarey, 1:355. Richard White refers to Wells as "a figure as thoroughly a product of the middle ground as any person in the *pays d'en haut*. White also states that Wells "served as Indian agent for the Miami confederation" (Richard White, *The Middle Ground: Indians, Empires, and Republics in the Great Lakes Region, 1650–1815* [Cambridge: Cambridge University Press, 1991], 500–501). Harvey Lewis Carter has demonstrated that Wells protected Little Turtle's Miami faction, and not the Miami people or confederation. Carter's *Life and Times of Little Turtle: The First Sagamore of the Wabash* (Urbana: University of Illinois Press, 1987) traces the rise of both Little Turtle and his son-in-law William Wells in great detail. Wells to Harrison, April 25, 1810, in *WHH Papers*, reel 3, 827; Wells to Harrison, August 20, 1807, ibid., reel 2, 900; Harrison to Dearborn, May 19, 1808, ibid., reel 3, 156; Prophet to Harrison, June 24, 1808, ibid., reel 3, 173; Message from the Shawnee Prophet, June 24, 1808, ibid., reel 3, 173; Harrison to the Prophet, June 24, 1808, ibid., reel 3, 178.

16. Trowbridge, *Meearmeear Traditions*, 4; Stewart Rafert, *The Miami Indians of Indiana: A Persistent People, 1654–1994* (Indianapolis: Indiana Historical Society Press, 1996), 58–76.

17. Stephen Warren and Randolph Noe, "'The Greatest Travelers in America': Shawnee Survival in the Shatter Zone," in *Mapping the Mississippian Shatter Zone: The Colonial Indian Slave Trade and Regional Instability in the American South*, ed. Robbie Ethridge and Sheri Shuck-Hall (Lincoln: University of Nebraska Press, 2009), 167. Warren argues that for the Shawnee, "Diplomatic considerations outweighed any long-standing attachments to homeland. The vicissitudes of trade and alliance determined migration patterns" (Stephen Warren and Randolph Noe, "'The Greatest Travelers in America': Shawnee Survival in the Shatter Zone," in *Mapping the Mississippian Shatter Zone: The Colonial Indian Slave Trade and Regional Instability in the American South*, ed. Robbie Ethridge and Sheri Shuck-Hall [Lincoln: University of Nebraska Press, 2009], 167). Eric Hinderaker, *Elusive Empires: Constructing Colonialism in the Ohio Valley, 1763–1800* (Cambridge: Cambridge University Press, 1997), 48; Sleeper-Smith, *Indian Women and French Men*, 87–89.

18. Cave, *Prophets of the Great Spirit*, 98. Cave states that Main Poc "rejected as well the call to Indian unity and brotherhood, 'insisting that he would become weak and lose his medicine power if he were to give up warfare against the Osage and other enemies'" (ibid.). James A. Clifton, *The Prairie People: Continuity and Change in Potawatomi Indian Culture, 1665–1965* (Lawrence: Regents Press of Kansas, 1977), 194; Sugden, *Tecumseh*, 217; Clifton, *Prairie People*, 194–95; Harrison to Eustis, April 23, June 6, and June 19. 1811, in *Messages and Letters of Harrison*, ed. Esarey, 506–10, 512–19; Lalime to William Clark, May 26, 1811, and Harrison to Clark, June 19, 1811, ibid., 511, 519–21; Cave, *Prophets of the Great Spirit*, 116; Edmunds, *The Shawnee Prophet*, 68–87.

19. Cave, *Prophets of the Great Spirit*, 97–98.

20. Ibid., 98; James A. Clifton, *The Prairie People: Continuity and Change in Potawatomi Indian Culture, 1665–1965* (Lawrence: Regents Press of Kansas, 1977), 194; Sugden, *Tecumseh*, 217; Clifton, *Prairie People*, 194–95; Harrison to Eustis, April 23,

June 6 and 19, 1811, in *Messages and Letters of Harrison*, ed. Esarey, 506–10, 512–19; Lalime to William Clark, May 26, 1811, and Harrison to Clark, June 19, 1811, ibid., 511, 519–21; Cave, *Prophets of the Great Spirit*, 116; Edmunds, *The Shawnee Prophet*, 68–87.

21. Willig, "Prophetstown on the Wabash," 125; Cave, *Prophets of the Great Spirit*, 95–100.

22. Wells to Harrison, Vincennes, April 8, 1809, in *Messages and Letters of Harrison*, ed. Esarey, 337; Cave, *Prophets of the Great Spirit*, 97; Johnston to Dearborn, Ft. Wayne, May 31, 1807, Potawatomi File, Great Lakes Indian Archives; Wells to Harrison, April 8, 1809, in *WHH Papers*, reel 3, 380.

23. Wells to Harrison, Vincennes, April 8, 1809, in *Messages and Letters of Harrison*, ed. Esarey, 337.

24. Harrison to Secretary of War, Vincennes, December 3, 1809, in *Messages and Letters of Harrison*, ed. Esarey, 393; Wells to Harrison, April 8, 1809, in *WHH Papers*, reel 3, 380; Carter, *Life and Times of Little Turtle*, 169–240; Wells to Harrison, August 20, 1807, in *WHH Papers*, reel 2, 901; Harrison to Eustis, December 3, 1809, ibid., reel 3, 668, 669.

25. Robert Owens, *Mr. Jefferson's Hammer: William Henry Harrison and the Origins of Indian Policy* (Norman: University of Oklahoma Press, 2007), 60–64; Jay Gitlin, "Old Wine in New Bottles: French Merchants and the Emergence of the American Midwest, 1795–1835," *Proceedings of the Thirteenth and Fourteenth Meetings of the French Colonial Historical Society*, ed. Philip P. Boucher (Lanham MD: University Press of America, 1990), 47.

26. Katherine Wagner Seineke, *The George Rogers Clark Adventure in the Illinois and Selected Documents of the American Revolution at the Frontier Posts* (New Orleans: Polyanthos, 1981), 333; Jennifer Harrison, "A Place in Between: The Story of a French and Miami Family" (master's thesis, Ball State University, 2001). Michel married a Miami woman with whom he had Tahquakeah (Jean Baptiste) and married Marie de Richardville when his first wife died. Susan Sleeper-Smith's *Indian Women and French Men* examines the significance of intercultural relationships and the multiethnic nature of the frontier. She also stresses the importance of cultural processes over the "formal structures of political power," which is a central tenet of this book. Gitlin, "Old Wine in New Bottles," 44, 40. Hamilton states that after capturing Michel Brouillet Sr., they discovered that he had written orders from both Lieutenant Governor Abbott (a British official) and Francois Bosseron (aide to George Rogers Clark) (Henry Hamilton's Journal, December 15, 1778); Vermillion County, *Biographical and Historical Record of Vermillion County, Indiana* (Chicago: Lewis, 1888), 192. In *The Journals and Indian Paintings of George Winter, 1837–1839* (Indianapolis: Indiana Historical Society, 1948), 44, George Winter states that Jean Baptiste Brouillet was the half brother of a fiddle player named Brouillet in Logansport. This was Michel Brouillet's son, Michel Bradamore Brouillet, who published *A Collection of Cotillions, Scotch Reels, &c. Introduced at the Dancing School of M B. Brouillett* (Logansport IN: Lasselle, 1834). Otho Winger, *The Lost Sister among the Miamis* (Elgin IL: Elgin Press, 1936), 142, lists Jean Baptiste Brouillet as born in 1796. His obituary in the *Lafayette Courier,* July 6, 1867, says he was born at Fort Harrison (near present-day Terre Haute): "his father was a Frenchman, and was made a captive when a youth." Harrison to Eustis, December 3, 1809, in *Messages and Letters of Harrison*, ed. Esarey, 395.

27. Harrison to Eustis, April 26, 1809, in *WHH Papers*, reel 3, 400; Harrison to Eustis, April 18, 1809, ibid., reel 3, 394; Harrison to Eustis, April 18, 1809, in *Messages and Letters of Harrison*, ed. Esarey, 340; R. David Edmunds, *The Potawatomis: Keepers of the Fire* (Norman: University of Oklahoma Press, 1978), 162-65; *Western Sun*, October 13, 1810; Edmunds, *The Shawnee Prophet*, 68, 87. Benjamin Stickney mentions a Potawatomi town six miles north of Prophetstown in a letter to Secretary of War Eustis in May 7, 1812. Gayle Thornbrough, ed., *Letter Book of the Indian Agency at Fort Wayne, 1809-1815* (Indianapolis: Indiana Historical Society, 1961), 116-17; Harrison to Eustis, May 3, 1809, in *WHH Papers*, reel 3, 409; Logan Esarey, ed., *A History of Indiana* (Indianapolis: B. F. Bowen, 1918), 1:29; Esarey, ed., *Messages and Letters of Harrison*, 337n.

28. Dubois had a trading post in Vincennes and had spent the late 1700s before the creation of Indiana Territory as a voyageur and middleman for the Lasselle trading network in the region. Harrison to Secretary of War, Vincennes, May 3, 1809, in *Messages and Letters of Harrison*, ed. Esarey, 345. Toussaint Dubois owned a trading store in Vincennes and worked several trading posts throughout the area (Helen L. Allen, "Sketch of the Dubois Family, Pioneers of Indiana and Illinois," *Journal of the Illinois State Historical Society* 5, no. 1 [April 1912]: 55). *St. Francis Xavier Parish Records*, vol. *1796-1808* (English translation), 19. William Wesley Woollen, Daniel Wait Howe, and Jacob Piatt Dunn, eds., *Executive Journal of Indiana Territory, 1800-1816* (Indianapolis: Indiana Historical Society, 1900), 186; Edmunds, *The Shawnee Prophet*, 77; Harrison to Eustis, April 26, 1809, in *WHH Papers*, reel 3, 399; Tanner, *Captivity and Adventures*; Esarey, ed., *Messages and Letters of William Henry Harrison*, 337. Lafontaine had moved from Detroit to trade among the Miamis and married a Miami woman with whom he had children who became Miami leaders.

29. Harrison to Secretary of War, Vincennes, March 3, 1803, in *Messages and Letters of Harrison*, ed. Esarey, 81; National Archives, Record Group No. 75 LR—1803 I O.I.T., Fort Wayne Factory; Patrick Griffin, *American Leviathan: Empire, Nation, and Revolutionary Frontier* (New York: Hill and Wang, 2007), 10-16; Harrison to Dearborn, March 3, 1805, in *WHH Papers*, reel 2, 104; Harrison and James Wilkinson to Dearborn, October 19, 1805, ibid. Harrison also believed that Indians could not be trusted, even identifying certain groups as "the most perfidious of their race" and Indians on the whole as "blood thirsty savages" (Harrison to Dearborn, February 18, 1808, ibid., reel 3, 113; Harrison to Indiana Territorial Assembly, October 17, 1809, ibid., reel 3, 583). Eustis routinely agreed with Harrison's assessments. Regarding the problems at Prophetstown in 1808, Eustis thanked Harrison for the "agreeable information of the dispersion of the hostile Combination of the Savages [Prophetstown] in your vicinity" (Eustis to Harrison, June 5, 1809, ibid., reel 3, 429; Harrison to Eustis, May 3, 1809, ibid., reel 3, 409; Harrison to Eustis, December 3, 1809, ibid., reel 3, 669; Harrison to Eustis, June 6, 1811, ibid., reel 4, 538). LaPlante was caught selling merchandise to the Indians without a license in 1808. Thomas Randolph to Harrison, July 19, 1808, ibid., reel 3, 209; Harrison to Eustis, April 25, 1810, ibid., reel 3, 827; Harrison to Eustis, June 6, 1811, ibid., reel 4, 538.

30. Harrison to Dearborn, March 3, 1805, in *WHH Papers*, reel 2, 104. Harrison also thought the French were too "ignorant" to be too much trouble. Harrison to Eustis, August 22, 1810, in *Messages and Letters of Harrison*, ed. Esarey, 462; Harrison to John Johnston, in *WHH Papers*, May 4-12, 1809, reel 3, 411, 413.

31. Johnston to the Prophet, May 3, 1809, in Thornbrough, ed., *Letter Book*, 49–52; Harrison to Eustis, May 16, 1809, in *WHH Papers*, reel 3, 424; Johnston to Eustis, July 1, 1809, M221, roll 24, 8062, National Archives; Cave, *Prophets of the Great Spirit*, 96; Johnston to Eustis, July 1, 1809, M221, roll 24, 8062, National Archives; Edmunds, *The Shawnee Prophet*, 79.

32. Harrison to Eustis, July 5, 1809, in *WHH Papers*, reel 3, 446. Harrison to Johnston, July 8, 1809, Jones Collection, Cincinnati Historical Society; Thornbrough, ed., *Letter Book*, 46–47; R. David Edmunds, "Forgotten Allies: The Loyal Shawnees and the War of 1812," in *The Sixty Years' War for the Great Lakes, 1754–1814*, ed. David C. Skaggs and Larry L. Nelson (East Lansing: Michigan State University Press, 2001), 341; Warren, *The Shawnee and Their Neighbors*, 14, 37–38.

33. Esarey, ed., *Messages and Letters of Harrison*, 369.

34. Mann, "The Silenced Miami," 405; "Copy of a Council held at Detroit 18th September 1774 by Pacan Chief of the Miamis Indians with Five Others of the Chiefs and Principal Men of his Nation in the Presence of Richard Berringer Lernoult Esquire Captain in the King's or 8th Regiment Commander of the Detroit and Its Dependencies," Thomas Gage Papers, American Series, vol. 123.

35. Mann, "The Silenced Miami," 411, 410. Indian Reports, *Western Sun*, June 23, 1810, July 7, 1810; John Johnston to Harrison, October 14, 1810, in *WHH Papers*, reel 4, 232, 231; John Shaw, Assistant Indian Agent's Translation, June 24, 1810, ibid., reel 4, 064; Harrison to Eustis, July 18, 1810, ibid., reel 4, 103.

36. Esarey, ed., *Messages and Letters of Harrison*, 446; White, *The Middle Ground*, 216; Mann, "The Silenced Miami," 415–27.

37. Henry Hamilton's Journal, October 17, 1778, November, 8, 1778, December 23, 1778, December 31, 1778; A. S. de Peyster, Detroit, to Lt. Col. Mason Bolton, June 27, 1780, in Michigan Pioneer and Historical Society, *Historical Collections: Collections and Researches Made by the Michigan Pioneer and Historical Society* (Lansing MI: Robert Smith, 1891), 19:501.

38. Harrison to Eustis, October 5, 1810, in *WHH Papers*, reel 4, 218; Harrison to Eustis, August 22, 1810, in *Messages and Letters of Harrison*, ed. Esarey, 459; ibid.

39. Mann, "The Silenced Miami," 408–12.

40. Harrison to Secretary of War, June 14, 1810, in *Messages and Letters of Harrison*, ed. Esarey, 425; Harrison to Eustis, June 14–19, 1810, in *WHH Papers*, reel 4, 040; Deposition of Michel Brouillet, June 30, 1810, ibid., reel 4, 083.

41. Harrison to Eustis, June 14–19, 1810, in *WHH Papers*, reel 4, 040; Deposition of Michel Brouillet, June 30, 1810, ibid., reel 4, 083. Elihu Stout posted a notice in the June 23, 1810, *Western Sun* that included the stories of the Frenchmen, their estimates of Prophetstown's military capability, and a statement requiring all citizens of Knox County to attend a meeting "to consult upon the best plan of avoiding the threatened war with the Indians, & of securing their several families" (*WHH Papers*, reel 4, 062). Harrison's speech to the Indiana Legislature (as edited by Stout), *Western Sun*, June 23, 1810.

42. Harrison's speech to the Indiana Legislature (as edited by Stout), *Western Sun*, June 23, 1810; *Western Sun*, July 7, 1810; John Johnston to Harrison, October 14, 1810, in *WHH Papers*, reel 4, 232, 231; John Shaw, Assistant Indian Agent's Translation, June 1810, ibid., reel 4, 064; Harrison to Eustis, July 18, 1810, ibid., reel 4, 103; Harrison to Eustis, November 7, 1810, ibid., reel 4, 255; Speech to Indiana Territorial Assembly, November 12, 1810, ibid., reel 4, 259.

43. John Johnston to Harrison, October 14, 1810, in *WHH Papers*, reel 4, 231; Johnston to Harrison, June 24, 1810, ibid., reel 4, 058.

44. Elihu Stout's "Report on Indian Affairs" in the *Western Sun* stated that "the Indians were collecting in very great numbers about the Prophet; that the Miamis [no distinction made between the factions] had been so intimidated as to agree to attend his council" (May 1– June 22, 1810, in *WHH Papers*, reel 3, 833). Harrison sent a speech to the Miami during August 1811 declaring that "all those who join the [Shawnee] Prophet & his party as hostile and call upon you to fulfil [sic] your engagements" (Message to the Miami, August 21, 1811, ibid., reel 4, 731). Elihu Stout's coverage of the Shawnee Prophet demonstrates not only his growing paranoia about the Indian threat but the extent to which his readers wanted to understand the situation (*Western Sun*, June 8, June 22, July 6, July 13, 1810). Harrison to Eustis, December 24, 1810, in *Messages and Letters of Harrison*, ed. Esarey, 497.

45. Harrison to Eustis, October 10, 1810, in *WHH Papers*, reel 4, 227; "Extra," *Western Sun*, October 18, 1810; Harrison to Eustis, October 17, 1810, in *WHH Papers*, reel 4, 241.

46. Deposition of Michel Brouillet, June 30, 1810, in *WHH Papers*, reel 4, 082; Deposition of Michel Brouillet, June 30, 1810, ibid., reel 4, 082; Harrison to Eustis, June 6, 1811, ibid., reel 4, 541.

47. Harrison to Eustis, June 6, 1811, in *Messages and Letters of Harrison*, ed. Esarey, 512; Harrison to Clark, June 19, 1811, ibid., 519.

48. Harrison to Eustis, July 10, 1811, in *Messages and Letters of Harrison*, ed. Esarey, 534–35. Harrison says: "Although I have no doubt that the mischief which has been done in the Illinois is to be attributed to the Prophet, I think it nevertheless extremely probable that his friends there have gone further than he intended and that he did not mean that more than one or two persons should be killed, for upon mature reflection and comparing a number of circumstances which I have learned relatively to his situation I do not think that he intended that the war should break out at this time. I may however be mistaken. Those circumstances which I mention as forming the ground of my opinion may have been artfully brought into view for the purpose of deception." Harrison to Eustis, July 24, 1811, ibid., 538; Harrison to Eustis, July 10, 1811, ibid., 531; Harrison to Eustis, October 28, 1811, in *WHH Papers*, reel 5, 019.

49. Harrison to Eustis, July 10, 1811, in *Messages and Letters of Harrison*, ed. Esarey, 532.

50. Pekka Hämäläinen and Samuel Truett, "On Borderlands," *Journal of American History* 98 (2011): 361.

51. Preston, *Texture of Contact*, 160. "The sources of American anger, fear, and hatred that fueled" frontier violence "are unclear" (James Merrel qtd. ibid., 160). This echoes a point recently made by Pekka Hämäläinen and Samuel Truett, who argue that "new work on borderlands violence highlights different networks; by showing how violence can simultaneously divide, connect, break, and revitalize societies, it demonstrates how borderlands communities could be locked into long-standing relationships that endured despite—and at times because of—the bloodshed" (Hämäläinen and Truett, "On Borderlands," 351).

4 / Vincennes, the Politics of Slavery, and the Indian "Threat"

1. For more information on the growth of violence in the region, see Richard White, *The Middle Ground: Indians, Empires, and Republics in the Great Lakes Region, 1650–1815* (Cambridge: Cambridge University Press, 1991). White's work focuses on the extent to which colonial cultures shaped Native peoples, but I am more focused on the ways in which Indians, as well as the French, shaped American policy by manipulating information about Prophetstown. At the same time, I use White's pathbreaking study of cultural misunderstandings as a springboard to discuss the role that villages and local identities played in the history of the Ohio Valley. White contextualizes Prophetstown and the American entrance into the Ohio Valley as ushering in the collapse of the middle ground and fueling a period of increased violence. White believes that the Americans bore the most responsibility for stoking up violence. My book makes a distinction, in that Indians and French traders/interpreters also spurred violence by spreading rumors and lies about Prophetstown, which ultimately facilitated the collapse of the middle ground through increased violence like that at the Battle of Tippecanoe. I believe that the actions of the French and Miamis represent purposeful and intentional misunderstandings rather than what White would call "creative misunderstandings," which were produced by cultures that could not quite understand each other. I recognize that there is a certain amount of creative misunderstanding occurring within the American community (Indian agents and the public never quite understanding the Miamis, the Shawnees, and the Potawatomies), but I do not see this happening within the French and Miami communities. Although White argues that the Americans failed to enter the middle ground, the growth of cultural misunderstandings continued. Rather than see the misunderstandings of Prophetstown as simply a product of people trying "to persuade others who are different from themselves by appealing to what they perceive to be the values and practices of those others," I argue that the French and Miami very much understood American diplomacy and intentionally created misunderstandings in order to shape William Henry Harrison's Indian policy. White further argues that "Americans invented Indians and forced Indians to live with the consequences of this invention." That is true, but incomplete. As my book demonstrates, Indians and French traders also invented Indians as they created an image of Prophetstown, and Indians also had to live with the legacy of those actions (ibid., x, xv, 449).

2. Robert Owens, *Mr. Jefferson's Hammer: William Henry Harrison and the Origins of Indian Policy* (Norman: University of Oklahoma Press, 2007), 66.

3. This is not to say that slavery in the region was new. In fact, different forms of slavery and captivity had existed in the region for more than a century, but the discussion of slavery in Vincennes was in many ways disconnected from the reality and history of slavery in the western Ohio Valley. For more on the relationship between Atlantic plantation slavery and the captive/sale exchange of the western Ohio Valley, see Brett Rushforth, *Bonds of Alliance: Indigenous and Atlantic Slaveries in New France* (Chapel Hill: University of North Carolina Press, 2014). Francis S. Philbrick, ed., *The Laws of Indiana Territory, 1801–1809* (Springfield: Illinois Historical Library, 1930), xxxvii–xxxviii. Judge Davis to the Attorney General, January 26, 1806, in *The Territorial Papers of the United States*, ed. Clarence Edwin Carter, vol. 7, *The Territory of Indiana, 1800–1810* (Washington DC: GPO, 1939), 335.

4. Owens, *Mr. Jefferson's Hammer*, 78.

5. Ibid., 92–93.

6. My use of the term "white" does not refer to a racial group but rather to the community of American, French, Swiss, and other cultural groups who lived in or near Vincennes. Using the term "American" would speak to only one aspect of the community and would by default exclude other cultural groups like the French from historical consideration.

7. Glenda Riley, "The Specter of a Savage: Rumors and Alarmism on the Overland Trail," *Western Historical Quarterly* 15, no. 4 (October 1984): 428; Glenda Riley, *Confronting Race: Women and Indians on the Frontier, 1815–1915* (Albuquerque: University of New Mexico Press, 2004), 96–97.

8. *Western Sun*, "Indian War," April 15, 1809, May 6, 1809, May 13, 1809; Riley, "Specter of a Savage," 428.

9. Riley, "Specter of a Savage," 428.

10. Owens, *Mr. Jefferson's Hammer*, 6–12.

11. Ibid., 25, 35–36.

12. Andrew R. L. Cayton, *Frontier Indiana* (Bloomington: Indiana University Press, 1996), 238–39.

13. This refers to reports that a small war party of Ottawa and Ojibwe Indians had killed an Indian woman at Prophetstown in the spring of 1809, as well as to a reported attack on Fort Madison by Sac and Ho-Chunk Indians in late 1808. R. David Edmunds, *The Shawnee Prophet* (Lincoln: University of Nebraska Press, 1983), 70–78; John Badollet to Albert Gallatin, November 13, 1809, in John Louis Badollet and Albert Gallatin, *The Correspondence of John Badollet and Albert Gallatin, 1804–1836*, ed. Gayle Thornbrough (Indianapolis: Indiana Historical Society, 1963), 114. Robert Owens discounts much of what Badollet says as simply exaggeration, but upon closer examination, Badollet's fears often ring true, and if Badollet is to be accused of exaggeration, this book demonstrates that so too should Harrison, Wells, and a host of other characters in the region who were also prone to lie and stretch the truth. Furthermore, through exaggeration and inflamed rhetoric about slavery and Indians, frontier diplomats and leaders engaged in a rhetorical process that made real the exaggerations and fears expressed by the inhabitants. Wells to Harrison, April 8, 1809, in *WHH Papers*, reel 3, 380–81; Carter, ed., *Territorial Papers*, 7:650.

14. Owens, *Mr. Jefferson's Hammer*, 200–208; Harrison to Eustis, April 18, 1809, in *WHH Papers*, reel 3, 394; Journal of the Treaty Negotiations with the Delawares, et al., September 24, 1809, ibid., reel 3, 504.

15. Gallatin to Harrison, September 27, 1809, in *WHH Papers*, reel 3, 513; Petition to Congress by Citizens of Harrison County, n.d., 1809, in Carter, ed., *Territorial Papers*, 7:703; Harrison to Gallatin, August 29, 1809, in *WHH Papers*, reel 3, 477.

16. *Western Sun*, October 21, 1809; Annual Message Third General Assembly, October 17, 1809, in *Messages and Letters of William Henry Harrison*, ed. Logan Esarey (Indianapolis: Indiana Historical Commission, 1922), 381; Harrison to Dearborn, February 18, 1808, in *WHH Papers*, reel 3, 113; Badollet to Gallatin, November 13, 1809, in Badollet and Gallatin, *Correspondence*, 114; Gayle Thornbrough and Dorothy L. Riker, eds., *Journals of the General Assembly of Indiana Territory, 1805–1815*, Indiana Historical Collections 32 (Indianapolis: Indiana Historical Bureau, 1950), 321–22; Owens, *Mr. Jefferson's Hammer*, 213–19. Michel Foucault calls this behavior a

"substantial component in the exercise of power" (Foucault, *Michel Foucault, Ethics: Subjectivity and Truth*, ed. Paul Rabinow [New York: New Press, 1994], 36).

17. Benjamin Stickney to Harrison, April 19, 1812, in *WHH Papers*, reel 5, 515; Riley, "Specter of a Savage," 431; Cayton, *Frontier Indiana*, 186.

18. Badollet to Gallatin, November 13, 1809, in Badollet and Gallatin, *Correspondence*, 119; William Wesley Woollen, *Biographical and Historical Sketches of Early Indiana* (Indianapolis: Hammond, 1883), 396-97. McNamee swore to local judge Henry Vanderburgh, a former lieutenant in the Continental Army, "that Thomas Randolph . . . challenged him to fight a duel" and that he feared "Thomas Randolph will take his life and do him some bodily harm" (Woollen, *Biographical and Historical Sketches*, 396-97). Badollet to Gallatin, November 13, 1809, in Badollet and Gallatin, *Correspondence*, 120; Carter, *Territorial Papers*, 7:667n2.

19. The treaty of which Small speaks is an addendum to the Fort Wayne Treaty of 1805. By the Fort Wayne Treaty, Governor William Henry Harrison acquired 2.9 million acres of land in the Wabash and White River Valleys. *Western Sun*, November 18, 1809.

20. Petition to the President and Senate by Citizens of Clark County, n.d., 1809, Indiana Territorial Papers, blue binder, p. 705; *Western Sun*, November 18, 1809.

21. Carter, *Territorial Papers*, 7:703, 705; Philbrick, *Laws of Indiana Territory*, xxxvii-xxxviii. The residents of the western portions of Indiana Territory, while more supportive of slavery, felt that they were not represented in the territorial government. Francis Philbrick states that the governor's "appointments to territorial offices were indeed made exclusively from his intimates of Knox County" (ibid., lvi, xliii, n1).

22. Randy Keith Mills, *Jonathan Jennings: Indiana's First Governor* (Indianapolis: Indiana Historical Society Press, 2005), 2; Harrison to Christopher G. Champlin, November 21, 1809, in *WHH Papers*, reel 3, 655; Jonathan Jennings, *Unedited Letters of Jonathan Jennings: With Notes by Dorothy Riker*, ed. Riker (Indianapolis: Indiana Historical Society Press, 1932), 172-74, 174.

23. Badollet to Gallatin, November 13, 1809, in Badollet and Gallatin, *Correspondence*, 114; Cayton, *Frontier Indiana*, 251-52; Owens, *Mr. Jefferson's Hammer*, xvi.

24. Edmunds, *The Shawnee Prophet*, 83, 151; Badollet to Gallatin, June 24, 1810, in Badollet and Gallatin, *Correspondence*, 161.

25. Judge John Johnson to Albert Gallatin, June 26, 1810, in Badollet and Gallatin, *Correspondence*, 165; John Johnson to John Badollet [enclosure], in Nathaniel Ewing to Albert Gallatin, June 26, 1810, ibid., 159, 165. Johnson heard the discussion over Dubois and suggested that "it would be well in doing this not to infringe on the prerogative of the Governor as he had the exclusive superintendence of Indian affairs. McIntosh and some other present said [they] did not intend to interfere with the proceedings of the Governor in any respect whatsoever." Nathaniel Ewing to Gallatin, June 26, 1810, ibid., 159; Badollet to Gallatin, June 24, 1810, ibid., 151.

26. Ewing to Gallatin, June 26, 1810, in Badollet and Gallatin, *Correspondence*, 159; Badollet to Gallatin, September 25, 1810, ibid., 166.

27. Badollet to Gallatin, September 25, 1810, in Badollet and Gallatin, *Correspondence*, 166; quote from Harrison to Eustis, April 18, 1809, in *WHH Papers*, reel 3, 392; Badollet to Gallatin, September 25, 1810, in Badollet and Gallatin, *Correspondence*, 166; quote from Harrison to Eustis, April 18, 1809, in *WHH Papers*, reel 3, 392;

Badollet to Gallatin, September 25, 1810, in Badollet and Gallatin, *Correspondence*, 166; Ewing to Gallatin, June 26, 1810, ibid., 159; *Western Sun*, June 23, 1810.

28. Elihu Stout's record of Tecumseh's visit, "Negotiations at an Indian Council," *Western Sun*, August 12–21, 1810, in *WHH Papers*, reel 4, 148; *Western Sun*, October 13, 1810.

29. Ewing to Gallatin, June 26, 1810, in Badollet and Gallatin, *Correspondence*, 159; *Western Sun*, June 26, 1810; Ewing to Gallatin, June 26, 1810, in Badollet and Gallatin, *Correspondence*, 163. Ewing recognized that peace north of Vincennes would be profitable for a man who at times traded with the local Indians (George E. Greene, *History of Old Vincennes and Knox County, Indiana* [Indiana: S. J. Clarke, 1911], 323).

30. Harrison to Eustis, August 28, 1810, in *WHH Papers*, reel 4, 180; Harrison to Eustis, August 22, 1810, in Esarey, ed., *Messages and Letters of Harrison*, 459; Philbrick, ed., *Laws of Indiana Territory*, 136–38; Badollet to Jennings, December 25, 1810, in Badollet and Gallatin, *Correspondence*, 175; Thornbrough and Riker, eds., *Journals of the General Assembly*, 352–55; Harrison to Eustis, July 4, 1810, in *WHH Papers*, reel 4, 79; Badollet to Jennings, December 25, 1810, in Badollet and Gallatin, *Correspondence*, 175; Thornbrough and Riker, eds., *Journals of the General Assembly*, 352–53, 355; Harrison to Eustis, August 28, 1810, in *WHH Papers*, reel 4, 179.

31. Harrison to Eustis, July 10, 1811, in *WHH Papers*, reel 4, 630, 632. Harrison wrote Secretary of War William Eustis and asked him to disregard any charges that his actions toward the Prophet had been "premature and unfounded." Harrison reminded Eustis that the president was "too just to censure an officer for an unintentional error or to lend a favorable ear the calumnies" produced by his enemies. Yet such comments reflect Harrison's fear that he might indeed be removed. Harrison to Eustis, August 28, 1810, in *WHH Papers*, reel 4, 178–79; Harrison to Eustis, July 10, 1811, ibid., reel 4, 629–32; Harrison to Gov. Charles Scott, December 13, 1811, ibid., reel 5, 146–47.

32. *Western Sun*, July 27, 1811. Edmunds suggests that Harrison's behavior toward Tecumseh was a product of "rumors that Tecumseh originally planned to murder him," and while this was likely true, the greater motivation may have been territorial politics and Harrison's effort to make real the threat he had spoken about in public (Edmunds, *The Shawnee Prophet*, 104). Badollet to Gallatin, August 6, 1811, in Badollet and Gallatin, *Correspondence*, 182–92, quote on 187; Harrison to Eustis, August 13, 1811, in *WHH Papers*, reel 4, 714. Harrison writes: "Heedless of futurity, it is only by placing the danger before his eyes, that a Savage is to be control'd. Even the gallant Tecumseh is not insensible to an argument of this kind. No courtier could be more complaisant, than he was upon his late visit. To have heard him one would have supposed, that he came here for the purpose of complimenting me. This wonderful Metamorphosis in manner, was entirely produced by the gleaming & clanging of arms, & by frowns of a considerable body of hunting Shirt men, which accidentally lined a road, by which he approached to the council." Badollet to Gallatin, August 6, 1811, in Badollet and Gallatin, *Correspondence*, 182–92, quote on 188.

33. Harrison to Eustis, July 10, 1811, in *WHH Papers*, reel 4, 630. Earlier that year, Jonathan Jennings had written to someone that he planned to impeach the governor. "The governor is very unpopular here and daily becomes more unpopular—I have received depositions and certificates with charges against Harrison and have shwen [*sic*] them to several members of Congress and they all tell I am bound to give them their usual cause and declare he ought to be out of office—His political career is ended.

I shall lay the groundwork of an impeachment before ten days. The above is confidence until I see you" (Jonathan Jennings to Solomon Manwarring, January 22, 1811, in Esarey, *Messages and Letters of Harrison*, 501-2). Ibid.

34. *Western Sun*, August 3, 1811; Resolutions Concerning Indians, July 31, 1811, in Esarey, *Messages and Letters of Harrison*, 541.

35. Harrison to Eustis, August 22, 1810, in *Messages and Letters of Harrison*, 462; Harrison to Eustis, November 7, 1810, in *WHH Papers*, reel 4, 255; Harrison to Eustis, January 15, 1811, ibid., reel 4, 322; Harrison to Eustis, April 23, 1811, in Esarey, *Messages and Letters of Harrison*, 509.

36. Harrison vs William McIntosh, April 10, 1811, in *WHH Papers*, reel 4, 474. Harrison recounted the events surrounding McIntosh, stating that Harrison "had commenced a suit against a certain Wm McIntosh, a Scotchman residing at this place, for slandering me in relation to my management of the Indian Department—The accusations which he brought against me were of the most serious nature—'Such as defrauding the Indians in the treaties I have made with them Making chiefs to answer my own particular purposes—Excluding the real Chiefs &c—By this and other conduct producing all the disturbances which have taken place in the Indian Country, & the Alarm produced in this &c'—This suit was tried in the Superior Court of this Territory on the 11 Inst:" (Harrison to Eustis, April 23, 1811, ibid., reel 4, 488).

37. Harrison to William Hull, August 20, 1811, in *WHH Papers*, reel 4, 726; Harrison to the Miami, et al., August 21, 1811, ibid., reel 4, 731-32; Harrison to John Johnston, August 23, 1811, ibid., reel 4, 738.

38. Speeches of Miami, et al. Chiefs, September 4, 1811, in *WHH Papers*, reel 4, 756, 757, 758.

39. Silver Heels to Harrison, speech, September 4, 1811, in *WHH Papers*, reel 4, 759. Other chiefs were as frustrated as Lapoussier. The Massassinway (Miami) chief Silver Heels emphasized his opposition to the Prophet but also claimed neutrality because his interests were first with the Miamis and concerned only secondly with the problems between the Prophet and the Americans.

40. Harrison to Eustis, September 17, 1811, in *WHH Papers*, reel 4, 785; Eustis to Harrison, July 20, 1811, ibid., reel 4, 655.

41. Benjamin Parke to Harrison, September 13, 1811, in *WHH Papers*, reel 4, 777.

42. Harrison to Gov. Charles Scott, December 13, 1811, in *WHH Papers*, reel 5, 146; Henry Swearingen, October 7, 1811, OM 0066, Indiana Historical Society, Indianapolis.

43. John Badollet to Albert Badollet, October 18, 1811, John Badollet Papers, Regional History Collection #6, Lewis Historical Library, Vincennes University, Vincennes IN; italics added; *National Intelligencer* (Washington DC), September 17, 1811; Badollet to Gallatin, October 15, 1811, in Badollet and Gallatin, *Correspondence*, 194, 195.

44. "For many migrants, rumor was far worse than reality. Their fears were seldom realized, and their trepidation proved to be largely unfounded. Most were actually harassed and plagued by their own angst more than they were by Indians" (Riley, "Specter of a Savage," 433).

45. Paul A. Gilje, *The Making of the American Republic, 1763-1815* (Upper Saddle River NJ: Pearson Prentice Hall, 2006), 275-76.

5 / The Battles of Tippecanoe

1. Sean Wilentz, *The Rise of American Democracy*, vol. 1, *The Crisis of the New Order, 1787–1815* (New York: Norton, 2007), 449; Richard White, *The Middle Ground: Indians, Empires, and Republics in the Great Lakes Region, 1650–1815* (Cambridge: Cambridge University Press, 1991), 517; Wilentz, *Rise of American Democracy*, 177. The Battle of Tippecanoe is hereafter called Tippecanoe. Alfred A. Cave states that the recent revisionist historiography concerning the Prophet has "left one major part of the old story untouched: Tenskwatawa's presumed disgrace at the Battle of Tippecanoe in 1811. Both textbooks and specialized histories still generally maintain that the Prophet's blundering and cowardice at Tippecanoe cost him the respect of his followers and the leadership of the movement, which was presumably then taken over by Tecumseh who transformed it from a religious crusade into a pragmatic political alliance" (Cave, "The Shawnee Prophet, Tecumseh, and Tippecanoe: A Case Study of Historical Myth-Making," *Journal of the Early Republic* 22, no. 4 [Winter 200]: 639).

2. James Buss brilliantly traces the ways in which Americans forgot about and even ignored Indians as they settled west in the period after 1820. Much of what happened concerning the memory of the Battle of Tippecanoe after 1820 reflects the patterns he identifies, yet, in Indiana, settlers could not simply ignore Indians, in particular the Miamis. Buss argues that placing "too much emphasis on the ability of Native leaders to shape the minds of American officials overlooks" people such as Harrison and other Americans who could simply "ignore" Indians at the end of the War of 1812. As my book demonstrates, Indians such as the Miamis did not simply vanish after the War of 1812, nor could they be ignored. And more importantly, the legacy of the fight over Prophetstown influenced the ways in which Harrison and other Americans thought about Native violence for years to come. So, yes, Harrison could ignore Indians, but he could not ignore the ways in which they had shaped his thinking or the ways in which ideas about Indians could be used to silence political adversaries (Buss, *Winning the West through Words: Language and Conquest through the Lower Great Lakes* [Norman: University of Oklahoma Press, 2011], 41).

3. Harrison to Eustis, July 10, 1811, in *WHH Papers*, reel 4, 630; Henry Swearingen, October 7, 1811, OM 0066, Indiana Historical Society, Indianapolis; Alfred Pirtle, *The Battle of Tippecanoe* (Louisville KY: J. P. Morton, 1900), 27, 29.

4. Pirtle, *Battle of Tippecanoe*, 29.

5. Ibid., 41.

6. Cave, "Historical Myth-Making," 653–54.

7. Lydia B. Bacon, journal, November 30, 1811, New York Historical Society; Cave, "Historical Myth-Making," 656; Cave, *Prophets of the Great Spirit: Native American Revitalization Movements in Eastern North America* (Lincoln: University of Nebraska Press, 2006), 133–35.

8. These scholars include Stephen Warren in *The Shawnees and Their Neighbors, 1795–1870* (Urbana: University of Illinois Press, 2005), 40; and R. David Edmunds in *The Shawnee Prophet* (Lincoln: University of Nebraska Press, 1983), 110–11.

9. Indian Speeches—Chiefs. Yealabahcah and the Prophet to Lewis Cass, 1816, Lewis Cass Papers, William L. Clements Library, University of Michigan, Ann Arbor; Cave, "Historical Myth-Making," 655; Indian Speeches—Chiefs. Yealabahcah and the Prophet to Lewis Cass, 1816, Cass Papers; Cave, *Prophets of the Great Spirit*, 118–23. Cave argues that the Prophet probably did not order an attack on Harrison's forces,

but he does so to critique historical conclusions that the Prophet lost his religious influence after the battle. I argue that he did not order an attack because he was unable to control his men and that such behavior was in concert with the way Prophetstown had always operated.

10. Lydia B. Bacon, journal, November 30, 1811, New York Historical Society.

11. Harrison to Charles Scott, November 19, 1811, in *WHH Papers*, reel 5, 147; Harrison to Eustis, December 28, 1811, ibid., reel 5, 219; John Badollet to Albert Gallatin, December 30, 1811, in John Louis Badollet and Albert Gallatin, *The Correspondence of John Badollet and Albert Gallatin, 1804-1836*, ed. Gayle Thornbrough (Indianapolis: Indiana Historical Society, 1963), 217; Badollet to Gallatin, December 4, 1811, ibid., 210.

12. Robert S. Lambert, "The Conduct of the Militia at Tippecanoe: Elihu Stout's Controversy with Colonel John P. Boyd, January, 1812," *Indiana Magazine of History* 51, no. 3 (September 1955): 239; Resolution adopted at a meeting of the Knox County Militia, December 7, 1811, in *WHH Papers*, reel 5, 159. This document is one of two enclosures in a December 18 letter from Harrison to Governor Scott (italics in original). Lambert, "Conduct of the Militia at Tippecanoe," 239, 240-41.

13. Harrison to Eustis, January 14, 1812, in *WHH Papers*, reel 5, 273.

14. Harrison to Stout, February 12, 1812, in *WHH Papers*, reel 5, 359.

15. Josiah Snelling to Harrison, February 17, 1812, in *WHH Papers*, reel 5, 375.

16. Statement by Officers, November 17, 1811, in *Messages and Letters of William Henry Harrison*, ed. Logan Esarey (Indianapolis: Indiana Historical Commission, 1922), 634. This document is a statement signed two weeks after the Battle of Tippecanoe by five militia officers and one Regular Army officer. Harrison to Scott, December 13, 1811, in Pirtle, *Battle of Tippecanoe*, 102; *New York Commercial Advertiser*, December 4, 1811.

17. *Western Sun*, January 18, 1812.

18. Ibid., January 25, 1812; Lambert, "Conduct of the Militia at Tippecanoe," 242-44.

19. Badollet to Gallatin, February 26, 1812, in Badollet and Gallatin, *Correspondence*, 224.

20. Snelling to Harrison, February 17, 1812, in *WHH Papers*, reel 5, 375; Snelling to Harrison, January 18, 1812, ibid., reel 5, 289.

21. George Hunt to Harrison, March 17, 1812, in *WHH Papers*, reel 5, 445; Badollet to Gallatin, April 29, 1812, in Badollet and Gallatin, *Correspondence*, 227; *Western Sun*, May 26, 1812; Badollet to Gallatin, May 19, 1812, in Badollet and Gallatin, *Correspondence*, 234; Badollet to Gallatin, April 29, 1812, ibid., 227.

22. Badollet to Gallatin, November 19, 1811, in Badollet and Gallatin, *Correspondence*, 209.

23. Badollet to Gallatin, May 6, 1812, in Badollet and Gallatin, *Correspondence*, 229; Harrison to Eustis, May 6, 1812, in *WHH Papers*, reel 5, 546; Harrison to Eustis, May 13, 1812, ibid., reel 5, 564.

24. Badollet to Gallatin, May 27, 1812, in Badollet and Gallatin, *Correspondence*, 236; Badollet to Gallatin, April 29, 1812, ibid., 227.

25. *Western Sun*, May 26, 1812.

26. Ibid.

27. Harrison to Eustis, July 8, 1812, in *WHH Papers*, reel 5, 668.

28. Badollet to Gallatin, June 7, 1812, in Badollet and Gallatin, *Correspondence*, 240–41.

29. Charles M. Franklin, *Indiana: War of 1812 Soldiers* (Indianapolis: Ye Olde Geneology Shoppe, 1984), 48–49; Jay Gitlin, "Old Wine in New Bottles: French Merchants and the Emergence of the American Midwest, 1795–1835," *Proceedings of the Thirteenth and Fourteenth Meetings of the French Colonial Historical Society*, ed. Philip P. Boucher (Lanham MD: University Press of America, 1990), 44–46.

30. Harrison to Eustis, April 25, 1810, in *WHH Papers*, reel 3, 827. Harrison states: "The friends of the French Traders amongst the Indians have advised them to separate themselves from the Americans in this town, lest they should suffer in the attack, which they meditate against the latter."

31. Franklin, *Indiana: War of 1812 Soldiers*, 48–49.

32. Benjamin Parke to Thomas Posey, December 7, 1814, in *Messages and Letters of William Henry Harrison, John Gibson, and Thomas Posey*, ed. Logan Esarey (Indianapolis: Indiana Historical Commission, 1922), 679; Posey to James Monroe, November 18, 1814, ibid., 669; Parke to Posey, December 21, 1814, ibid., 680; Parke to Posey, February 15, 1815, ibid., 686.

33. Brouillet was a regular at Fort Harrison, and LaPlante is relatively absent from the record.

34. Posey to James Monroe, November 18, 1814, Jeffersonville, Indiana Territory, in *Messages and Letters of Harrison, Gibson, and Posey*, ed. Esarey, 669.

35. John Bradbury, *Travels in the Interior of America* (Liverpool: Smith and Galway, 1817), 263–64; David Thomas, *Travels through the Western Country in the Summer of 1816: Including Notices of the Natural History, Antiquities, Topography, Agriculture, Commerce and Manufacturers* (Auburn NY: David Rumsey, 1819), 143; Denise Marie Wilson, "Vincennes: From French Colonial Village to American Frontier Town, 1730–1820" (PhD diss., West Virginia University, 1997), 343; Mary A. Brouilette, "The Creole (French) Pioneers at Old Post Vincennes," in *The Federal Writers' Project District 5 (Vincennes Office)*, ed. Doyle Joyce, Loy Followell, Elizabeth Kargacos, Bernice Mutchmore, and Paul R. King (Vincennes IN: Works Progress Administration, 1930), n.p.

36. *Western Sun*, June 2, 1812.

37. Ibid.; Brouilette, "The Creole (French) Pioneers," n.p.; Patrick Hutton, *History as an Art of Memory* (Hanover NH: University Press of New England, 1993), 128.

38. Cave, "Historical Myth-Making," 656. Cave states that Little Eyes "may well have endeavored to mislead the Americans about the Prophet's actual status after Tippecanoe." Cave offers this conclusion based on tenuous reports that Little Eyes was "reputedly an ally of the Prophet," but I argue that it was more likely, given the ways in which the Miami utilized Prophetstown to protect their interests, that Little Eyes was an ally neither of the Prophet nor of the Americans.

39. John Sugden, *Tecumseh: A Life* (New York: Henry Holt, 1998), 230. Peter Mancall and James Merrell agree with Cave (Mancall and Merrell, eds., *American Encounters: Natives and Newcomers from European Contact to Indian Removal* [New York: Routledge, 2000], 392).

40. Harrison to Eustis, April 15, 1812, in *WHH Papers*, reel 5, 495.

41. Harrison to Eustis, December 24, 1811, in *WHH Papers*, reel 5, 200; Badollet to Gallatin, May 19, 1812, in Badollet and Gallatin, *Correspondence*, 233.

42. Harrison to Eustis, December 24, 1811, in *WHH Papers*, reel 5, 200.

43. Ibid.; Harrison to Secretary of War, January 7, 1812, in *Governors Messages and Letters*, vol. 2 of *Indiana Historical Collections* (Indianapolis: Indiana Historical Commission, 1922), 5.

44. Wells to Harrison, July 30, 1812, in *WHH Papers*, reel 5, 730.

45. Speeches of Indians at Massassinway, May 15, 1812, in *Messages and Letters of Harrison, Gibson, and Posey*, ed. Esarey, 50, 53.

46. Paul A. Gilje, *The Making of the American Republic, 1763–1815* (Upper Saddle River NJ: Pearson Prentice Hall, 2006), 280.

47. Harrison to Eustis, September 3, 1812, in *WHH Papers*, reel 6, 076; Harrison to Eustis, September 21, 1812, ibid., reel 6, 203; Clark to Eustis, August 10, 1812, ibid., reel 5, 801.

48. Pierre Andrie to Thomas Posey, February 8, 1815, in *Messages and Letters of Harrison, Gibson, and Posey*, 686; Benjamin Parke to Posey, May 25, 1815, ibid., 691.

49. Parke to Posey, February 6, 1816, in *Messages and Letters of Harrison, Gibson, and Posey*, ed. Esarey, 716; Posey to William Crawford, April 20, 1816, ibid., 725; Benjamin Stickney, Indian agent at Fort Wayne, to Thomas L. McKenney, superintendent of Indian affairs, August 27, 1817, qtd. in Wallace A. Brice, *History of Fort Wayne* (Fort Wayne, IN: D. W. Jones and Son, 1868), 291; Stewart Rafert, *The Miami Indians of Indiana: A Persistent People, 1654–1994* (Indianapolis: Indiana Historical Society Press, 1996), 80; Posey to Crawford, April 20, 1816, in *Messages and Letters of Harrison, Gibson, and Posey*, ed. Esarey, 725.

50. Treaty of Greenville of 1814; Parke to Posey, February 6, 1816, in *Messages and Letters of Harrison, Gibson, and Posey*, ed. Esarey, 716; Resolution of the Constitutional Convention, June 29, 1816, ibid., 728.

51. Harlow Lindley, ed., *Indiana as Seen by Early Travelers: Collection of Reprints from Books of Travel, Letters and Diaries Prior to 1830* (Indianapolis: Indiana Historical Commission, 1916), 66.

52. Harrison to Secretary of War, March 22, 1814, in *Messages and Letters of Harrison, Gibson, and Posey*, ed. Esarey, 637.

53. Federal Writers' Project, *Indiana: A Guide to the Hoosier State* (New York: Reprint Services Corp., 1941), 198; Rafert, *The Miami Indians* 107, 135.

54. Rafert, *The Miami Indians*, 113.

55. An act of March 3, 1819, provided funds for Indians to learn the "habits and arts of civilization," which in total amounted to ten thousand dollars, of which the Miamis were given a portion. William Lee to Tipton, May 17, 1823, and footnote 13 in *U.S. Statutes at Large* 3:516–17. Statements of expenditures from the fund are printed in *American State Papers. Indian Affairs*, 2:368. 370, 443. John Tipton, *The John Tipton Papers*, vol. 1, *1809–1827*, ed. Nellie Armstrong Robertson and Dorothy L. Riker (Indianapolis: Indiana Historical Bureau, 1942), 307; Rafert, *The Miami Indians*, 87.

56. Rafert, *The Miami Indians*, 107–8.

57. Ibid., 90.

58. Ibid., 92; Tipton, *John Tipton Papers*, 1:400.

59. Ana Maria Alonso, "The Politics of Space, Time and Substance: State Formation, Nationalism, and Ethnicity," *Annual Review of Anthropology* 23 (1994): 394–95.

60. Tipton, *John Tipton Papers*, 1:275.

61. John Tipton, *The John Tipton Papers*, vol. 2, *1828–1833*, ed. Nellie Armstrong Robertson and Dorothy L. Riker (Indianapolis: Indiana Historical Bureau, 1942), 2:833, 832 (italics added).

62. Ibid., 2:833.

63. The phrase "invention of tradition" references the processes in which "societies create historical narratives or rituals to suit contemporary political or cultural conditions" (Kammen, *Mystic Chords of Memory*, 117–32; Kelman, *A Misplaced Massacre: Struggling over the Memory of Sand Creek*, 73). Thomas A. Chambers argues that "Americans imagined a past rooted in martial sacrifice, which provided the basis for a shared nationalism" (Chambers, *Memories of War: Visiting Battlegrounds and Bonefields in the Early American Republic* [Ithaca: Cornell University Press, 2012], 16).

64. "The Presidency," *Western Sun and General Advertiser*, October 31, 1835.

65. Geoffrey Cubitt, *History and Memory* (Manchester: Manchester University Press, 2007), 141–42.

66. Francois Furstenberg has challenged the prevailing interpretation that the violence of the Ohio Valley was simply a by-product of the conflict that arose from British imperialism and American nationalism. Instead, Furstenberg situates the violence of the Ohio Valley within the debates of the Seven Years' War, thereby extending both its geographical and temporal interpretations. My book also expands the temporal and geographical frameworks of violence in the western Ohio Valley by situating the conflict within the Miami borderland in the mid-eighteenth century. Like Furstenberg, my book maintains a focus on the French and indigenous peoples of the region, who typically fall out of the story after the Seven Years' War, but as part of the prevailing influences of the Miami world rather than the entire Ohio Valley (Furstenberg, "Anglo-America and Its Borderlands," in *Major Problems in the History of North American Borderlands*, ed. Pekka Hämäläinen and Benjamin Johnson [Boston: Wadsworth, 2012]).

67. Benjamin Drake, *Life of Tecumseh and His Brother the Prophet with a Historical Sketch of the Shawanoe Indians* (Cincinnati OH: E. Morgan, 1850), 153, 154.

68. John Tipton, *The John Tipton Papers*, ed. Nellie Armstrong Robertson and Dorothy L. Riker, 2 vols. (Indianapolis: Indiana Historical Bureau, 1942), 2:832–33.

69. R. David Edmunds, *The Shawnee Prophet* (Lincoln: University of Nebraska Press, 1983), 160; William MacDonald, ed., *Select Documents Illustrative of the History of the United States, 1776–1861* (New York: Ayer, 1968), 197.

70. Lewis Cass to John C. Calhoun, November 21, 1819, Cass Papers, Burton Collection, Detroit Public Library; Cass to Calhoun, December 25, 1819, Shawnee File, Great Lakes Indian Archives; Johnson to Cass, November 9, 1816, ibid.; Alexander Wolcott to Cass, November 14, 1819, in *Territorial Papers of the United States*, ed. Clarence Edwin Carter, vol. 10, *The Territory of Michigan, 1805–1820* (Washington DC: GPO, 1942), 855–57; Edmunds, *The Shawnee Prophet*, 168.

71. Edmunds, *The Shawnee Prophet*, 185–88.

72. Isaac Rand Jackson, *A Sketch of the Life and Public Services of William Henry Harrison* (Columbus OH:, I. N. Whiting, 1840); S. J. Burr, *The Life and Times of William Henry Harrison* (New York: L. W. Ransom, 1840); James Hall, *A Memoir of the Public Services of William Henry Harrison of Ohio* (Philadelphia: Key and Biddle, 1836); Caleb Cushing, *Outlines of the Life and Public Services, Civil and Military, of William Henry Harrison* (Boston: Weeks, Jordan, 1840); Richard Hildreth, *The People's Presidential*

Candidate; or, The Life of William Henry Harrison of Ohio (Boston: Weeks, Jordan, 1839); Captain Miller, *Hero of Tippecanoe; or, The Story of the Life of William Henry Harrison* (New York: J. P. Giffing, 1840); Jacob Bailey Moore, *The Contrast; or, Plain Reasons Why William Henry Harrison Should Be Elected President of the United States: And Why Martin Van Buren Should Not Be Re-Elected* (New York: J. P. Giffing, 1840).

73. Robert Vincent Remini, *The Jacksonian Era* (Arlington Heights IL: H. Davidson, 1997), 78; Jacob Piatt Dunn, "Indiana Geographical Nomenclature," *Indiana Magazine of History* 8, no. 3 (September 1912): 113.

74. Miller, *Hero of Tippecanoe*, 72; William McCarty, *Songs, Odes, & Other Poems, on National Subjects; Compiled from Various Sources* (Philadelphia: W. McCarty, 1842), 249; John P. Bowes, *Exiles and Pioneers: Eastern Indians in the Trans-Mississippi West* (Cambridge: Cambridge University Press, 2007), 255–60; Theda Perdue and Michael D. Green, *The Cherokee Nation and the Trail of Tears* (New York: Penguin, 2008), 42–69.

75. Edmunds, *The Shawnee Prophet*, 187.

76. Susan Sleeper-Smith, *Indian Women and French Men: Rethinking Cultural Encounters in the Western Great Lakes* (Amherst: University of Massachusetts Press, 2001), 119.

77. Ibid., 135–36.

78. Ibid., 129, 139.

79. Ann Laura Stoler, ed., *Haunted by Empire: Geographies of Intimacy in North American History* (Durham NC: Duke University Press, 2006), 3.

80. Joshua Piker, "Lying Together: The Imperial Implications of Cross-Cultural Untruths," *American Historical Review* 116 (2011): 985.

Bibliography

Archives and Manuscript Materials

Badollet, John. Papers. Lewis Historical Library. Vincennes University, Vincennes IN.

Bentley Historical Library. University of Michigan, Ann Arbor.

Cass, Lewis. Papers. Burton Historical Collection. Detroit Public Library, Detroit MI.

Cass, Lewis. Papers. William L. Clements Library. University of Michigan, Ann Arbor.

Court of Common Pleas for Knox County. Indiana State Archives. Indianapolis.

Gage, Thomas. Papers. William L. Clements Library. University of Michigan, Ann Arbor.

Great Lakes Indian Archives. Indiana University. Bloomington.

Indiana Historical Society. Indianapolis.

Jones Collection. Cincinnati Historical Society. Cincinnati OH.

New York Historical Society. New York NY.

Pennsylvania Historical Society. Philadelphia.

St. Francis Xavier Parish Records, vol. *1796–1808*.

United States National Archives. Washington DC.

Wayne, Anthony. Papers. Historical Society of Pennsylvania. Philadelphia.

William H. English Collection. University of Chicago Library.

Published Works

Adelman, Jeremy, and Stephen Aron. "From Borderlands to Borders: Empires, Nation-States, and the Peoples in Between in North American History." *American Historical Review* 104, no. 3 (1999): 814–41.

Allen, Helen L. "Sketch of the Dubois Family, Pioneers of Indiana and Illinois." *Journal of the Illinois State Historical Society* 5, no. 1 (April 1912): 50–65.

Alonso, Anna Maria. "The Politics of Space, Time, and Substance: State Formation, Nationalism, and Ethnicity." *Annual Review of Anthropology* 23 (1994): 379–405.

Alvord, Clarence Walworth, and Clarence Edwin Carter, eds. *Collections of the Illinois State Historical Library*. Vol. 11, *The New Régime, 1765–1767*. Springfield: Illinois State Historical Society, 1916.

American State Papers: Indian Affairs and the Northwest Indians, March 3, 1789 to March 3, 1815. Vol. 1. Washington DC: GPO, 1832.

Anson, Bert. *The Miami Indians*. Norman: University of Oklahoma, 1970.

Appleby, Joyce. "Republicanism and Ideology." *American Quarterly* 37, no. 4 (Autumn 1985): 461–73.

Badollet, John Louis, and Albert Gallatin. *The Correspondence of John Badollet and Albert Gallatin, 1804–1836*. Edited by Gayle Thornbrough. Indianapolis: Indiana Historical Society, 1963.

Barnhart, John D., ed. *Henry Hamilton and George Rogers Clark in the American Revolution*. Crawfordsville IN: R. E. Banta, 1951.

Barnhart, John D., and Dorothy L. Riker., eds. *Indiana to 1816: The Colonial Period*. Indianapolis: Indiana Historical Bureau, 1971.

Beckwith, H. W., ed. *Collections of the Illinois State Historical Library*. Vol. 1. Springfield IL: R. W. Rokker, 1903.

Biggs, William. *Narrative of the Captivity of William Biggs among the Kickapoo Indians in Illinois in 1788*. Metuchen NJ: C. F. Heartman, 1922.

Birzer, Bradley J. "French Imperial Remnants on the Middle Ground: The Strange Case of August de la Balme and Charles Beaubien." *Journal of the Illinois State Historical Society* 93 (Summer 2000): 135–54.

Blackhawk, Ned. *Violence over the Land: Indians and Empires in the Early American West*. Cambridge: Harvard University Press, 2008.

Blasingham, Emily J. "The Depopulation of the Illinois Indians." *Ethnohistory* 3, no. 4 (Autumn 1956): 361–412.

Bodley, Thomas, and John Wade. "Notes on the Wabash in 1795." Edited by Dwight L. Smith. *Indiana Magazine of History* 50, no. 3 (September 1954): 277–90.

Bottiger, Patrick. "Stabbed in the Back: Vincennes, Slavery, and the Indian 'Threat.'" *Indiana Magazine of History* 107 (June 2011): 89–122.

Bowes, John P. *Exiles and Pioneers: Eastern Indians in the Trans-Mississippi West*. Cambridge: Cambridge University Press, 2007.

Boyd, Steven, ed. *The Whiskey Rebellion: Past and Present Perspectives*. Westport CT: Greenwood, 1985.

Bradbury, John. *Travels in the Interior of America*. Liverpool: Smith and Galway, 1817.

Brice, Wallace A. *History of Fort Wayne*. Fort Wayne IN: D. W. Jones and Son, 1868.

Brouillett, Michel Bradamore. *A Collection of Cotillions, Scotch Reels, &c. Intro-duced at the Dancing School of M. B. Brouillett.* Logansport IN: Lasselle, 1834.

Brouilette, Mary A. "The Creole (French) Pioneers at Old Post Vincennes." In *The Federal Writers' Project District 5 (Vincennes Office)*, edited by Doyle Joyce, Loy Followell, Elizabeth Kargacos, Bernice Mutchmore, and Paul R. King. Vincennes IN: Works Progress Administration, 1930.

Burr, S. J. *The Life and Times of William Henry Harrison.* New York: L. W. Ransom, 1840.

Calloway, Colin G. *The Shawnees and the War for America.* New York: Viking, 2008.

Carter, Clarence Edwin, ed. *Territorial Papers of the United States.* Vols. 2 and 3, *The Territory Northwest of the River Ohio, 1787–1803.* Washington DC: GPO, 1934.

———, ed. *The Territorial Papers of the United States.* Vol. 7, *The Territory of Indiana, 1800–1810.* Washington DC: GPO, 1939.

———, ed. *Territorial Papers of the United States.* Vol. 10, *The Territory of Michigan, 1805–1820.* Washington DC: GPO, 1942.

———, ed. *The Territorial Papers of the United States.* Vol. 14, *The Territory of Louisiana-Missouri, 1806–1814.* Washington DC: GPO, 1949.

Carter, Harvey Lewis. *The Life and Times of Little Turtle: First Sagamore of the Wabash.* Urbana: University of Illinois Press, 1987.

Cave, Alfred A. *Prophets of the Great Spirit: Native American Revitalization Movements in Eastern North America.* Lincoln: University of Nebraska Press, 2006.

———. "The Shawnee Prophet, Tecumseh, and Tippecanoe: A Case Study of Historical Myth-Making." *Journal of the Early Republic* 22, no. 4 (Winter 2002): 637–73.

Cayton, Andrew R. L. *Frontier Indiana: A History of the Trans-Appalachian Frontier.* Bloomington: Indiana University Press, 1996.

———. *The Frontier Republic: Ideology and Politics in the Ohio Country, 1780–1825.* Kent OH: Kent State University Press, 1986.

———. "Race, Democracy, and the Multiple Meanings of the Indiana Frontier." In *Indiana Territory: A Bicentennial Perspective*, edited by Darrel E. Bigham, 47–71. Indianapolis: Indiana Historical Society, 2001.

Chambers, Thomas A. *Memories of War: Visiting Battleground and Bonefields in the Early American Republic.* Ithaca: Cornell University Press, 2012.

Clifton, James A. *The Prairie People: Continuity and Change in Potawatomi Indian Culture, 1665–1965.* Lawrence: Regents Press of Kansas, 1977.

Cockrum, William Monroe. *Pioneer History of Indiana: Including Stories, Incidents, and Customs of the Early Settlers.* Oakland City IN: Press of Oakland City Journal, 1907.

Cushing, Caleb. *Outlines of the Life and Public Services, Civil and Military, of William Henry Harrison.* Boston: Weeks, Jordan, 1840.

Cutler, Jervase. *A Topographical Description of the State of Ohio, Indiana Territory, and Louisiana*. Boston: Charles Williams, 1812.

Dain, Bruce. *A Hideous Monster of the Mind: American Race Theory in the Early Republic*. Cambridge: Harvard University Press, 2003.

Davidson, Alexander, and Bernard Stuve. *A Complete History of Illinois from 1673 to 1873*. Springfield: Illinois Journal Co., 1877.

Davis, David Brion. *The Slave Power Conspiracy and the Paranoid Style*. Baton Rouge: Louisiana State University Press, 1969.

Dawson, Moses. *A Historical Narrative of the Civil and Military Services of Major-General William H. Harrison, and a Vindication of His Character and Conduct as a Statesman, a Citizen, and a Soldier*. Cincinnati OH: M. Dawson, 1824.

Denny, Ebenezer. *Military Journal of Major Ebenezer Denny*. Philadelphia: Lippincott, 1859.

Dixon, David. *Never Come to Peace Again: Pontiac's Uprising and the Fate of the British Empire in North America*. Norman: University of Oklahoma Press, 2005.

Dowd, Gregory Evans. "The French King Wakes up in Detroit: 'Pontiac's War' in Rumor and History." *Ethnohistory* 37, no. 3 (Summer 1990): 254–78.

———. "The Panic of 1751: The Significance of Rumors on the South Carolina-Cherokee Frontier." *William and Mary Quarterly* 53, no. 3 (July 1996): 527–60.

———. *A Spirited Resistance: The North American Struggle for Unity, 1745–1815*. Baltimore: Johns Hopkins University Press, 1990.

Drake, Benjamin. *Life of Tecumseh and His Brother the Prophet with a Historical Sketch of the Shawanoe Indians*. Cincinnati OH: E. Morgan, 1850.

Dunn, Jacob Piatt. "Indiana Geographical Nomenclature." *Indiana Magazine of History* 8, no. 3 (September 1912): 109–14.

———. *The Mission to the Ouabache*. Indiana Historical Society Publications 3, no. 4. Indianapolis: Bowen-Merrill, 1902.

———, ed. *Slavery Petitions and Papers*. Indiana Historical Society Publications 2, no. 12. Indianapolis: Bowen-Merrill, 1894.

DuVal, Kathleen. *The Native Ground: Indians and Colonists in the Heart of the Continent*. Philadelphia: University of Pennsylvania Press, 2007.

Edmunds, R. David. "Forgotten Allies: The Loyal Shawnees and the War of 1812." In *The Sixty Years' War for the Great Lakes, 1754–1814*, edited by David C. Skaggs and Larry L. Nelson, 337–51. East Lansing: Michigan State University Press, 2001.

———. *The Potawatomis: Keepers of the Fire*. Norman: University of Oklahoma Press, 1978.

———. *The Shawnee Prophet*. Lincoln: University of Nebraska Press, 1983.

Esarey, Logan, ed. *A History of Indiana from Its Exploration to 1850*. Indianapolis: B. F. Bowen, 1918.

———, ed. *Messages and Letters of William Henry Harrison*. Indianapolis: Indiana Historical Commission, 1922.

———, ed. *Messages and Letters of William Henry Harrison, John Gibson, and Thomas Posey*. Indianapolis: Indiana Historical Commission, 1922.

Foucault, Michel. *Ethics: Subjectivity and Truth*. Edited by Paul Rabinow. New York: New Press, 1994.

Franklin, Charles M. *Indiana: War of 1812 Soldiers*. Indianapolis: Ye Olde Geneology Shoppe, 1984.

Furstenberg, Francois. "Anglo-America and Its Borderlands." In *Major Problems in the History of North American Borderlands*, edited by Pekka Hämäläinen and Benjamin Johnson, 189–98>. Boston: Wadsworth, 2012.

Gabrielson, Teena. "James Madison's Psychology of Public Opinion." *Political Research Quarterly* 62, no. 3 (September 2009): 431–44.

Gibson, Arrell. *The Kickapoos: Lords of the Middle Border*. Norman: University of Oklahoma Press, 1976.

Gilje, Paul A. *The Making of the American Republic, 1763–1815*. Upper Saddle River NJ: Pearson Prentice Hall, 2006.

Gitlin, Jay. *The Bourgeois Frontier: French Towns, French Traders, and American Expansion*. New Haven CT: Yale University Press, 2010.

———. "Old Wine in New Bottles: French Merchants and the Emergence of the American Midwest, 1795–1835." In *Proceedings of the Thirteenth and Fourteenth Meetings of the French Colonial Historical Society*, edited by Philip P. Boucher, 37–52. Lanham MD: University Press of America, 1990.

———. "On the Boundaries of Empire: Connecting the West to Its Imperial Past." *Under an Open Sky: Rethinking America's Western Past*, edited by William Cronon, George Miles, and Gitlin, 71–90. New York: Norton, 1992.

Glenn, Elizabeth J. "Miami and Delaware Trade Routes and Relationships in Northern Indiana." In *Native American Cultures in Indiana: Proceedings of the First Minnetrista Council for Great Lakes Native American Studies*, ed. Ronald Hicks. Muncie IN: Minnetrista Cultural Center and Ball State University, 1992.

Gonella, Michael P. "Myaamia Ethnobotany." PhD diss., Miami University, 2007.

Goodman, Alfred T, ed., *Journal of Captain William Trent from Logstown to Pickawillany*. Cincinnati: Robert Clarke, 1871.

Greene, George E. *History of Old Vincennes and Knox County, Indiana*. Chicago: S. J. Clarke, 1911.

Greer, Allen. "Commons and Enclosure in the Colonization of North America." *American Historical Review* 117, no. 2 (April 2012): 365–86

Griffin, Patrick. *American Leviathan: Empire, Nation, and Revolutionary Frontier*. New York: Hill and Wang, 2007.

Hall, James. *A Memoir of the Public Services of William Henry Harrison of Ohio*. Philadelphia: Key and Biddle, 1836.

Hämäläinen, Pekka, and Samuel Truett. "On Borderlands." *Journal of American History* 98, no. 2 (2011): 338–61.

Harrison, Jennifer. "A Place in Between: The Story of a French and Miami Family." Master's thesis, Ball State University, 2001.

Harrison, William Henry. *The Papers of William Henry Harrison, 1800–1815.* Edited by Douglas E. Clanin and Ruth Dorrel. Indianapolis: Indiana Historical Society, 1994.

Hildreth, Richard. *The People's Presidential Candidate; or, The Life of William Henry Harrison of Ohio.* Boston: Weeks, Jordan, 1839

Hinderaker, Eric. *Elusive Empires: Constructing Colonialism in the Ohio Valley, 1673–1800.* Cambridge: Cambridge University Press, 1997.

Houck, Louis, ed. *The Spanish Regime in Missouri.* 2 vols. Chicago: R. R. Donnelley and Sons, 1909.

Hunter, William A., ed. "John Badollet's 'Journal of the Time I Spent in Stony Creek Glades,' 1793–1794." *Pennsylvania Magazine of History and Biography* 104, no. 2 (April 1980): 162–99.

Hutchins, Thomas. *A Topographical Description of Virginia, Pennsylvania, Maryland, and North Carolina, Comprehending the Rivers Ohio, Kenhava, Sioto, Cherokee, Wabash, Illinois, Mississippi.* London: Burlington House, 1778.

Hyde, Anne F. *Empires, Nations, and Families: A New History of the North American West, 1800–1860.* Lincoln: University of Nebraska Press, 2011.

Jackson, Isaac Rand. *A Sketch of the Life and Public Services of William Henry Harrison.* Columbus OH: I. N. Whiting, 1840.

Jacoby, Karl. *Shadow at Dawn: An Apache Massacre and the Violence of History.* New York: Penguin, 2009.

James, James Alton, ed. *Collections of the Illinois State Historical Library.* Vol. 8, *George Rogers Clark Papers, 1771–1781.* Springfield: Illinois State Historical Library, 1912.

Jennings, Jonathan. *Unedited Letters of Jonathan Jennings: With Notes by Dorothy Riker.* Edited by Dorothy L. Riker. Indianapolis: Indiana Historical Society Publications, 1932.

Jennings, Matthew. *New Worlds of Violence: Cultures and Conquests in the Early American Southeast.* Knoxville: University of Tennessee Press, 2011.

Jones, Henry, ed. *Journal of the Proceedings: Indian Treaty, Fort Wayne, September 30th, 1809.* Connersville IN: Knights of Columbus Council 861, 1910.

Jortner, Adam. *The Gods of Prophetstown: The Battle of Tippecanoe and the Holy War for the American Frontier.* New York: Oxford University Press, 2012.

Joutel, H. *A Journal of the last voyage perform'd by Monsr. De la Sale, to the Gulph of Mexico, to find the mouth of the Mississippi River.* London: A. Bell, B. Lintott, and J. Baker, 1714.

Kappler, Charles J., ed. *Indian Affairs: Laws and Treaties.* Washington DC: GPO, 1904.

Kinnaird, Lawrence, ed. *Spain in the Mississippi Valley.* Vol. 2, *Post War Decade, 1782–1791.* Washington DC: AHA, 1945.

Lambert, Robert S. "The Conduct of the Militia at Tippecanoe: Elihu Stout's Controversy with Colonel John P. Boyd, January, 1812." *Indiana Magazine of History* 51, no. 3 (September 1955): 237–50.

Larrabee, Charles. "Lieutenant Charles Larrabee's Account of the Battle of Tippecanoe, 1811." Edited by Florence G. Watts. *Indiana Magazine of History* 57, no. 3 (September 1961): 225–47.

Lindley, Harlow, ed. *Indiana as Seen by Early Travelers: A Collection of Reprints from Books of Travel, Letters and Diaries Prior to 1830.* Indianapolis: Indiana Historical Commission, 1916.

MacDonald, William, ed. *Select Documents Illustrative of the History of the United States, 1776–1861.* New York: Ayer, 1968.

MacLean, John Patterson. "Shaker Mission to the Shawnee Indians." *Ohio Archaeological and Historical Publications* 11 (June 1903): 215–29.

Mancall, Peter C., and James Hart Merrell, eds. *American Encounters: Natives and Newcomers from European Contact to Indian Removal.* New York: Routledge, 2000.

Mann, Robert. "The Silenced Miami: Archaeological and Ethnohistorical Evidence for Miami-British Relations, 1795–1812." *Ethnohistory* 46 (Summer 1999): 399–427.

Marrero, Karen. "'She Is Capable of Doing a Good Deal of Mischief': A Miami Woman's Threat to Empire in the Eighteenth-Century Ohio Valley." *Journal of Colonialism and Colonial History* 6, no. 3 (Winter 2005): 1–20

McCarty, William. *Songs, Odes, & Other Poems, on National Subjects; Compiled from Various Sources.* Philadelphia: W. McCarty, 1842.

Merrell, James. "Some Thoughts on Colonial historians and American Indians." *William and Mary Quarterly* 69 (July 2012): 94–119.

Michigan Pioneer and Historical Society. *Historical Collections: Collections and Researches Made by the Michigan Pioneer and Historical Society.* Vol. 19. Lansing, MI: Robert Smith, 1891.

———. *Pioneer Collections: Collections and Researches Made by the Pioneer and Historical Society of the State of Michigan.* Vol. 10. Lansing MI: Wynkoop, Hallenbeck, Crawford, 1908.

———. *Pioneer Collections: Collections and Researches Made by the Pioneer Society of the State of Michigan.* Vol. 11. Lansing MI: Thorp and Godfrey, 1888.

Miller, Captain. *Hero of Tippecanoe; or, The Story of the Life of William Henry Harrison.* New York: J. P. Giffing, 1840.

Mills, Randy Keith. *Jonathan Jennings: Indiana's First Governor.* Indianapolis: Indiana Historical Society Press, 2005.

Moore, Jacob Bailey. *The Contrast; or, Plain Reasons Why William Henry Harrison Should Be Elected President of the United States: And Why Martin Van Burn Should Not Be Re-Elected.* New York: J. P. Giffing, 1840.

Mulkearn, Lois, ed., *George Mercer Papers: Relating to the Ohio Company of Virginia*. Pittsburgh: University of Pittsburgh Press, 1954.

Owens, Robert. *Mr. Jefferson's Hammer: William Henry Harrison and the Origins of Indian Policy*. Norman: University of Oklahoma Press, 2007.

Pease, Theodore Calvin, and Ernestine Jenison, eds. *Collections of the Illinois State Historical Library*. Vol. 29, *Illinois on the Eve of the Seven Years' War, 1747–1755*. Springfield: Illinois State Historical Library, 1940.

Pennsylvania Historical Society. *Memoirs of the Historical Society of Pennsylvania*. Vol. 7, *Record of Upland, and Denny's Military Journal*. Philadelphia: Lippincott, 1860.

Perdue, Theda, and Michael D. Green. *The Cherokee Nation and the Trail of Tears*. New York: Penguin, 2008.

Philbrick, Francis S., ed. *Laws of Indiana Territory, 1801–1809*. Springfield: Illinois State Historical Library, 1930.

Piker, Joshua. "Lying Together: The Imperial Implications of Cross-Cultural Untruths." *American Historical Review* 116 (2011): 964–86.

———. *Okfuskee: A Creek Indian Town in Colonial America*. Cambridge: Harvard University Press, 2003.

Pirtle, Alfred. *The Battle of Tippecanoe*. Louisville KY: J. P. Morton, 1900.

Preston, David L. *The Texture of Contact: European and Indian Settler Communities on the Frontiers of Iroquoia, 1667–1783*. Lincoln: University of Nebraska Press, 2009.

Provincial Council of Pennsylvania. *Minutes of the Provincial Council of Pennsylvania*. Vol. 5, *Containing the Proceedings of Council from December 17th, 1745, to 20th March, 1754*. Harrisburg: Theo. Fenn, 1851.

Putnam, Rufus. *The Memoirs of Rufus Putnam and Certain Official Papers and Correspondence*. Edited by Rowena Buell. Boston: Houghton Mifflin, 1903.

Quaife, M. M. *Fort Wayne in 1790*. Indiana Historical Society Publications, no. 7. Greenfield: William Mitchell, 1921.

———, ed. *A Narrative of Life on the Old Frontier: Henry Hay's Journal from Detroit to the Mississippi River*. Madison: Historical Society of Wisconsin. 1915.

Rafert, Stewart. *The Miami Indians of Indiana: A Persistent People, 1654–1994*. Indianapolis: Indiana Historical Society Press, 1996.

Remini, Robert Vincent. *The Jacksonian Era*. Arlington Heights IL: H. Davidson, 1997.

Riley, Glenda. "The Specter of a Savage: Rumors and Alarmism on the Overland Trail." *Western Historical Quarterly* 15, no. 4 (October 1984): 427–44.

Rushforth, Brett. *Bonds of Alliance: Indigenous and Atlantic Slaveries in New France*. Chapel Hill: University of North Carolina Press, 2014.

Schoolcraft, Henry Rowe. *Information Respecting the History, Condition, and Prospects of the Indian Tribes in the United States*. 6 vols. Philadelphia: Lippincott, 1853–57.

Schultz, Jeffrey D., Kerry L. Haynie, Anne M. McCulloch, and Andrew L. Aoki, eds. *Encyclopedia of Minorities in American Politics.* Vol. 2, *Hispanic Americans and Native Americans.* Phoenix: Oryx, 2000.

Seineke, Katherine Wagner. *The George Rogers Clark Adventure in the Illinois and Selected Documents of the American Revolution at the Frontier Posts.* New Orleans: Polyanthos, 1981.

Shoemaker, Nancy. "How Indians Got to Be Red." *American Historical Review* 102 (June 1997): 625–44.

———. *A Strange Likeness: Becoming Red and White in Eighteenth-Century North America.* New York: Oxford University Press, 2004.

Silver, Peter. *Our Savage Neighbors: How Indian War Transformed Early America.* New York: Norton, 2008.

Silverman, David. *Red Brethren: The Brothertown and Stockbridge Indians and the Problem of Race in Early America.* Ithaca: Cornell University Press, 2008.

Sleeper-Smith, Susan. *Indian Women and French Men: Rethinking Cultural Encounters in the Western Great Lakes.* Amherst: University of Massachusetts Press, 2001.

Smith, William Henry, ed. *The St. Clair Papers.* Cincinnati: Robert Clark, 1882.

Stevens, Sylvester K., and Donald H. Kent, eds. *The Papers of Col. Henry Bouquet.* Ser. 21648. Pt. 1. Philadelphia: Pennsylvania Historical Commission, 1942.

Stoler, Ann Laura, ed. *Haunted by Empire: Geographies of Intimacy in North American History.* Durham NC: Duke University Press, 2006.

Strezewski, Michael, Robert G. McCullough, Dorothea McCullough, Craig R. Arnold, Joshua J. Wells, James R. Jones, and Leslie Bush. *Report of the 2006 Archaeological Investigations at Kethtippecanunk (12-t-59), Tippecanoe County, Indiana.* Fort Wayne: IPFW Archaeological Survey, Indiana University–Purdue University, 2007.

Sugden, John. *Tecumseh: A Life.* New York: Henry Holt, 1998.

Tanner, Helen Hornbeck. "The Glaize in 1792: A Composite Indian Community." *Ethnohistory* 25, no. 1 (Winter 1978): 15–39.

Tanner, John. *Narrative of the Captivity and Adventures of John Tanner during Thirty Years Residence among the Indians in the Interior of North America.* New York: G. C. H. Carvill, 1830.

Thomas, David. *Travels through the Western Country in the Summer of 1816: Including Notices of the Natural History, Antiquities, Topography, Agriculture, Commerce and Manufacturers.* Auburn NY: David Rumsey, 1819.

Thornbrough, Emma Lou. *The Negro in Indiana: A Study of a Minority.* Indianapolis: Indiana Historical Bureau, 1957.

Thornbrough, Gayle, ed. *Letter Book of the Indian Agency at Fort Wayne, 1809–1815.* Indianapolis: Indiana Historical Society, 1961.

———, ed. *Outpost on the Wabash, 1787–1791: Letters of Brigadier General Josiah Harmar and Major John Francis Hamtramck, and Other Letters and Docu-*

ments *Selected from the Harmar Papers in the William L. Clements Library*. Indiana Historical Society Publications 19. Indianapolis: Indiana Historical Society, 1957.

Thornbrough, Gayle, and Dorothy L. Riker, eds. *Journals of the General Assembly of Indiana Territory, 1805–1815*. Indianapolis: Indiana Historical Bureau, 1950.

Thwaites, Reuben Gold, ed. *Early Western Travels, 1748–1846*. Vol. 1. Cleveland OH: A. H. Clark, 1904.

———, ed. *The French Regime in Wisconsin*. Pt. 1, *1634–1727*. Collections of the State Historical Society of Wisconsin 16. Madison: Wisconsin State Historical Society Press, 1902.

———, ed. *The French Regime in Wisconsin*. Pt. 2, *1727–1748*. Collections of the State Historical Society of Wisconsin 17. Madison: Wisconsin State Historical Society, 1906.

Tipton, John. *The John Tipton Papers*. 2 vols. Edited by Nellie Armstrong Robertson and Dorothy L. Riker. Indianapolis: Indiana Historical Bureau, 1942.

Trowbridge, C. C. *Meearmeear Traditions*. Edited by W. Vernon Kinietz. Occasional Contributions from the Museum of Anthropology of the University of Michigan 7. Ann Arbor: University of Michigan Press, 1938.

———. *Shawnese Traditions*. Edited by W. Vernon Kinietz and Erminie Wheeler-Voegelin. Occasional Contributions from the Museum of Anthropology of the University of Michigan 9. Ann Arbor: University of Michigan Press, 1939.

Vermillion County, Indiana. *Biographical and Historical Record of Vermillion County, Indiana*. Chicago: Lewis, 1888.

Villerbu, Tangi. "Pouvoir, religion et societe en des temps indecis: Vincennes, 1763–1795." *Revue D'Histoire de L'Amerique Francaise* 62, no. 2 (Autumn 2008): 185–214.

Volney, C. F. *A View of the Soil and Climate of the United States of America: With Supplementary Remarks upon Florida; on the French Colonies on the Mississippi and Ohio, and in Canada; and on the Aboriginal Tribes of America*. Philadelphia: J. Conrad, 1804.

Warner, Michael. *The Letters of the Republic: Publication and the Public Sphere in Eighteenth-Century America*. Cambridge: Harvard University Press, 1992.

Warren, Stephen. *The Shawnee and Their Neighbors, 1795–1870*. Urbana: University of Illinois Press, 2008.

———. *The Worlds the Shawnees Made: Migration and Violence in Early America*. Chapel Hill: University of North Carolina Press, 2014.

Warren, Stephen, and Randolph Noe. "'The Greatest Travelers in America': Shawnee Survival in the Shatter Zone." In *Mapping the Mississippian Shatter Zone: The Colonial Indian Slave Trade and Regional Instability in the American South*, edited by Robbie Ethridge and Sheri Shuck-Hall, 163–87. Lincoln: University of Nebraska Press, 2009.

Wheeler-Voegelin, Erminie, Emily J. Blasingham, and Dorothy R. Libby, eds. *An Anthropological Report on the History of the Miamis, Weas, and Eel River Indians—Summary of Piankashaw Locations.* 2 vols. New York: Garland, 1974.

White, Richard. *The Middle Ground: Indians, Empires, and Republics in the Great Lakes Region, 1650–1815.* Cambridge: Cambridge University Press, 1991.

Winter, George. *The Journals and Indian Paintings of George Winter, 1837–1839.* Indianapolis: Indiana Historical Society, 1948.

Wilentz, Sean. *The Rise of American Democracy.* Vol. 1, *The Crisis of the New Order, 1787–1815.* New York: Norton, 2007.

Willig, Timothy D. "Prophetstown on the Wabash: The Native Spiritual Defense of the Old Northwest." *Michigan Historical Review* 23, no. 2 (Fall 1997): 115–58.

———. *Restoring the Chain of Friendship: British Policy and the Indians of the Great Lakes, 1783–1815.* Lincoln: University of Nebraska Press, 2008.

Wilson, Denise Marie. "Vincennes: From French Colonial Village to American Frontier Town, 1750–1820." PhD diss., West Virginia University, 1997.

Winger, Otho. *The Lost Sister among the Miamis.* Elgin IL: Elgin Press, 1936.

Woollen, William Wesley. *Biographical and Historical Sketches of Early Indiana.* Indianapolis: Hammond, 1883.

Woollen, William Wesley, Daniel Wait Howe, and Jacob Piatt Dunn, eds. *Executive Journal of Indiana Territory, 1800–1816.* Indianapolis: Indiana Historical Society, 1900.

Xavier, Pierre Francois. *The History and General Description of New France.* Vol. 5. New York: John Gilmary Shea, 1866.

INDEX

Page numbers in italics indicate illustrations.

accommodation, 12, 25, 189n28
accommodationist-nativist interpretive
    framework, xv, 46, 173
Adams, John, 43
African Americans, 74–75, *74*, 125, 157
agriculture: Miami, 18, 19, 38, 165–
    66, 187n16; as power source, 19; at
    Prophetstown, 86; at Vincennes, 29,
    189n33
alcohol, 62, 64, 92, 158
Alderman, Jeremy, xviii, 6–7
Algonquian languages, 16, 185n9
Algonquian peoples, 54, 195n16
alliances, 8, 9
America, early, American Indian history
    and, xvi
"American" (term), 112, 208n6
American army, 25, 114, 155, 168
American borderland, 135, 167, 168, 172, 179
American colonialism, 9, 44
American empire, 7, 9, 184n11
American expansion: groups facilitating,
    173; history of, xvi, 181n4; *vs.* Indian
    resistance and nationalism, xvi,
    181n4; measures promoting, 60–
    61; Miamis, impact on, 172, 179;
    narratives, 5, 10, 25, 168, 183n8,
    189n28; national values centered on,
    176–77; political advancement and,
    64–65; presupposing, limitations of,
    xv; Shawnee attitudes concerning,

55; through Indian land cessions,
    94–95; through treaties, 84; violence
    connected with, 4; William Wells's
    views on, 56, 93
American hegemony, 97
American identity, 79, 81, 114, 199n58
Americanism, birth of, 168–69
American Leviathan (Griffin), xvi, 11, 181n4
American militia, 66
American missionaries, 52, 177
American nation, growth of, 10
American nationalism, xvi, 5, 179, 181n4
American-nativist dichotomy, 155
American peacekeeping missions, 33–34
American policy, 110, 207n1
American political ideologies, 46
American republic, xvi, 4, 37, 114, 133–34
American Revolution, xvi–xvii, 71, 77,
    78–79, 114
Americans: boundaries' defense, 155;
    British contrast with, 14, 285n4;
    cultural agenda of, 47; divisions
    among, 47; as ethnic group, 10; French,
    relationship with, 62, 63, 65–66, 94–97,
    151, 153–55; Indians, relations with, 5, 44,
    50, 64–65, 151, 183n8; lies, participation
    in spreading, 83–84; Miamis, relations
    with, 41, 49, 100–101, 164–65; Miamis'
    world threatened by, xiv, 33; militancy,
    debate over, 54; misinformation from,
    107; official history created by, 10;

relationship with, 5, 58–59; Miamis'
borderland, destruction attempts,
xv; militancy, 131; in Mississinewa
River council, 157; nativist settlement
established by, 45; nativist vision,
83, 85, 179, 200n3; overemphasis on,
dangers of, 173; pan-Indian movement
advocated by, 100; patterns and
relationships preceding, xiv; peace
overtures by, 45–46; post-Tippecanoe
years, 173, 174–75, 177; Prophetstown
(ks) established by, 176, 177; as
Prophetstown (in) leader, xiv, 82,
85, 132, 137, 138; as religious debate
participant, 5, 182–83n7; revisionist
historiography concerning, 136, 212n1;
rumors about, 53, 102–3, 115–16; as
Shawnee society reformer, 53; stories
about, 156; threat, perceived posed by,
6, 55–56; in Tippecanoe battle, 136,
139–40, 212n1; trade restricted by, 94;
visions and plan of, 2–3; in War of 1812,
159; war plot, alleged by, 105, 122, 123,
125, 126; white invasion watched by, 2;
whites' destruction predicted by, 56–57;
William Henry Harrison and, 5, 45, 48,
90, 106–7, 123, 129–30, 132, 137, 138, 156–
57, 182–83n7; witch-hunts by, 54
The Texture of Contact (Preston), xiv–xv,
5, 182n7
Thames, Battle of, 161, 176
"third peoples," boundary shaping role
of, 12
Tippecanoe: burials and monument
at, 167–68; debate over, 140–49;
destruction and rebuilding of, 38;
historic context of, 176–77; Indian
migration to, 58, 90; lies surrounding,
168; memories of, 161, 173; narrative of,
136, 167–70, 179; settlements at, 22; term
usage, 176–77; trading houses, burning
of, 66; violence at, 4, 11, 47, 109, 134, 135,
137–40, 145; W. H. Harrison campaign
theme, 176
Tippecanoe, Battle of: aftermath of,
45–46, 164–67; causes of, xiv, 2, 83,
107; conditions paving way for, 6; as
denouement, 135; historical memory
skewed by, 135, 171–72; land cession
treaties and, 152; overview and scope
of, 136–37; postwar boundaries, 161;

reaction to, 159; reinvention and re-
remembering of, 4, 154, 167–69, 171, 177;
scholarly examinations of, 9; struggles
before and after, 11–12; Tenskwatawa at,
136, 212nn1–2; tropes, 10; victories in, 12
Tippecanoe River, Indian resettlement
near, 174
Tipton, John, 165, 167, 168
trade: avenues facilitating, 7; boundaries
of, 21; complicated history of, 7;
etiquette observed in, 15; local *versus*
nationalist interests, 8; violence
connected with, 62
trade network: control, contest for, 31;
dominance of, 19; protecting, 65;
relationship to local, 8; Tenskwatawa
confrontation of, 84; violence shaped
through, 24
trade wars, French *vs.* British, 22, 47,
188n20
Trans-Mississippi West, 60, 161–62
treaties, 67, *152. See also individual treaties*
Trowbridge, C. C., 13, 16, 59, 88
Truett, Samuel, xviii, 5–6, 108, 109, 206n51

Uncommon Defense (Hall), 5, 183n7
United States: army, 25, 114, 155, 168;
development as nation, 70–71; Indian
country, boundary with, 54, 195n16;
northern boundaries of, 168, 172;
territorial expansion (*see* American
expansion); western boundary,
securing, 154
U.S.–Great Britain conflict, 45, 56–57, 158,
169, 170. *See also* Revolutionary War;
War of 1812
Utes, 5, 183n8

Vigo, Francis, 51, 127
Vincennes, Sieur de, 19, 94
Vincennes in: after Tippecanoe, 140–
49, 153; alcohol sales regulation at,
9; American control of, 43, 44, 59,
84; American troops at, 33; attack
plans, rumored, 105, 122; boundaries,
defining, 67; characteristics of, 133;
communication with people in, 83; as
contested place, 29, 60–81; convention,
1805 at, 51; cultural hegemony, vying
for, 59; culture of lying in, 113; defense
of, 137; education at, 67; enemies,

www.ingramcontent.com/pod-product-compliance
Lightning Source LLC
Chambersburg PA
CBHW030410100426

42812CB00028B/2900/J